SOCIAL ECONOMICS

THE CAMBRIDGE ECONOMIC HANDBOOKS

General Editors

J. M. KEYNES (Lord Keynes)	1922–1936
D. H. ROBERTSON (Sir Dennis Robertson)	1936–1946
C. W. GUILLEBAUD	1946–1956
C. W. GUILLEBAUD ⎱ MILTON FRIEDMAN ⎰	1956–

SOCIAL
ECONOMICS

By

WALTER HAGENBUCH, M.A.
Fellow of Queens' College, Cambridge

DIGSWELL PLACE
JAMES NISBET & CO. LTD.
CAMBRIDGE
AT THE UNIVERSITY PRESS

First Published 1958
Reprinted . . 1959

James Nisbet and Company Limited
Digswell Place, Welwyn, Herts
and the Cambridge University Press
in association with the University of Chicago Press

INTRODUCTION

TO THE CAMBRIDGE ECONOMIC HANDBOOKS
BY THE GENERAL EDITORS

SOON after the war of 1914–18 there seemed to be a place for a series of short introductory handbooks, 'intended to convey to the ordinary reader and to the uninitiated student some conception of the general principles of thought which economists now apply to economic problems'.

This Series was planned and edited by the late Lord Keynes under the title 'Cambridge Economic Handbooks' and he wrote for it a General Editorial Introduction of which the words quoted above formed part. In 1936 Keynes handed over the editorship of the Series to Mr. D. H. Robertson, who held it till 1946, when he was succeeded by Mr. C. W. Guillebaud.

It was symptomatic of the changes which had been taking place in the inter-war period in the development of economics, changes associated in a considerable measure with the work and influence of Keynes himself, that within a few years the text of part of the Editorial Introduction should have needed revision. In its original version the last paragraph of the Introduction ran as follows:

'Even on matters of principle there is not yet a complete unanimity of opinion amongst professional economists. Generally speaking, the writers of these volumes believe themselves to be orthodox members of the Cambridge School of Economics. At any rate, most of their ideas about the subject, and even their prejudices, are traceable to the contact they have enjoyed with the writings and lectures of the two economists who have chiefly influenced Cambridge thought for the past fifty years, Dr. Marshall and Professor Pigou.'

Keynes later amended this concluding paragraph to read:

'Even on matters of principle there is not yet a complete unanimity of opinion amongst professional students of the subject. Immediately after the war (of 1914–18) daily economic events were of such a startling character as to divert attention from theoretical complexities. But today, economic science has recovered its wind. Traditional treatments and traditional solutions are being questioned, improved and revised. In the end this activity of research should clear up controversy. But for the moment controversy and doubt are increased. The writers of this Series must apologize to the general reader and to the beginner if many parts of their subject have not yet reached to a degree of certainty and lucidity which would make them easy and straightforward reading.'

Many though by no means all the controversies which Keynes had in mind when he penned these words have since been resolved. The new ideas and new criticisms, which then seemed to threaten to overturn the old orthodoxy, have, in the outcome, been absorbed within it and have served rather to strengthen and deepen it, by adding needed modifications and changing emphasis, and by introducing an altered and on the whole more precise terminology. The undergrowth which for a time concealed that main stream of economic thought to which Keynes referred in his initial comment and to which he contributed so greatly has by now been largely cleared away so that there is again a large measure of agreement among economists of all countries on the fundamental theoretical aspects of their subject.

This agreement on economic analysis is accompanied by wide divergence of views on questions of economic policy. These reflect both different estimates of the quantitative importance of one or another of the conflicting forces involved in any prediction about the consequences of a policy measure and different value judgments about the desirability of the predicted outcome. It still remains as true today as it was when Keynes wrote that—to quote once more from his Introduction:

'The Theory of Economics does not furnish a body of settled conclusions immediately applicable to a policy. It is a method rather than a doctrine, an apparatus of the mind, a technique of thinking, which helps its possessor to draw correct conclusions.'

This method, while in one sense eternally the same, is in another ever changing. It is continually being applied to new problems raised by the continual shifts in policy views. This is reflected in the wide range of topics covered by the Cambridge Economic Handbooks already published, and in the continual emergence of new topics demanding coverage. Such a series as this should accordingly itself be a living entity, growing and adapting to the changing interests of the times, rather than a fixed number of essays on a set plan.

The wide welcome given to the Series has amply justified the judgment of its founder. Apart from its circulation in the British Empire, it has been published from the start in the United States of America, and translations of the principal volumes have appeared in a number of foreign languages.

The present change to joint Anglo-American editorship is designed to increase still further the usefulness of the Series by expanding the range of potential topics, authors and readers alike. It will succeed in its aim if it enables us to bring to a wider audience on both sides of the Atlantic lucid explanations and significant applications of 'that technique of thinking' which is the hallmark of economics as a science.

G. W. GUILLEBAUD

April 1957

PREFACE

EVER since I began to take a special interest in social problems I have been conscious of the need for a textbook in this field suitable for students taking a degree in economics. There is no lack of books on economic theory, the structure of industry, the monetary and banking system, and international trade. Nor is the labour field, as such, short of literature, but it is a strictly labour field, consisting of wages, trade unions and industrial relations. Other social problems, instead of being studied as a group, have been dealt with piecemeal, partly in textbooks on the traditional branches of economics and partly in specialised books and articles unsuitable for, often inaccessible to, the general run of students.

The shape of the literature is reflected in the shape of syllabuses and lecture courses. Social problems, other than labour problems, tend to be pushed rather uncomfortably into one or other of the main categories. Population is sometimes treated as an offshoot of economic theory, sometimes as an aspect of labour, sometimes as an element in the structure of industry. Housing and working conditions are often ignored or regarded as relevant only to the course in economic history. The social services have until recently been confined to courses in social administration, where they are usually considered from the descriptive and administrative angles; and the analysis of their economic implications has scarcely begun.

In this book social problems are discussed in the light of elementary economic theory and with the aid of such historical, statistical and descriptive material as is appropriate. The topics are selected (some obvious candidates, notably the distribution of incomes and education, have been excluded for lack of space); and each of the Chapters II to VII, and the group of Chapters VIII to X, is self-contained. Nevertheless, they are bound together, not only by frequent cross-references, but also by a similarity of treatment and, for good or ill, by the author's attitude and point of view.

Some knowledge of elementary economic theory is assumed, and some of the concepts relevant to the general approach are discussed in the first chapter. (This chapter is, however, more sober than the rest, and may safely be skipped by the impatient and the initiated.) There is no attempt to apply advanced theoretical techniques and no extensive treatment of the theoretical aspects, as distinct from the social aspects of, for example, population and unemployment. Two further limitations should be mentioned: labour problems, apart from references in the chapter on working conditions, have been excluded; and the factual material is almost entirely confined to Great Britain.

My indebtedness to other writers is great, and equalled only by my anxiety lest I have misunderstood or misrepresented them. If the works of Marshall and Pigou seem unduly prominent in my references, it may be worth saying that I was brought up on them, and that I am not unaware that a great deal has been written since.

I humbly acknowledge the generous help and friendly encouragement received from teachers, colleagues and students in Cambridge and elsewhere. Some have read earlier drafts of odd chapters and made valuable amendments; some have offered suggestions and corrected errors in the course of discussion; some have spurred me on by merely repeating that the need to fill the gap becomes daily more urgent. If I do not recite their names, it is because they are so many and not because I am unmindful of their kindness.

Some particular acknowledgements must however be made. Sir Dennis Robertson read rather more than half the chapters at an early stage and provided a host of constructive comments. Mr. C. W. Guillebaud has far exceeded his stint as general editor and sustained me with general and detailed advice and help throughout. Mr. H. J. Mackenzie Wood, as publisher, has displayed greater patience in the face of repeated delays than I had ever thought possible. Mr. S. R. Dennison, who has not seen the manuscript, has yet contributed immeasurably by his genius for offering a word of encouragement when it is most needed. My wife has taken more than her share of the burden, in all its forms and at every stage. Her economic wisdom has been affectionately devoted to teaching me the elementary lesson which I have never learnt for myself: how to allocate the scarce resources of time and energy among the insatiable demands of teaching, lecturing, reading, writing, College duties, outside interests, home and family.

I am grateful to the Editor of *Lloyds Bank Review* for permission to reprint, as an Epilogue to this book, the substance of an article published in the *Review* in July 1953.

WALTER HAGENBUCH

February 1958

CONTENTS

CHAPTER III

HOUSING

CHAPTER IV

WORKING CONDITIONS

CHAPTER V

UNEMPLOYMENT

CHAPTER VI

POVERTY

CHAPTER VII

VOLUNTARY SOCIAL SERVICES

CHAPTER VIII

PUBLIC SOCIAL SERVICES—THEIR STRUCTURE AND HISTORY

CHAPTER IX

NATIONAL INSURANCE AND ASSISTANCE

CHAPTER X

OTHER PUBLIC SOCIAL SERVICES

EPILOGUE

CHAPTER I

SCOPE AND MEANING OF SOCIAL ECONOMICS

§ 1. Economics and Social Economics. Economics is a social science. It belongs to a group of sciences concerned with human behaviour in society, and it concentrates on one aspect of that behaviour which Marshall described as 'mankind in the ordinary business of life'. This may not be the most important aspect, but it is probably the most amenable to scientific study because so many of its values can be expressed quantitatively, in terms of goods or money. By observing and interpreting the facts of the economic world, the economist has been able to build up an apparatus of thought which we call economic theory and which helps in the understanding and discussion of social phenomena. But he must always be conscious of the limitations of his approach.

'There is a large debatable ground,' said Marshall, 'in which economic considerations are of considerable but not dominant importance; and each economist may reasonably decide for himself how far he will extend his labours over that ground. He will be able to speak with less and less confidence the further he gets away from his central stronghold, and the more he concerns himself with conditions of life and with motives of action which cannot be brought to some extent at least within the grasp of scientific method.'[1]

Something of this caution and humility must characterise any attempt to define the special field of social economics. It does not matter that it should be defined precisely; it would be quite sufficient to say that social economics is whatever social

[1] *Principles of Economics*, 8th Edition, 1920, p. 780.

1

economists study, and to point to the chapter headings of this book. What does matter is that the social economist should realise that his study is essentially a frontier activity, and that in pursuing it he may often cross and recross the boundary of neighbouring social sciences without jumping a fence or climbing a stile. In these territories the economist may have a great deal to say, but the last word may properly rest with the politician, or the psychologist or the moralist. And yet, a little farther on, he may be back on his own ground, where the other social scientists have a great deal to say, but the balance of authority is in favour of the economist.

To say that social economics is whatever social economists study, however, does not absolve us from describing our activities in greater detail; and they can usefully be considered from four points of view: (1) as a branch of applied economics: the application of economic theory to social problems; (2) as a branch of applied statistics: the numerical measurement of the extent and constitution of social problems; (3) as the study of the social causes of economic behaviour, which might be called economic ecology; (4) as the study of the social consequences of economic behaviour, which some would call welfare economics. Let us look at these more carefully.

§ 2. A Branch of Applied Economics. First, what constitutes a 'social problem'? Our society does not stand still, but is continually changing and developing. This change implies that the social structure must constantly adapt itself to new circumstances. But the structure is made up of institutions, organisations and social groups of various kinds which are not always adaptable, so that when changes are big or sudden the strain of adjustment is serious and gives rise to a social problem. Many of these changes are economic, most of them have economic repercussions of one kind or another; the institutions are often business units, and the groups are often associations of workers, employers or consumers. The economist can therefore contribute a great deal to the explanation of social problems. His knowledge of economic theory has acquainted him with some of the general principles on which the social mechanism works and his application of that theory to particular social problems may, at the worst, prevent ignorant remedial action on the part of politicians and social reformers and, at the best, suggest effective measures for solving the problems.

The social problem of unemployment is an obvious example. No one wants to be unemployed or to see others unemployed. It is true that some people, sometimes, would like to have nothing to do, especially if they are paid for doing it; but, for the most part, they revolt against unemployment not only because it threatens their livelihood, but also because of its psychological and social effects. Few things are more demoralising than the feeling of not being wanted; few more depressing than the sight of depression. Suppose now that in a small town, whose principal industry is the weaving of cloth, sudden and substantial unemployment occurs among the weavers. Public sympathy may be moved by the obvious signs of distress and may try to express itself by the setting up of soup kitchens or the collection of a relief fund. But these would be mere palliatives. If the cause of the unemployment were sought, it might be found that a new type of loom, requiring only one weaver for every twenty looms, had been introduced in place of the old looms which required one weaver for every four looms. One way of curing the unemployment could be to break up the new looms and enforce the continued use of the old. This kind of policy has been advocated, not only by the Luddites of 150 years ago but also in quite recent times; whenever, in fact, an increase in efficiency threatens security of employment. Alternatively, it might be found that the demand for cloth had suddenly slumped, and voices would be raised for some Government agency to step in and place large orders, even if this meant accumulating excessive stocks of fabrics normally purchased by the Government, or stocks of cloth not required for any known purpose.

The moral of this example is that the obvious ways of alleviating the effects or removing the causes of unemployment may not be consistent with the efficient working of the economic system as a whole. For it can be argued that without new machines there would be no economic progress, and that it would be better if the unemployed could be set to work making goods that are currently required, rather than goods that may never be required at all.

These problems will be studied in more detail in Chapter V. For the present we have simply shown that human sympathy, though it may be the mainspring of social policy, is by itself not enough. It must be supported by economic knowledge. This application of economic theory to social problems is, then, the first task of social economics.

§ 3. **A Branch of Applied Statistics.** When we turn to the second aspect of our study, namely, the measurement of the extent of social problems, we find the field in which the social economist has probably made his most valuable and significant contributions to human knowledge and welfare. When Charles Booth undertook his social survey of the extent and causes of poverty in London at the end of the nineteenth century, he laid the foundations of modern social economics. There had been, as will be seen in Chapter VI, studies of poverty before the time of Booth. Many of them contained a wealth of statistical detail and were written with passionate conviction. But it is Booth's distinction that he was the first to present an accurate and objective account of the extent and causes of poverty in a convincing and manageable form. Since his time 'the measurement of social phenomena', as Professor Bowley has called it, has grown in scope and respectability. The twentieth century has witnessed an unprecedented growth in the official and unofficial collection of social statistics, and there are now few social problems whose scope cannot be assessed with objectivity and reasonable accuracy, as a basis for formulating social policy. Indeed social scientists are occasionally in danger of forgetting that their subject matter is not merely statistical units, but human beings.

The development of this technique of analysis applies,

however, to the whole field of social studies; to such widely different problems as the incidence of juvenile crime and the use of baths for storing coal.   This book concerns only those problems which have an economic aspect and are fairly closely connected with the getting and spending of incomes.   The study of the social services, for example, is concerned with schemes and organisations whose sole purpose is to supplement or replace privately earned income by income which is either shared communally (as in the case of public parks and libraries) or received through some communal organisation (a Friendly Society or the National Assistance Board).   Before discussing the operation of the social services, therefore, it is necessary to know why private income is insufficient.   Is it because earning power is low, as in the case of unskilled or exploited labour?   Or is it because needs are exceptionally high as in the case of wage-earners with large families or dependent relatives?   Or is it because the income is mis-spent, so that although in total it would satisfy the essential needs of the family, too much is allocated to inessentials and luxuries? Clearly the whole form and structure of the social services depends on the answers to these questions; and they are questions of fact, calling for the analysis of household expenditure, labour mobility, family size and other social phenomena. We shall have recourse to the results of statistical enquiry in every part of the field of social economics, but most of all in the study of poverty and the social services in Chapters VI to X.

§ 4. The Study of Social Causes.   The third task of social economics is to fill in the broad background of social conditions against which the narrower economic forces play their part. The economist begins his work in the market, where prices are determined through the interaction of demand and supply. He then stands back, as it were, to see what lies behind these demand and supply forces, to study the costs and expectations which help to explain the producers' behaviour and the utilities and choices which help to explain that of the consumers.

All this time he is concerned with values which are, in principle at any rate, measurable and amenable to analytical treatment. But it is also useful to know something of the social environment in which people play their part as producers and consumers, to study, for example, living conditions and working conditions; for these not only have a profound influence on the ability to earn and spend income, they are themselves the subject of social legislation, which implies the control of some part of individual earning and spending in the wider interests of society.

Chapters II, III and IV, concerned with Population, Housing and Working Conditions, belong, for the most part, to this branch of social economics. Particularly is this true of population. The whole tenor of economic behaviour may be changed according to whether the environment is one of expanding, stationary or declining population. At the time of writing it appears that in Great Britain the growing proportion of old people in the population is likely to provide one of the social problems of the next thirty years. Their retirement from productive work will affect the national income; their pensions will affect the budget; their demand for suitable accommodation will affect the housing and health service programmes; their need for companionship and personal care, in an age in which the number of children per family and their capacity to look after their aged parents are declining, will make unprecedented demands on the voluntary and public social services.

Here the main task of the social economist is descriptive rather than statistical, but he can, nevertheless, give some account of the relative importance of social influences. He may not be able to estimate precisely the real cost of old age pensions (the additional resources of labour and capital, that is, which are used up as a result of the pensions schemes); or the real benefits of factory legislation (the increase in efficiency resulting from the greater security and better health of the workers); but he can do much to put these matters in their proper perspective, to show that some social influences have economic effects much greater than is popularly supposed, while others are exaggerated in the popular imagination and may need to be soft-pedalled or even exploded as what Professor Cannan used to call 'economic scares'.

§ 5. The Study of Social Consequences.   We have been considering the influence of social conditions on economic behaviour.   But there is a fourth and equally important aspect of social economics, namely the study of the social *consequences* of economic behaviour.   Most economic decisions, whether people take them as business men, as workers or as consumers, are taken having regard to their own advantage or the advantage of those for whom they have a direct responsibility: their families, their workpeople or some group or organisation to which they belong.   It is clear, however, that in any closely-knit society, be it a tribal village or a modern industrial nation, individual economic decisions inevitably have secondary effects on other people and groups, and perhaps on the whole society.   Social economics, and, in a narrower sense, welfare economics, take account of these secondary effects.

Before analysing them, however, we must deal with two popular misconceptions.   First, there is no moral judgment implied in the statement that individuals or groups make economic decisions having regard to their own advantage only. It is simply a factual statement about the way in which the economic world works.   It may be that, as business men, people would like to do what is best, not merely for themselves, but for society as a whole, or what is sometimes called the 'national interest'.   But the further afield they look, the more it becomes impossible to take account of the social effects of their behaviour, partly because they cannot measure them, and still more because, even if they could measure them, the costs and benefits involved would not appear in their own profit and loss accounts—if they did they might cease to be business men.   Similarly, as workers, people may wish wholeheartedly to modify their wage claims or their choice of a job in accordance with some wider interest than their personal or family or trade union advantage; and for some people, for a period, this is possible. For most people, most of the time, however, it is not, again chiefly because of the difficulty of measurement, but also because, as has been pointed out, the social or moral or political values, even if they could be measured, are not consistently reflected in their wages and salaries. Even in wartime, when the State lays down the ingredients of the national interest and directs and rewards each person's work accordingly, there is not always universal agreement with the official interpretation of this wider interest and it is accepted only temporarily and at the cost of giving up a considerable amount of personal freedom and trade union independence. Again, as consumers, people may wish to take account of the social consequences of their spending, but their decisions in this matter are difficult enough as it is, and if their consciences were further burdened in this way, the spending of money would require greater intellectual and moral gymnastics than most people are capable of. The analysis of the social effects of economic behaviour does not, then, carry any implication that individual and group decisions are right or wrong, still less that they are in any way anti-social.

Nor does it imply that the social effects are necessarily different from, or in conflict with, the direct economic effects which are taken into account in individual decisions.   Indeed, as we shall presently see, the basis of welfare economics is that in many cases an increase in individual economic welfare will represent an equivalent increase in general social welfare.

What are these social effects? Let us suppose that a new factory is set up, in a town in which there was previously considerable unemployment, to produce razor blades in a new type of container designed both for the rapid unloading of new blades and the safe disposal of used ones. The increased welfare of the manager, the shareholders and the workers in that factory will be measured by the rewards which they receive for their contributions to its output; and the net output of the factory (the value of its gross output less the value of materials which it buys from other firms) will constitute an increase in the economic welfare of the country as a whole.   But there is more to it than this.   The *general* welfare of both the workers in the factory and the consumers of the product may be increased by much more than the increase in their *economic* welfare as measured by figures of wages and net output.   For the workers were previously unemployed, and the security value of their employment is much greater than can be measured by the wage they now receive.   The consumers, for their part, not only have a new product for which there has long been a latent demand.   They are generally happier, as any reader will testify who has unpacked a new razor blade on a late morning or been secretly worried for years about how to get rid of the old ones.   Moreover, the *social* welfare (the economic welfare of the community as a whole) will probably be increased by more than the increase in the *private* welfare of those who receive an income from the operation of the factory. The increased traffic into and out of the town may justify the opening of a branch line which can be used by all the other firms in the district and enables them to achieve 'external economies' in the form of lower transport costs.   Allowance must also be made for the 'multiplier effect' of the increase in incomes resulting from the setting up of the factory.   Not only will those directly concerned enjoy increased prosperity and optimism.   They will pass it on to the shopkeepers and others on whose goods and services they spend their incomes; and these in turn will pass it on to wholesalers and manufacturers; so that there may be several 'rounds' of increased activity and employment, and social welfare may be increased far beyond the reckoning of those who first set up the factory.

But of course it does not always happen this way.   The increase in social welfare, instead of being equal to, or greater than, the increase in private welfare, may fall short of it.   If the factory were to emit a large volume of black smoke, the effect on the atmosphere of the town and on the health and laundry bills of its citizens would represent a social cost which the factory promoters would not have to pay but which the social economist must take account of.

The same problems arise in the case of a decrease in welfare. If it were a question, not of opening a new factory, but of closing an existing one, the cost to the community in terms of loss of income, social distress and change in economic and psychological outlook could be greater than the value of the net output of that factory (as the Census of Production measures it) or the difference between the revenue which he loses and the costs which he avoids by closing down (as the entrepreneur would measure it in such circumstances).

§ **6. Social Economics and Welfare Economics.** So far from wandering about in the spacious territory of social economics, we are now coming close to one of the citadels of modern economic theory. For, since the publication of Professor Pigou's *Economics of Welfare*,[1] economists have felt it incumbent upon them not only to explain how the economic system works, but also to seek to throw light on the effects of economic changes upon welfare. This book is not about the theory of welfare economics, but we have defined one aspect of social economics as the 'study of the social consequences of economic behaviour' and welfare economics is very much concerned with those social consequences which can be, in principle at any rate, objectively measured and handled with the analytical tools of economic theory. It is necessary, therefore, to give a brief account of some aspects of welfare economics and show roughly at what points it overlaps with social economics.[2]

To begin with the individual consumer. We are concerned with his economic welfare, that is, the satisfaction or utility which he derives from his income. Is it possible to measure the total of this satisfaction? The answer, as we shall presently see, is no. But two very important things can be said about

[1] First published under the title of *Wealth and Welfare* in 1912.

[2] It should be made clear at the start that, although welfare economics has its strictly scientific side, as Pigou and many later writers so ably demonstrate, it does inevitably give rise to value judgments. Some at least of the conclusions on problems of welfare reached by any individual economist (and this holds good also for the writer of this book) are likely to have been influenced by his own personal and subjective reactions to the issues involved.

it: first, that the more of any commodity or service he has, the less additional satisfaction he will derive from another unit of it—this is the law of diminishing marginal utility; secondly, that he will endeavour so to arrange his expenditure that he derives the greatest possible total satisfaction from it—this will occur when the marginal utility to him of each commodity is proportionate to its price. All that is assumed here is that the amount of money the consumer pays for a *marginal* unit of a commodity is a measure of the *additional* satisfaction he derives from it. This is a reasonable assumption and it enables us to analyse his behaviour and to correlate it with the general working of the price system.

Why can we not measure the total satisfaction which his income yields? This grand total would be the sum of the total satisfactions derived from each commodity, which in turn would be the sum of the marginal satisfactions derived from each successive unit of each commodity. But although he pays the same price for every unit of a commodity, that price measures only the satisfaction derived from the marginal unit. The other units (because of the law of diminishing marginal utility) yield a surplus of satisfaction above what he pays for them; and the surplus may be very large indeed for some units of some commodities. He may buy five loaves a week when bread is 6*d*. a loaf, but if bread went up to 10*s*. a loaf he might still buy one loaf rather than have no bread at all. Thus when the price is 6*d*. he has a consumers' surplus of 9*s*. 6*d*. on the first loaf and smaller surpluses on the second, third and fourth. Clearly, it is hardly a sensible procedure to add all these surpluses to what the consumer actually pays and call the total the measure of the satisfaction he derives from his entire consumption of bread. The surpluses are not without significance: it would be sensible to add them up if this addition excluded those initial units of some commodities for which the consumer would pay extremely high prices in desperate circumstances. It would also be sensible in the case of commodities on which he would in any event spend only a very small proportion of his income. But, beyond these limits, the measurement of the total satisfaction derived from a single commodity is an unsatisfactory business, and the addition of such totals to produce a measure of the total utility of income as a whole may be quite meaningless; the cumulation of surpluses would yield a figure many times greater than the total money income and the consumer would begin to wonder whether he had inherited a fortune without knowing it.

So far, then, we have established two propositions. On the one hand, because of the existence of consumers' surplus, total expenditure does not measure total satisfaction. This is so because the consumer arranges his expenditure in such a way that the marginal utility of each commodity is equal to its price. It is worth repeating that, from the consumer's point of view, the price is equated to the *marginal* utility, not to the *average* utility. If he is found buying four loaves when the price is 9*d*. and five when the price is 6*d*. the implication is that the fourth loaf gives him nine pennyworth of added satisfaction and the fifth six pennyworth. This being so, consumers' surplus does exist and total expenditure does not measure total satisfaction. On the other hand, the inclusion of surpluses in the measurement of total satisfaction is significant only if we take a sensible starting point.

In short, the concepts of marginal utility and consumers' surplus are less useful for purposes of addition than for purposes of comparison. This is important because in practice the consumer is rarely faced with fundamental changes in his pattern of consumption, such as the exclusion of a commodity on which he has been used to spending a substantial part of his income. Most of his choices consist of spending a little more on this and a little less on that. They are marginal choices, and it is within these limits that the concepts of utility and consumers' surplus play a significant part, not indeed for the consumer only, but also for the Chancellor of the Exchequer, in such matters as the allocation of indirect taxes and subsidies.

Nevertheless, there are two ways in which the money value of the consumer's income can be used in the analysis of satis-

faction and welfare.   It is sometimes useful, and not unreasonable, to assume that people whose money incomes are roughly
the same will suffer roughly similar gains or losses in satisfaction from a given increase or decrease in income.   Moreover, just as, in the case of a single commodity, although it is
not usually possible to measure the total utility, it is possible
to measure the marginal utility and, aided by the law of diminishing marginal utility, to make considerable progress in systematic analysis; so, in the case of whole incomes, the inability
to measure total satisfaction does not prevent analysis at the
margin.   For the law of diminishing marginal utility applies
to income as a whole, and, with certain qualifications, it is
reasonable and useful to say that in general an income of £3,000
a year does not yield twice as much satisfaction as an income of
£1,500 a year, and that an extra £50 is likely to mean much
more to a poor man than to a rich man.

We can now extend our analysis of the economic welfare
of the individual consumer to that of the whole community.
Corresponding to the individual's income we have a national
income, which, while it does not measure the nation's economic
welfare in any absolute sense, is an invaluable concept for
comparative analysis, for working out, that is, whether certain
economic behaviour or policy is likely to increase or diminish
the nation's welfare.   Marshall defined the national income
by saying that 'The labour and capital of the country, acting on
its natural resources, produce annually a certain net aggregate
of commodities, material and immaterial, including services of
all kinds. . . . This is the true net annual income, or revenue
of the country.'[1]   Professor Pigou fastened on this annual
flow of goods and services, this real national income, and made
it the focus of the economic system.   A fundamental principle
of welfare economics is that, subject to certain reservations,
the larger the national income and the more equally it is distributed among persons, the greater will the economic welfare
of the community be.   This statement is of course a very
rough one, and among the many reservations, the chief would

[1] *Principles*, p. 523.

be that where a given change makes the total national income smaller but distributes it more equally, it will sometimes be difficult and often impossible to assess the combined effect on economic welfare. The technique of welfare economics, then, has been to work out, by logical analysis, the effects of certain causes on the size and distribution of the national income. In particular it has concentrated on those aspects of the economic system, such as the immobility of labour and capital, the influence of monopoly, and the extremes of poverty and wealth, which hindered the allocation of resources in such a way as to achieve the maximum economic welfare, interpreted either as the largest possible national income or as the fairest possible distribution of a given national income. A good deal of present-day economic and social legislation can be traced back to the influence of *Economics of Welfare*, though the book itself is somewhat austere and appears to be less concerned with the real world than Marshall's *Principles*, where the atmosphere of the market, the workshop and the kitchen can be smelt as one turns the pages.

It will already be obvious that the social economist must make considerable use of the techniques of welfare economics. They will help him to distinguish between the effect of actions and policies on the economic welfare of the persons who initiate them and their effects on the economic welfare of the community as a whole. They will help him to distinguish between the effects on the economic welfare only, and the effects on the general welfare of the community, in so far as he can reasonably assess it. They will show him why it is worth while for him to study the working of social institutions, and assist his judgment on the efficacy of these institutions in solving social problems.

Since the study of welfare economics began, however, two important extensions to its territory have created a further area of overlap with the field of social economics. The first is the preparation and publication, on an elaborate scale, of national income statistics, and the growth of a new branch of study called social accounting. The second is the development

of employment theory, and the study of the nature and
causes of economic progress.   We must say something about
both of these subjects, not with the intention of summarising
the vast literature concerning them, but simply in order to
show their connection with social economics.

§ 7. The National Income and Social Accounting.

While the
technique of welfare economics consists in working out *in
principle* the effect of certain causes on the size and distribution of the national income, and thus on the economic welfare
of the community, this has been supplemented in the last
twenty or thirty years by the *actual* statistical calculation of the
total national income and its distribution in Great Britain and
many other countries.   The first estimate of the national income of England was probably made by Gregory King in
1696, and, as so often happens in social affairs, an enormous
amount of pioneering work was done by private investigators
before the full weight of Government authority and the full
range of official records were lent to the publication of a series
of national income statistics.   Similar work has been done in
other countries and the United Nations publish comparative
national income statistics, of varying reliability and usefulness,
for most countries of the world.

A number of the problems which have arisen in the course
of this development of national income accounting are of
interest to the social economist.   The chief problem is what to
include in the estimate of the national income; and this will
depend on the purpose for which the estimate is required and
the extent to which the common measuring rod of money is
applicable to the items we should like to include.   If we are
concerned with the spending habits of the community: how
much of their income people use to pay taxes, how much to
save, and how much to spend on different kinds of consumer
goods, all of which is of special interest to the social economist,
the national income may be simply defined as the sum total of
all personal incomes, whether they are earned or not.   But if
we are concerned with the taxable capacity of the community,

it is necessary to add to the total those incomes which do not accrue to individual persons but are nevertheless possible sources of tax revenue, namely, undistributed business profits. This definition of the national income is sometimes called private income, to distinguish it from personal income and to show that it does not include any Government, or public, income. For the purpose of measuring economic welfare, the real national income, the annual flow of goods and services, or, looked at from the point of view of output, the gross national product, is required. Social problems relating to the standard of living all turn, ultimately, on the size and division of this stream of real income. It can only be measured, however, in money terms, and this is done by adding up the money incomes of all those who have contributed to it—the earnings of the owners of the factors of production (that is why it is sometimes called national income at factor cost). Most of these incomes will accrue to individual persons but care must be taken to exclude personal income in such forms as pensions or interest on the National Debt, which does not correspond to goods and services currently produced. On the other hand, it must include, not only the undistributed profits of businesses, but also the incomes of Government and local authorities from their own productive activities, such as the rent on houses owned by the local authority.

Two further questions of scope and definition immediately arise. First, what is to be done about real income which people enjoy through their own use of their own property? If Smith and Jones lived in each other's (identical) houses and paid each other rent, the payments would figure in the national income; if they lived in their own houses they would not, unless a special adjustment were made to the estimates. Such an adjustment is in fact made in the case of house-room and it is quite small in relation to the total national income. In the discussion of housing problems, however, the size and basis of this adjustment would be of importance. Secondly, what about real services for which no payment is made? The most important of these are the services of the housewife, but it has not been found possible to make any reasonable estimate of the value of these or of any other voluntary services, from the work of the scoutmaster to the domestic efforts of the home handyman. Consequently the national income estimates may change when in fact the total annual output of goods and services has not changed, simply because of some change in social custom which brings activities hitherto performed voluntarily into the sphere of exchange values. Normally such changes are not important, but they would become important, for example, in discussing an extension of the public social services, organised by paid social workers, to replace voluntary services hitherto provided without reward.

National income estimates are meaningless in isolation; comparative figures for two or more years are necessary before any useful conclusions can be drawn. But the statement that an increase in the national income, or an improvement in its distribution, represents an increase in economic welfare, must still be made with caution. First, since measurement is in terms of money, allowance must be made for changes in the value of money, that is, in the general level of prices. The real national income, the quantities of goods and services produced, might be identical in two years, while the money value of the national income might be twice as great in the second year, simply because all the prices had doubled. An adjustment is therefore made by using an index of prices; but a second precaution must be to ensure that the index is 'representative'. It must be suitably 'weighted', so that, for instance, an increase of 50 per cent in the price of hairpins, on which people spend a very small part of their incomes, does not count for as much as a similar increase in the price of milk, on which they spend a much larger part. If applied to a change in the distribution of the national income from rich to poor, the index may have to take account of the fact that the prices of goods and services bought by the poor have increased proportionately more than the prices of goods and services bought by the rich. In this case the effect on welfare of the redistribution might be more than offset by the change

3

in relative prices. A third precaution when comparing the national income for two different years is to look at the general quality of goods produced. The quantity of goods and services produced could be precisely the same in the two years—so many chairs, so many newspapers, so many haircuts; but economic welfare might have changed because of a general improvement or deterioration in quality—a typical daily newspaper, for example, might have more or fewer pages. A fourth precaution is to take account of changes in the stock of capital and in the size of the population over the period we are considering. Not only individuals but nations can live off their capital (it was done on an enormous scale during the war) and, to obtain a truer picture of economic welfare, it is necessary to set aside that part of the income which ought to be devoted to maintaining capital intact. With regard to population, a distinction must be made between a change in *total* real income from one year to another, and a change in real income *per head*; and a great deal depends on whether the heads are young or old or middle-aged. Finally, one highly important constituent of welfare, namely leisure, does not figure in the national income statistics. It is always open to a community to take out part of a rising standard of living in the form of increased leisure, and it must not complain that the real national income has not increased if, over the same period, the average working week has fallen from, say, 44 to 40 hours.

This hedging about with qualifications need not deter us from making frequent use of national income statistics. They are now the everyday tools of the social economist, and the important thing is not to be able to recite and evaluate all the possible modifications but to know in what circumstances each of them is significant. Nevertheless, there has been a growing distaste among economists for the simple correlation of national income changes with changes in welfare, and this may be one reason why the statisticians have increasingly diverted their energies into the more specialised study of social accounting.

In a broad sense social accounting is merely a more learned

phrase for the tabulation of national income statistics, but in a narrower sense it means the application of the methods of accountancy to the flows of money which take place *within* the general framework of the national income.   Every transaction represents income for one person, or firm, or group, or sector of the economy, and expenditure to another.   It is therefore possible to build up a set of social accounts showing how the transactions balance as between different persons, firms, groups or sectors.   This method of exposition is extremely valuable for demonstrating the effect on the distribution of the national income of the operations of, for example, the National Insurance Fund.   It can follow the course of the various currents and counter-currents in the general national income stream; and it will clearly be of increasing value to the social economist as more detailed information, e.g. figures of local income and expenditure for regions, industries and small social communities, is collected and analysed.

§ 8. Economic Planning and Social Policy.

We have seen that the social consequences of economic behaviour can often be worked out in terms of its effect on the economic welfare of the community and on the objective counterpart of that economic welfare—the real national income.   But we considered only two aspects of the national income; its size and its distribution.   The objection to this type of analysis is that it is too 'static'; it assumes that the total amount of resources available to produce the national income remains much the same from year to year; and that cyclical fluctuations—the alternation of periods of prosperity and depression in which these resources are very fully or very inadequately employed—are simply, so to speak, a nuisance: economic welfare would be greater if employment were steady rather than fluctuating, but there is nothing more to it than that.   This does not imply that from the beginning welfare economics did not regard unemployment as a serious problem.   Indeed the suggestions in the earliest edition of Professor Pigou's work regarding the dominant causes of unemployment and possible remedies for it are remarkably modern. But it was not clear at that time that, even if the fluctuations were ironed out, the resultant steadier flow of output might still leave a considerable pool of unemployed resources, in other words that there could be equilibrium at less than full employment. In more recent times two facts have become clearer which call for a more 'dynamic' approach to the analysis of social consequences, as we have called it. One is that the activities of individual producers and consumers can be, and often need to be, influenced and supplemented by the economic policy of the State in order to maintain, not only a *stable* level of employment and output but also a *high* level of employment and output. The other is that economic progress is not simply a matter of improving the size or distribution of the national income, and therefore of economic welfare, by removing hindrances to the efficient utilisation of given resources. It is much more a matter of increasing the stock of one type of resource, namely productive capital, and achieving the co-operation of the other resources in such a way that the national income rides, so to speak, on a steadily rising wave. Moreover, there is evidence that cyclical fluctuations in the shorter term, and economic progress in the longer term, are not unconnected, in the sense that they both have something to do with the rate of investment, the pace at which the stock of capital is replaced and added to. These matters will be referred to in Chapter V. For the present it is clear that some social problems such as unemployment and poverty may require for their solution not only the removal of hindrances to the best use of given resources and a redistribution of the product of those resources: they may also require deliberate supervision by the State of the movement of total income, output, investment and a number of other 'aggregates' with a view to the achievement of full employment and economic progress. In this way national income statistics become both the tools of economic analysis and the 'barometers' of economic and social policy, indicating what is happening to the economic weather.

CHAPTER II

POPULATION

§ **1. Population and Social Economics.** 'With every mouth God sends a pair of hands' runs the old saying, implying that, whatever other sorts of problem may arise in connection with population, the economic problem has been providentially solved. For economics is concerned with the behaviour of human beings as producers and consumers, and the proverb says that every new child brings with it the power not only to consume but also to produce. There is even a suggestion, for those of simple faith, that the latter power should exceed the former: we are blessed with only *one* mouth, but with *two* hands.

Nevertheless, there are economic problems connected with population, and especially with changes in the size and structure of the population; and it is not necessary to look far, or indeed show any lack of faith or irreverence, to discover how such problems arise. While each member of the population is initially provided with the means both to produce and to consume, the ability to exercise those powers varies enormously according to age, sex, intelligence, training and opportunity; and the willingness to do so varies according to taste, character and circumstance. Even if in total the hands produced enough to satisfy all the mouths, there would still be the problem of redistributing the product. As things are, the mouths are insatiable, the hands are reluctant; in other words, the potential demand of consumers for goods and services of all kinds is unlimited; the potential supply of those goods and services is restricted, partly by the ability and the willingness of people to work, partly by the limitations of the land, materials and equipment with which they work.

This general problem of scarcity in relation to demand is of course the basis of all economic study. The particular task of the present chapter is to isolate, as far as possible, the influence upon it of the size and composition of the population. We may assume that the economic welfare of a country can be roughly measured in terms of real national income per head, that is, the value, at constant prices, of the total national output of goods and services, divided by the total population. We must then ask in what sense a country's population may be too small or too large, and what effects a growing or declining population is likely to have on real national income per head. Finally, we shall describe the population structure of Great Britain and discuss the changes that are taking place.

Before proceeding, however, two further points should be noted. To take real national income per head as the measure of economic welfare is to emphasise the effect of population changes on the *production* of the national income rather than on its *distribution* among consumers. This is not to say that population changes do not influence both the distribution of income before taxation and its redistribution after taxation.

The other point is that the study of population problems leads very quickly to the frontiers of economics. The description of population changes and the analysis of their effect on the national income is well within the province of the social economist. He soon finds it necessary, however, to go one stage further and ask why the population changes themselves occur. Here he finds himself face to face with a whole host of social forces, the assessment of some of which can be more competently undertaken by the sociologist, the demographer, the statistician and the biologist. Why do people have larger or smaller families? Why do they marry earlier or live longer? Why do they emigrate? Which influences are likely to be permanent and which temporary? Are the temporary influences likely to recur? . . . and so on.[1]

[1] Professor Bowen provides a useful classification of the forces determining population change in his *Population* (Cambridge Economic Handbooks, 1954), pp. 10–12 and Table I.

Some of these forces are economic. In consequence, there may emerge an endless chain of cause and effect: changes in the size and distribution of the national income may affect population growth, which in turn may influence the national income. The Malthusian theory of population, in its simplest form, is based on this interaction.

Thus, population is only one of the determinants of national income, and economic forces are only part of the complex of forces which cause populations to grow, decline or stand still.

§ 2. The Size of the Population.

In what sense may the population of a country be too small? The extreme case is not difficult to envisage. An isolated community, consisting of only a few people, would necessarily have a primitive and undeveloped economy. The search for food would probably occupy most of their time and energies, but even if they lived in a Garden of Eden, some tasks, such as the construction of large buildings or bridges, would be impossible through sheer lack of manpower (as anyone who has been in charge of a camp of small boys and had to put up a fairly large marquee will testify).

More significant, however, would be the restricted scope for specialisation, or the division of labour. Even within the smallest social unit, the family, some specialisation is possible, and the result is that far more of the necessary work gets done than if everybody did everything for himself. As a society becomes larger, the advantages of specialisation increase. Workers with special aptitudes can work full time at their specialised tasks and so increase the total output proportionately more than the increase in numbers, and the larger society also provides a larger *market* for the product of the specialised worker. A village becomes large enough to support a whole-time baker; a town becomes large enough to support a whole-time fire brigade; a country becomes large enough to support whole-time specialists in diseases of the eye. The specialised worker might be able to perfect his skill in a smaller community, but he would not have enough customers to make it worth while for him to exercise that skill continuously. He would have to spend some of his time in unspecialised, or diverse, activities, and so reduce his total output.

Output is produced, however, not by labour alone, but by labour working on land and with capital. Capital and land may also be put to specialised uses, with advantages similar to those that accrue to specialised labour. If therefore a larger population were accompanied by a larger amount of land of the same quality and a larger stock of capital of suitable kinds, there would be unlimited economies of large-scale production and the only threat to a continually rising real income per head would perhaps be the danger of a breakdown in the increasingly complex organisation of the economic system.

For various reasons, however, the availability of larger amounts of suitable land and capital is restricted, and this is why the population of a country may be too large. First, there are physical restrictions. There was a time when, within the total area of land available on the earth's surface, large tracts of agricultural land were unoccupied; now, the most fertile land has been cultivated. Other things remaining the same, larger populations can obtain larger food supplies only by cultivating less fertile land or by working the existing agricultural land more intensively. Be it noted that this is not necessarily a situation of food shortage. Certainly, in some parts of the world, where the standard of living is very low, the pressure of a large population on a limited area of cultivable land is the obvious cause of poverty. But the principle would apply equally in a very rich country: other things remaining the same, a larger population would enjoy a lower real income per head—say, fewer motor-cars and television sets—than a smaller population, because the limited amount of agricultural land calls for more resources in order to yield the same amount of food per head.

As with agricultural land, so it is with one particular form of capital, namely, the raw materials of industry. The total known supply is limited and the additional requirements of a larger population may be obtainable only by exploiting less fertile sources.

Could not such restrictions be overcome by the advance of technical knowledge? New ways of doing things are continually being invented and applied, both in agriculture and in industry; and in fact the dangers of over-population have often been avoided in the past by the application of new techniques which increased the yield of a given amount of land or capital. But the state of technical knowledge at any time and place may nevertheless be a restrictive force. An area may be over-populated which, if it could make use of more advanced techniques of production and organisation (without necessarily any change in the *amount* of land and capital per head), would be able to raise output per head to the level it enjoyed with a smaller population.

A third restrictive force is that of time. Even assuming no technical progress, the creation of additional capital for the use of a larger population (whether in agriculture or industry) takes time and can be speeded up only to the extent that people refrain from current consumption. The problem is most serious in countries where the population is living 'from hand to mouth' and where any increase in output, instead of providing an addition to the stock of capital goods, seems to be immediately swallowed up, almost mortgaged in advance, by the urgent demands of consumers. But it could also arise in a country with a high standard of living that the growth of population took place faster than the growth of capital equipment.

To introduce the element of time, however, is to alter the whole nature of the analysis. Given time, not only the amount of capital equipment, but also the state of technical knowledge and economic organisation, the knowledge of sources of raw materials, even the natural fertility of land, may change. Moreover, once we begin to discuss a *growing* population, rather than simply compare a larger with a smaller population, we ought to take account of the changes in population structure that accompany growth. In short, we have been engaged in a static and not a dynamic analysis. We have assumed that one component, the size of the population, changes, while everything else, land, capital, technique and so on, remains fixed.

The static analysis is, however, a good starting point, for it does show that *at any one time*, in relation to the existing resources of land and capital and the existing state of technique and organisation, the population may be too large or too small; and in certain countries the size of the population is the main economic problem. Just as a machine may produce its maximum output per worker when it has a team of five workers, but a lower output per worker when it has a team of four or six, and a much lower output with one or ten, so there is in theory an optimum population for getting the most out of the resources of a country at any one time: it is the population which produces the maximum output per head. A larger or smaller population would mean a lower national income per head, or, to put it another way: up to this point an increase in population would yield increasing returns, beyond this point an increase in population would yield diminishing returns.

There is one further complication. No country is self-contained, and to the extent that a country engages in international trade the advantages of specialisation increase beyond the limits set by its own population and resources. A country which, in relation to its internal resources of land, capital, technique and so on had been over-populated, might find that, as a result of developments in international transport, or the removal of tariff barriers, or the advent of a stable government in another country, its horizon was extended so that it could with a larger population enjoy a higher real income per head. Similarly the impoverishment of overseas markets or the erection of new barriers could transform a country from a condition of under-population to one of over-population. The existing possibilities of international trade must therefore be combined with the existing internal resources of a country in order to complete the environment in which its population is set.

What is external to any country, however, is an internal factor from the point of view of the world as a whole, and here we meet one of the special difficulties of the concept of world-population. It is possible, in theory, to say that the world as a whole is over-populated or under-populated, using the same static analysis as in the case of a single country. But the optimum world population is of little significance apart from its distribution among different regions, some of which may be relatively over-populated and some relatively under-populated; and the movement of people and resources between different parts of the world, unlike that between parts of a particular country, is restricted.

The conclusion is not that, if there were completely free international trade and migration, there would be no population problem. It is rather that changes in the structure and distribution of the population are of more interest than changes in its total numbers.

§ 3. The Measurement of Population Change.

Before turning from the simple discussion of population size to that of population growth or decline, it is useful to examine some of the techniques of measuring population changes. Such knowledge is helpful both for understanding the past and for forecasting the future. As regards the past, much light has been shed on the course of economic history by the more careful interpretation of population statistics. Forecasts of future population, on the other hand, have often generated more heat than light, and more and more elaborate indices of population change have been devised in an attempt to distinguish the fundamental, or long-run trends in population from those which are temporary or abnormal. This section describes some of these indices.

The simplest procedure is to take the figures of a country's total population over a period of years, and work out an *annual rate of change*, that is, show that the total population increases or decreases at so many per cent per annum (it is usual to express the rate as so many per thousand) between the years for which figures are available. This by itself will indicate certain trends not immediately apparent in the original figures. It might show, for example, that although the total population was continually increasing, the rate of increase was slowing down; or, in a table of figures from several countries, that the rate of increase was much higher in some countries than in others.

The annual rate of change cannot be explained, however, nor can it be said whether it is likely to continue in one direction or another, unless it is broken down into its constituent parts. Changes in the total population result from net emigration or net immigration, and from natural increase (more births than deaths) or natural decrease (the opposite). Migration has been all-important in the development of some countries at certain periods of their history, and it has at times occurred in recognisable waves or cycles. But natural increase or decrease is a more permanent and fundamental element in population change. The other indices are all concerned with the measurement of births and deaths.

The *crude birth rate* is the number of births per year for each thousand of the total population. Similarly the *crude death rate* is the number of deaths per year for each thousand of the population. The gap between them is the annual rate of natural increase or decrease, which obviously cannot be explained, nor can any forecast be attempted, without asking what is happening to birth and death rates respectively. The rate of natural increase might, for example, be constant over a period of years, either because birth and death rates were both constant, or because they were both falling, or because they were both rising. But one question leads to another. If the birth rate is falling, is it because people are less willing to have children, or because there are fewer women of child-bearing age, though the willingness to have children remains the same? Similarly if the death rate is rising, is it because mortality is increasing or because there are more people in the age-groups which normally have a high mortality rate? A change in the crude birth rate, in other words, is the combined result of changes in fertility and in the age-distribution of the population; likewise a change in the crude death rate results from changes in mortality and in age-distribution. With given fertility and mortality rates the change in the age-structure of the population can be worked out fairly reliably from one generation to the next. Fertility and mortality are the unpredictable elements in population change.

Thus the next stage is to work out *age-specific fertility rates*, showing the number of births per year for each thousand persons of each age; and *age-specific mortality rates*, showing the number of deaths per year for each thousand persons of each age. In Great Britain the tendency has been for mortality rates to fall steadily over a long period; so that the basic variable item in the population pattern seems to be the fertility rate. Consequently *the fertility rate* is often expressed as a single figure of the number of births per year for each thousand women of child-bearing age (which is assumed to be 15 to 45).

Since the 1930's a new device, which seems to give a simple answer to the simple question 'Is the population replacing itself?' has been widely used in preference to the fertility rate. This is the *reproduction rate*. It shows to what extent that heroic band of women from 15 to 45 is replaced from one generation to the next. Briefly, the calculation consists of taking 1,000 baby girls born in, say, 1954, and following through their life history to the age of 45, applying year by year the age-specific fertility rates of 1954. The result is a new generation of children, from which the boys have to be eliminated. If there remain 1,000 girls in this new generation, the *gross reproduction rate* for 1954 is 1, if there remain 1,200 girls it is 1·2, if 800 it is 0·8, and so on. The *net reproduction rate* is obtained by applying also the age-specific mortality rates for 1954 to the original 1,000 babies in order to eliminate those likely to die before reaching the age of 45. A net reproduction rate of 1 means that the population is just replacing itself. The Registrar General for England and Wales, in his annual Statistical Review, introduces a further refinement by allowing for the probable continuation of the long-period fall in mortality rates. His device, called the *effective reproduction rate*, is therefore higher than the net reproduction rate because it results from applying, not the actual mortality rates of 1954, but the estimated mortality rates for each of the subsequent forty-five years.

A net reproduction rate of 1 was for many years popularly accepted as the simple indicator of a healthy population. Yet recently this device also has come into disfavour. The calculation is made with the aid of age-specific fertility rates of a recent year. These rates may in fact fluctuate from year to year, and the net reproduction rate with them, even though the ultimate degree of replacement remains the same. If people decide to postpone marriage because of a depression, or to space their children at longer intervals, fertility rates will fall over the period in which these changes occur. Conversely a wave of early marriages, such as occurred in Britain after the war, or a speeding-up of the rate at which families are completed will bring a temporary increase in fertility rates. But if the ultimate size of families is not altered, replacement is not affected and the movements of the net reproduction rate are misleading.

Accordingly the statisticians have developed 'marriage-standardised' reproduction rates which allow not only for the likelihood of survival but also for the likelihood of marriage at different ages. But, although this last point may be of vital interest to some readers, they must be warned that information about it, as well as information about the average size of completed families, can be obtained only by studying the history of the last generation. The demographic habits of the present generation may be different; and we shall not know for another decade or two.

Meanwhile there is no harm in saying that a *persistent* rise in the net reproduction rate would probably represent an eventual increase in the average size of family; and in Britain at least, many people would regard such an increase as desirable.

§ **4. The Problems of an Expanding Population.** It follows from what has been said above that an expanding population is not simply one in which the birth rate is higher than the death rate. In addition, the fertility and mortality rates must be such as to ensure replacement. Given such an expanding population, there are several reasons why the economy will tend to be buoyant and national income per head will tend to increase.

If resources other than labour are in fixed supply but are not fully utilised, an expanding population will probably yield increasing returns up to the point of full employment of all resources: in other words, 10 per cent increase in the labour force alone may result in more than 10 per cent increase in total output. If the other resources are not fixed in supply but can be expanded together with the population there may be increasing returns to scale: 10 per cent increase in all the factors of production may result in more than 10 per cent increase in total output because of the economies of large-scale production. At the same time the expanding population will provide a growing market and greater opportunities of specialisation. A high level of employment is likely to be maintained because of the continuous growth in total demand: in particular the danger of a decline in investment and in the incomes of those who are producing investment goods will be avoided if expanding population provides a continuing demand for *new* houses, machines and factories. Structural changes in industry will take place more smoothly, and unemployment on this account will be less likely, if the whole economy is expanding; that is, the movement of labour and capital from declining to expanding industries will more easily be absorbed in the general flow of resources into and out of industry as a whole. Finally, the growth of output results not only from the employment of more labour and capital of the existing types and qualities, but also from the development of more efficient techniques of production and the invention of new machines; and here also an expanding population is likely to be more efficient because of the high proportion of young and enterprising workers and entrepreneurs in industry.

Nevertheless it is clearly possible for population to expand too rapidly and output per head to decline, if other resources do not expand fast enough. In a country that already has a high standard of living, such a situation would require the diversion of resources from producing consumer goods to producing capital goods, in order to maintain or increase the amount of capital per head of the working population and, ultimately, the flow of consumer goods. In a subsistence economy, either there is no margin of consumption to allow of such a diversion, or any small increase in output achieved by new investment is immediately swallowed up by the increase in population. This was the spectre that haunted Thomas Robert Malthus.

Malthus published his first *Essay on the Principle of Population* in 1798 and his second and much more elaborate version in 1803.

He believed that there was an inherent tendency for population to increase faster than the supply of food. This being so, an increase in food production would yield no permanent increase in the standard of living, because the increase in population would overtake it and the amount of food per head would again be sufficient only for bare subsistence. The tendency for population to increase would therefore be periodically checked, either by actual food shortage, i.e. death through famine, under-nourishment and disease, which he called 'positive checks' or 'misery'; or by practices resorted to under threat of a food shortage, such as the postponement or prevention of the birth of children, which he called 'preventive checks' or 'vice'. In the second edition of his Essay he added a further check, called 'moral restraint'; which was his only hope of keeping the population in balance with the supply of food without the intervention of misery and vice.

The basis of Malthus's belief cannot be discussed here.[1] But it is worth pointing out, since he is so often misunderstood, that he thought he was making adequate allowance for im-

[1] An elaborate critique will be found in Bowen, *op. cit.*, Chapter IV.

provements in agricultural production and variations in the import of food. His theory was not based on diminishing returns from land; nor on a mistaken assumption that the birth rate was rising. His causal relationship was not entirely that the food supply determined population: he allowed for the possibility that population would itself influence the food supply; there would, he thought, be a periodic fall in the price of labour and a consequent increase in employment and labour productivity in agriculture. But whatever might happen for a time, population would outstrip the food supply and the growing numbers be reduced by misery or vice, *unless* the power of population to increase could be curbed by moral restraint. And by moral restraint he meant the postponement of marriage until such a time as people could maintain a family at a reasonable standard of comfort. He abhorred the practices which have since been wrongly called 'Neo-Malthusianism'.

As the nineteenth century advanced, England was able to draw on food supplies undreamed of, in kind as well as in quantity, by Malthus, and the growth in population did not take place at the rate that he envisaged. Even so, it was a spectacular growth and our ability to feed it was providential. The birth rate fell, however, and with it the average size of the family, from the middle of the nineteenth century onwards. The *motives* underlying this decline are numerous and most of them would come under the heading of an increased responsibility on the part of parents and would earn Malthus's approval. Whether the *methods* of family limitation would have been classified by him as 'moral restraint' or 'vice' is another matter.

The problems of an expanding population are not now discussed in relation to the industrial nations of the West, but to the so-called 'under-developed countries'. In these countries the problem is not unlike that of Britain 150 years ago. As medical knowledge spreads, mortality rates fall, and food supplies must keep pace with the growing population. Indeed food supplies must grow *faster* than population in order to

4

relieve the under-nourishment of the existing population. Many calculations have been made of the probable trends in world population and world food production, and some of them point to a divergence as serious as that envisaged by Malthus. But we now have knowledge and experience which Malthus did not have, and it may well be that the problem will again be solved, partly by the application of vastly increased scientific knowledge to the task of food production, partly by the spread of 'moral restraint' in all its forms as the people of these countries attain higher standards of living and education. In addition, the twentieth century has a new characteristic: a conviction that these problems are an international responsibility and that their solution is a matter for international co-operation.

§ 5. **The Population Pattern of Great Britain.** We must now look at the population structure of Britain and see what is happening to its total numbers, how it is distributed by age and sex, where people live, and in what industries and occupations they work. Most of the information on these questions comes from three sources: The *Census of Population* has actually counted the heads every ten years since 1801 (except in 1941) and classified them according to place of residence and place of birth, age, sex, civil status and occupation. The *Registrar General's Statistical Review* provides annual estimates based on information about births, deaths and migration since the previous Census. The *Ministry of Labour Gazette* publishes monthly tables relating to the working population, showing how the total manpower is distributed among industries, how many are unemployed, how many in the Forces, and so on. The principal figures on these and many other subjects are published regularly by the Central Statistical Office in its *Monthly Digest of Statistics* and *Annual Abstract of Statistics*. In using these documents the student must be careful to note whether the figures relate to England and Wales or to Great Britain (including Scotland) or to the United Kingdom (including Northern Ireland).

(a) *Total population.* It is most convenient to begin with the figures for Great Britain. Table I shows the census totals from the first census in 1801 to the most recent in 1951.

Table I. Population in Great Britain

Year	Population (millions)	Percentage increase on preceding total
1801	10·5	
1811	12·0	14
1821	14·1	18
1831	16·3	16
1841	18·5	13
1851	20·8	12
1861	23·1	11
1871	26·1	13
1881	29·7	14
1891	33·0	11
1901	37·0	12
1911	40·8	10
1921	42·8	5
1931	44·8	5
1941	46·6[1]	4
1951	48·9	5

[1] Estimated. No census was taken in 1941.

It is clear at a glance that the total population increased with amazing rapidity between 1801 and 1841, a little less rapidly from 1841 to 1911, and at a distinctly slower pace from 1911 to 1951.

The part played by migration in this growth of total population was that a net loss by migration slightly reduced the rate of growth except during the decade 1931–1941, when there was a net gain by migration. There has long been a substantial flow of immigrants from Ireland, and from time to time a much smaller flow from Europe; but in the late nineteenth and early twentieth centuries these gains were more than offset by emigration to the United States and the Dominions. Had there been no net loss by migration in the sixty years 1851–1911, the Census in the latter year would probably have registered about 44 millions instead of 40·8. In the 1930's the outflow to the United States and the Dominions became insignificant, but it was resumed in the ten years following the second world war. A movement which is concealed in the figures for Great Britain is the continuous net emigration from Scotland, both across the border and overseas. Between 1901 and 1951 the net loss of the Scottish population by migration amounted to 63 per cent of the natural increase for that period (compared with 12 per cent for Great Britain as a whole), and in the decade 1921–1931 the loss by migration was greater than the natural increase. Patriotic Scots view this movement with mixed feelings. They are proud of their reputation as colonisers. They are alarmed at the fact that the proportion of males, and young and energetic males at that, is higher among the emigrants than in the population as a whole. In an expanding population this would not matter. But when the rate of expansion is slowing down, as it is in all parts of Great Britain, the export of young men has two unfavourable consequences: it reduces the number of eligible bachelors, and it lowers the proportion of the working to the dependent population.

To return to our Table: the great expansion of the nineteenth century was not the result, as was once supposed, of a rising birth rate. The birth rate was high and remained high until the 1880's, but the major cause of population growth was an almost continuous fall in the death rate. This decline began in the mid-eighteenth century and has been maintained up to the present day. It is difficult to give comparable figures over long periods, but the measure of the change is that in 1750 the death rate was probably between 25 and 30 per thousand, in 1850 it was between 20 and 25 per thousand, and in 1950 it was 12 per thousand. Better standards of nutrition and clothing, improved sanitation and public health services, and the growth of medical science have all contributed to this remarkable change, the more remarkable when we look at mortality rates (i.e. death rates for particular age groups) and see that, for example, mortality of children under 4 is only one-tenth of what it was eighty years ago.

While the death rate has continued to fall, however, it is to the birth rate that we must look for an explanation of the most recent trends in total population. In the century from 1780 to 1880 the birth rate moved roughly between 30 and 35 per thousand. Between 1880 and 1930 it fell to about 15 per thousand, and, following a slight jump during and after the war, settled at 15–16 in the early 1950's. There is not general agreement about the causes of this decline. They are certainly not entirely economic. But the fall in the birth rate has been accompanied by a fairly continuous rise in the standard of living and by significant developments in education, and the interaction of higher incomes and better education may account for a great deal. Compulsory education makes the upbringing of children more expensive, because, even if it is free, it postpones the day when they can supplement the family earnings. And to the extent that it is not free, there comes a stage at which parents who have discovered the benefits of education make great sacrifices, even limiting the size of their families, in order to purchase it for their children. On the other hand higher incomes, which would enable parents to support larger families at a given standard, may be used to provide, instead, higher material standards for themselves or higher educational standards for their (smaller) families. The widespread use of contraceptives, though often assumed to be a cause of family limitation, is not itself a cause, but rather a means by which such limitation has been achieved.

When we turn to examine the present position, we need, for reasons explained in section 3, to use more reliable indices than birth and death rates. We must take account of the changes in age distribution which characterise a declining population—and from this point of view it does not matter whether the total number is decreasing, or increasing at a diminishing rate.

(b) *Age and sex distribution.* The most useful ages for dividing the population are 15, 45 and 65. It is generally true that the under 15's and the over 65's constitute the dependent population, who consume more than they currently produce; and even if the school-leaving age and the retiring age are not fixed, the numbers and proportions of the population in these groups are of obvious significance. A division at the age of 45 is also valuable because it separates the younger from the older working population and, in the case of the women, isolates the age-group from which the next generation of children must come. Table II shows how these groups have moved in relation to one another in the last fifty years.

Here is the evidence that Britain has an ageing population. Since 1901 the percentage of males over 45 has increased from 18 to 32, of females from 20 to 37. When the age-structure changes in this way, the modal age-group, i.e. the age-group with most people in it, moves up, year by year, from the bottom of the age-scale. This is why the birth and death rates, being related to the total population, are less reliable as indicators of fundamental trends than are fertility and mortality rates. The substantial fall in the birth rate which we have already discussed was in fact less than the fall in the fertility rate, at least until 1931. In the early years of this century, although fertility was falling, the number and proportion of women in the child-bearing age-group was still increasing, partly because the modal age-group was moving up into the 15–45 range, partly because the fall in mortality rates was most effective among infants, so that many more children survived beyond the age of 15. Between 1870 and 1930 the birth rate fell by about 55 per cent, the fertility rate by about 65 per cent.

Similar arguments apply to the relative behaviour of mortality rates and death rates. In the past the combination of a rapidly falling infant mortality rate with a high proportion of the population in the lowest age groups probably meant that the death rate for the population as a whole was falling more rapidly than the mortality rate for the population as a whole. In the next few decades, while general mortality rates may continue to fall, the death rate will rise because of the growing proportion of people in the higher age groups.

Table II.　Age Distribution of the Population of Great Britain

Age-group	Number in 000's			Percentage of Total		
	1901	1931	1951	1901	1931	1951
MALES						
0–14	6,022	5,466	5,588	34	25	24
15–44	8,522	10,036	10,249	48	47	44
45–64	2,609	4,532	5,426	14	21	23
65 and over	749	1,425	2,188	4	7	9
Total	17,902	21,459	23,450	100	100	100
FEMALES						
0–14	6,019	5,359	5,360	32	23	21
15–44	9,204	10,980	10,620	48	47	42
45–64	2,889	5,105	6,280	15	22	25
65 and over	985	1,892	3,145	5	8	12
Total	19,097	23,336	25,404	100	100	100

Thus, whatever happens to fertility and mortality, there seems no escape, in the next decade or so, from two unfavourable consequences of the ageing population: (1) a shrinkage in the age-group 15–45, where fertility rates are effective; (2) an expansion in the age-group 65 plus, where mortality rates are high. To look further ahead, we should have to engage in the exciting game of population forecasting on a much more elaborate scale than is possible in this chapter.[1] But we can at least take note of what is happening to the index that purports to measure long-term replacement: the net reproduction rate. This index, which in the late 1930's showed no sign of rising above 0·8 (i.e. 20 per cent below replacement), rose to 1·1 in 1946 and remained above 1·0 right up to 1953. It is too early to say whether or not this indicates a permanent increase in fertility, for the main cause was a substantial increase in the marriage rate in the years 1945–1948, an increase that did not continue in subsequent years. The arrival of the first and second children of these post-war marriages is bound to raise the fertility rate, and the net reproduction rate, for a time; but in due course the rate will revert to less than 1 unless there is an increase in the average size of completed families.

In mid-Victorian times the average size of family was five or six children; nowadays it is just over two. This last figure, however, is based on a census, carried out in 1946, of marriages in 1925. It may be that the completed families of post-war marriages will average three, four or five children. It is sometimes maintained that the last generation of parents was exceptionally conscious of the disadvantages of the large Victorian families in which they had grown up; and that the present generation of parents is equally conscious of the disadvantages of the small families in which *they* grew up; with the result that larger families are again fashionable. But there is as yet no evidence of this.

For statistical purposes, one interesting consequence of the 'post-war baby boom' is that, if the population is divided into age-groups of five years, the lowest age-group, of children aged 0–4, was in 1951 the most thickly populated, the next largest being the age-group 40–44. This explains why in Table II the actual numbers of children aged 0–14 were higher in 1951 than in 1931, and the percentages only slightly lower.

Before leaving Table II we should notice the main features of the sex distribution of Britain's population. Each year

[1] The reader is referred to the *Report of the Royal Commission on Population* (1949), Chapters 8 and 9; and Bowen, *op. cit.*, Chapter III, Section 1.

more boys are born than girls, but the infant mortality rate is higher for boys, with the result that from the age of about 15 onwards the females predominate. Moreover, the females show greater relative powers of survival in later years: in the age-group 65 and over, we find in 1951 nearly 50 per cent more women than men. They seem to have greater ability to resist the diseases and stresses of life, and of course they are less exposed to occupational and other hazards.

(c) *Geographical distribution.* The Census of Population naturally provides complete information about where people live, or at least where they were living at 12 o'clock on the night of the Census. These facts about locality are of interest to demographers, geographers, town-planners, market research officers and students in many branches of the social sciences. To give one fascinating example: a report on the cost of the National Health Service published in 1956 analysed the hospital population on the night of the Census in order to find out what sorts of people require hospital care. Comparisons between one Census and another will of course show significant changes in the relative importance of different regions, districts, towns and so forth. Such changes may occur through differences in the rates of natural increase in different parts of the country, but they are more likely to be the result of migration, and the main reason for internal migration is economic: people move to the places where they find suitable work.

By taking a brief look at the geographical distribution as it is summarised in the *Annual Abstract of Statistics*, we can add one or two interesting features to our sketch of the population pattern of Great Britain. If we examine the distribution between 'urban and rural districts', we find that in 1951, 81 per cent of the population of England and Wales lived in towns. In 1851, only 50 per cent were town-dwellers; in 1911, 78 per cent. In Scotland, the distribution is different, and so is the language. There, in 1951, 70 per cent lived in 'cities and burghs' and 30 per cent in 'landward areas'; but the trend is similar, the percentage of town-dwellers having increased from 52 in 1851 and 66 in 1911.

When we turn to the regional distribution, we find evidence of the so-called 'drift to the south'. Forty years ago the Scottish, Northern, E. and W. Riding, North-Western and North Midland Regions together accounted for 48 per cent of the total population of Great Britain. In 1951 their share had fallen to 45 per cent.

The distribution between urban and rural areas, though it shows to what a striking degree the people of this country live in towns, may be misleading because of the definitions used. Quite small towns are classed as urban areas, and it must not be imagined that four-fifths of the population cannot see a tree or a field from their bedroom windows. We can probably obtain a more realistic picture of the concentration in towns by taking certain areas which have come to be known as 'conurbations', where 'a number of separate towns have grown into each other or become linked by such factors as a common industrial or business interest or a common centre for shopping or education'. The Census distinguishes seven conurbations: Greater London, West Midlands, West Yorkshire, South-east Lancashire, Merseyside, Tyneside and Central Clydeside. In 1951 these areas together contained 18·7 million people, and Greater London, with 8·3 million, was by far the largest.

(d) *Distribution by industry.* In the discussion of Table II, a rough division of the population into 'producers' and 'dependants' was suggested by placing those aged 15–65 in the first category and those under 15 and over 65 in the second. By this definition the 'producers' of 1951 totalled 15·7 million males and 16·9 million females. To complete our study we must ask in what industries and activities the producers are engaged; but for this purpose the total needs to be defined more precisely, to exclude those who are not yet earning their living, even if they are over 15, and to include those who are still at work even though they are above the usual retiring age of 65. The women present a special difficulty, not only because from one point of view, that of pensions, the usual retiring age is 60, but chiefly because we can only take account of those who do *paid* work, and the majority of women are engaged in the vital but for our purposes unrecognised activity of unpaid housekeeping. The injustice of this is not lessened by the fact that even after their husbands have retired and they themselves have reached pensionable age, they are expected to remain active as unpaid housekeepers, with the menfolk as unpaid assistants.

The two most useful sets of figures relate to the 'occupied population', as defined in the census, and the 'working population', as defined by the Ministry of Labour. The occupied population consists of all persons gainfully employed in the country at the time of the Census; and it is classified both by industry and by occupation. In many cases the headings and the figures in these two classifications do not differ greatly, but for questions relating to the mobility of labour, the differences may be quite important: a man occupied as a carpenter, for example, may be employed in a steelworks or a textile factory, so that if he became unemployed it would be much easier for him to find another job than would appear from the industrial classification. For the study of larger problems relating to changes in the structure of industry, however, the industrial classification is the more relevant. It should also be remembered that all questions of labour distribution are liable to be influenced by trade union membership, which is sometimes on a craft or occupational basis, sometimes on an industry basis, and sometimes on a general basis covering a wide range of industries and occupations.

The big disadvantage of the Census figures is that they appear only every ten years. For discussion of current problems the analysis of the working population, published monthly by the Ministry of Labour, must be used. These statistics also relate to persons 'who work for pay or gain' but they are derived from other sources, principally the cards stamped week by week for the purposes of the National Insurance Scheme. It was not until 1948 that the insurance scheme covered the whole occupied population. Thus, although the Ministry of Labour has for many years supplemented its insurance figures by returns from other sources, a consistent and comprehensive set of estimates of the working population has been available only since 1948.

Here are some of the total manpower figures that we have been discussing:

Great Britain: Manpower in millions

	Males	Females	Total
Total population aged 15–64:			
1951 Census	15·7	16·9	32·6
Occupied population (excluding unemployed): 1951 Census . . .	15·3	6·8	22·1
Working population (including unemployed): June 1951	15·9	7·3	23·2
Working population (including unemployed): December 1956 . . .	16·2	7·9	24·1

Thus the total working population has now reached 24 millions and, according to most estimates, is not likely to vary much either above or below that total in the next twenty years, unless the proportion of women doing paid work (at present about 40 per cent of those aged 15–64) shows a substantial change. The occupied population is less than the working population chiefly because it excludes the unemployed[1] and anyone out of the country at the time of the Census; and there are many minor snags in dealing with these figures—in particular the definition of a part-time worker.

In making long-period comparisons of the distribution of labour among industries two further hazards must be borne in mind: that the official classification of industries changes frequently[2]; and that the householder's description, on his census form, of his occupation and industry may be vague, misleading or even deceptive. Nevertheless, the broad pat-

[1] For the first time in 1951. In the 1931 and earlier censuses, persons 'seeking gainful employment' but not actually employed were included.

[2] A Standard Industrial Classification has now been adopted both for the Census and for the Ministry of Labour Statistics.

terns of social change stand out fairly clearly. Let us take six groups which account for most of the occupied population and see what changes have occurred since the beginning of the century. First, the extractive industries, of which the most important are agriculture and coalmining, have declined from employing about 20 per cent to employing about 10 per cent of the labour force. Secondly, the whole range of manufacturing and building industries have increased their share from 35–40 to 40–45 per cent, and within this range the textile and clothing industries have lost the leading place and been superseded by the engineering and vehicle industries. The increased number of women in these expanding industries is especially noticeable. Thirdly, distribution and commerce (including transport, finance and wholesale and retail trade) still absorb, as they did fifty years ago, between 20 and 25 per cent of the labour force, and here again the increasing proportion of women is very marked. To the question where the women have come from, the answer is: partly from their homes, where they have fewer children and more leisure, partly from the textile and clothing industries, and partly from our fourth category, domestic service. It is difficult to realise that, in any Census taken at the end of the nineteenth century, domestic service was the second largest occupation[1] in the classified list, agriculture being the first. Now, private domestic service accounts for only 2 per cent of the occupied population or, if hotels and catering establishments are included, about 4 per cent. Lastly, we notice two categories which have been growing in numerical importance and probably even more in influential importance: public administration (central and local government service) and the professions—ministers, doctors, nurses, teachers, lawyers. Each of these employs between 5 and 10 per cent of the occupied population.

Against the background of historic change revealed in the Census statistics may be placed a recent analysis of the working population published by the Ministry of Labour and summarised in Table III.

[1] Occupations and industries were not at that time distinguished.

Table III.   Distribution of the Working Population of
Great Britain in December 1956

	Numbers in 000's	Percentage of Total
Civil Employment		
Agriculture, forestry and fishing	994	4
Mining and quarrying	859	4
Manufacturing industries	9,226	39
Building and contracting	1,491	6
Gas, electricity and water	378	2
Transport and communication	1,712	7
Distributive trades	2,904	12
Professional, financial and miscellaneous services	4,131	17
Public administration	1,294	5
Total civil employment	22,989	96
H.M. Forces	767	3
Unemployed	331	1
Total Working Population	24,087	100

If the industries are arranged in groups as above, it is easy to remember that for every 100 members of the working population, the distribution of activities is as follows:

Extracting	8	Serving	.	22
Manufacturing	47	Soldiering	.	3
Distributing	19	Nothing	.	1

This kind of mnemonic is especially useful as a reminder that, although Britain is a manufacturing nation, less than half the workers work in factories; and that two-fifths are engaged in taking goods from the factory to the consumer and providing services of all kinds.

It is also useful for the student of current affairs to have a rough idea of the orders of magnitude (a modern word meaning round figures) of employment in certain special industries. Some of these are conveniently near to multiples of 250,000, and a list is given below. Of course, they may change by the time this page is read, and the reader may modify the list by reference to the latest *Monthly Digest of Statistics* or *Economic Survey*; but it is surprising how constant, over the years, some of the orders of magnitude are. Incidentally the Ministry of Labour's figures for particular industries relate to employees only, while the analysis of the working population includes employers and self-employed persons. Here is the list for December 1955.

Unemployed, about	$\frac{1}{4}$ million
Coal, agriculture, H.M. Forces, each about . . .	$\frac{3}{4}$ million
Textiles and leather, together about. . . .	1 million
Vehicles, public administration, each about . . .	$1\frac{1}{4}$ million
Building, about	$1\frac{1}{2}$ million
Engineering, shipbuilding and electrical goods, together about	2 millions
Wholesale and retail distribution, together about . .	$2\frac{1}{4}$ millions

These account for $11\frac{3}{4}$ millions out of the total working population of 24 millions.

§ 6. **The Problems of an Ageing Population.** We have already seen that, because the rate of increase of the population of Great Britain is slowing down, the proportions of young and old are changing. Britain has an ageing population. In discussing its possible consequences we should bear in mind the forecasts of the Royal Commission of 1949 in regard to (i) the total population, (ii) the ratio of producers to dependants, (iii) the ratio of the young (under 15) to the old (over 65) among the dependants.

The Royal Commission makes its principal estimates on four assumptions: that the average size of family remains at its pre-war level; that marriage rates continue to be between the low level of 1942–4 and the high level of 1945–7: that mortality rates continue to decline; and that there is no net migration. On this basis it forecasts that the total population will continue to rise until about 1977, when it will reach a peak of 50·7 millions. On the same assumptions, the distribution among age-groups will change as shown below (the Census figures for 1951 have been inserted for comparison):

Percentage of Total Population in each Age-group

	0–14	15–40	41–64	65 *and over*
1947	21	37	31	11
1951	22	35	32	11
1977	19	34	31	16

From some points of view, a settling down of the total number of the population may be advantageous. Ours is a crowded island; it could not possibly be self-sufficient in food supplies, and every increase in numbers makes it more dependent on success in international trade for maintaining and increasing its standard of living. What is more, the experience of the post-war years suggests that any given volume of imports may become increasingly expensive. The raising of living standards in other parts of the world seems likely to increase the price of the foodstuffs that we import relatively to that of the manufactured goods that we export. At the same time our ability to maintain our share of world exports, even without a relative increase in import prices, is threatened by the resurgence of powerful competitors. In the one case the terms of trade move against us, because import prices in general rise relatively to export prices in general. In the other case our competitors' export prices fall relatively to ours. Then there is the question of investment. The resources devoted to producing new capital goods, instead of being absorbed in providing given amounts of capital per head for a growing population, can be used to provide larger amounts per head for a stable population.

On the other hand, as the total number of the population becomes stable, we lose the advantages of growth. There is less opportunity for specialisation of labour. The home market ceases to expand. Structural changes become more awkward because the diversion of resources from declining to expanding industries is less likely to be absorbed by diverting the flow of *new* capital and labour into industry as a whole. In other words, in a contracting population, more industries will have to contract absolutely instead of merely ceasing to expand. There is less buoyancy in the economy, less business optimism, less pressure for new capital and new houses, and more difficulty in maintaining investment and employment, when the number of consumers ceases to grow. Fundamental to the whole problem is the fact that a nation in which the average size of family is too small for replacement is probably a nation that is becoming weaker, not only in numbers and in relative economic strength, but in many other respects as well.

Fortunately the symptoms of absolute decline have not yet begun to appear, and there is still time for the increase of 6 per cent in the average size of family which, according to the Royal Commission, would enable the total population to go on increasing beyond 1977. In the intervening years there will be much less concern about the total than about its age distribution. The most disquieting of the figures on page 48 is the increase in the proportion of people over 65 from 11 to 16 per cent in the years 1947 to 1977. The 'growing army of pensioners' was the subject of several official enquiries and many pamphlets and articles between 1950 and 1955. With the passage of time their conclusions, like those of the Royal Commission on the same subject, appear more gloomy than they need have been. In discussing them, therefore, we may strike a less pessimistic note.

Three broad questions need to be considered. The first may be called the national income question. Referring again to the figures on page 48, we see that the 'producers' aged 15–65 will decrease from 68 to 65 per cent and the dependants,

5

young and old, will increase from 32 to 35 per cent of the total population.[1] The number of consumers per producer will rise from 100/68 to 100/65: an increase of $4\frac{3}{4}$ per cent. Productivity must increase by $4\frac{3}{4}$ per cent in order to support the larger number of dependants without a fall in the standard of living. On the basis of past experience, technical progress in all its forms should yield, over a period of thirty years, an increase in productivity of the order of 50 per cent. Thus, about one-tenth of the expected increase in the national income is, as it were, mortgaged on account of the ageing population. Put like this, it appears an appreciable but not an unmanageable problem.

Of course this calculation is too simple; but of the many qualifications that could be made, a large number would cancel out. For example, many of the 'producers' in the 15–65 age-group are married women, whose productivity is not measured and, if it were, would not increase with productivity in paid occupations. But, on the other hand, they do not retire from their unpaid work, and household gadgets do increase their productivity and provide more leisure or more opportunity to do outside work, all of which constitutes the enjoyment, if not the production, of a higher standard of living. Again, the workers are growing older and may produce less; but so are the consumers, and they may consume less. Again, the development of national, occupational and private pensions schemes may place an increasing proportion of purchasing power in the hands of the dependent population at the expense of the living standards of the producers. But the rise in prices, if it continues, works in the opposite direction: wages rise faster than pensions. Again, if pensions are provided by the State out of money raised by progressive taxation, the incentive of producers to increase their productivity may be adversely affected. If they are provided by business firms, the

---

[1] It should be noted that, although the proportion of producers is falling, it is abnormally high when compared with the situation in an expanding population, which has fewer old people but many more children. From 1841 to 1891 the proportion of producers was about 59 per cent, of under 15's about 36 per cent, of over 65's about 5 per cent.

employees may be more content and their productivity increase.

The second question relating to the problems of an ageing population may be called the budget question. The increased output which the producers must produce in order to support more dependants may not appear large in relation to the whole national income. But if the transfer takes place through the medium of State benefits—pensions, family allowances, education grants and the like—if, that is to say, it is all channelled through the budget, it may be very large in relation to the budget. Suppose, for example, that 30 per cent of the national income is redistributed annually through the Exchequer. Then an increase of 5 per cent in the national income, all of which is redistributed through the Exchequer, means an increase of 15 per cent in the budget. Something like this is in fact occurring, and it is this aspect of the ageing population that has been the main theme of a number of official reports.

There are several reasons why the budgetary question is more serious than the national income question. In the first place, women receive retirement pensions at 60 (not 65) and this, combined with the fact that there are many more women than men in the higher age-groups, increases the pensionable population substantially. The Report of the Phillips Committee[1] sums it up neatly by saying that whereas in 1911 the number of men and women of pensionable age was 1 in every 15 of the total population, in 1954 it was 2 in every 15, and in 1979 it will be 3 in every 15.

In the second place, the national insurance scheme, for reasons that will be explained in Chapter IX, has worked out in such a way that the whole of the increase in the cost of retirement pensions after 1955 will fall on the general taxpayer, while before that date a large part of the revenue was obtained from contributions to the National Insurance Fund. In 1955 these pensions cost £360 millions, and the Exchequer

[1] Committee on the Economic and Financial Problems of the Provision for Old Age, December 1954.

paid £70 millions towards the cost of these and all other benefits provided through the Insurance Fund. In 1979 pensions, *at the present rates of benefit*, will cost £660 millions and the Exchequer will have to pay £440 millions.[1]

In the third place, the other types of income which are financed by the budget may also, on balance, increase. There will, it is true, be fewer children, but the demands for higher standards in respect of health and welfare services, education grants, and family allowances may more than offset the fall in numbers. In all these calculations, however, we must be careful to remember that an increase in the national income will automatically bring some increase in budget revenue, without any change in the rates of taxation. The budgetary question only becomes more serious if the benefits provided through the mechanism of the budget increase, in number or in quality, more than correspondingly. In this connection it may be added that the budget is a political instrument. Marginal adjustments in taxation and benefits generate a disproportionate amount of heat. Pensioners have votes, and so do parents.

The third question, covering a number of aspects of the ageing population, may be called the efficiency question. Will the British economy become less efficient, either from the point of view of costs, or from the point of view of employment? That is to say, will resources be put to the wrong use, or remain unused and be wasted, as a consequence of the changing population structure?

With regard to the first kind of efficiency, it could be said that an older working population is likely to be less enterprising. New ideas, the taking of risks, improvements in technique and organisation, adaptability in changing market conditions, are associated with the young vigorous entrepreneur. Even if the higher costs of the less efficient were tolerated in the home market, they would not be so in the export market. At the same time structural changes in

[1] *Report by the Government Actuary on the First Quinquennial Review of the National Insurance Scheme*, November 1954.

industry may need to be more frequent and more radical in order to meet the demands of elderly consumers.

Such arguments are easily magnified to appear more serious than they are. The figures on page 48 show some movement towards an older working population, but not a great deal. Young workers may be energetic, but they do not reach the height of their skill for several years. Young men may have ideas and invent new techniques, but it is the older men who have the managerial authority and control of capital which are necessary to put them into practice. As for structural changes, of all the changes in demand that business men have to deal with, those resulting from changes in the age distribution of the population are the most predictable. The switch from producing prams to producing bath chairs does not have to take place overnight.

Lastly, what of the employment aspect? Will there be more unemployment, more unused resources? It was pointed out earlier that when the *total* population ceased to grow, structural unemployment (delay in transferring labour ·from declining to expanding industries) would become more serious. Since at the same time the working population is becoming older, the difficulties of adjustment may increase. The Watkinson Committee[1] drew attention to the fact that, although the total number of unemployed in the post-war years was astonishingly low, both the rate of unemployment and the duration of unemployment increased considerably with age. In 1952, 60 per cent of those who had been continuously unemployed for more than a year were over 50.

Allied to this is the question of the retiring age. For various reasons,[2] many people are now better able, and quite anxious, to continue working beyond the age of 65, but are forced to retire because this is the rule in their profession or firm. The insurance scheme regulates retirement pensions in a way

[1] National Advisory Committee on the Employment of Older Men and Women. First Report, October 1953; Second Report, December 1955.

[2] See, for example, *Reasons given for Retiring or Continuing at Work*: Report of an enquiry by the Ministry of Pensions and National Insurance, November 1954.

that is intended to encourage people to work beyond the retiring age: and the Phillips Committee suggested 68 as a more suitable age in the present conditions than 65. Much of the discussion on this subject, however, misses the point. The case for later retirement is not that it would reduce the cost of pensions or that the national interest requires people to work till they drop. It is that people who wish to go on working should be free to do so and that employment policy should aim to provide a job for all those who want to work, whatever their age. They may still retire early if they wish. And if the gap between the retiring salary and the retirement pension is too wide, a gradual tapering off with less intensive and part-time work should be possible. In Great Britain standards of health and standards of living have been achieved that would permit freedom of choice between work and leisure for the growing body of people who, as a result of population trends, will find themselves in the higher age-groups.

CHAPTER III

HOUSING

§ 1. The Housing Market. This chapter and the next are mainly concerned with the conditions in which people live and work. Living conditions are not simply a matter of housing. They depend chiefly on such intangible and immeasurable forces as personal relationships in the household and the family. Harmony and goodwill in these relationships may triumph over all sorts of physical limitations and discomforts; and disharmony may bring unhappiness in the most luxurious surroundings. But although physical amenities are not essential to happiness, they do contribute substantially towards it. There is no doubt that the stresses of domestic life are more readily overcome in a comfortable than in a squalid environment. The study of this environment, of housing conditions and housing problems, is part of the province of the social economist.

We must begin by recognising that house-room is a highly peculiar commodity and that the housing market has a number of special characteristics that make it quite unlike any other. Some of the peculiarities lie in the nature of the commodity itself, others in the attitude of people towards it.

Shelter, like food and clothing, is one of the prime essentials of life. But shelter in the form of housing differs from food and clothing in its extreme durability. In certain cases food may be preserved, by modern methods of refrigeration, for a very long time. Some clothes may be handed down from generation to generation, while shelter is sometimes provided by temporary structures. As a rule, however, food and clothing are classed as 'single-use consumer goods' and houses as 'durable consumer goods'; so durable that the supply of housing accommodation is much more closely linked with the supply of various forms of capital equipment than with the consumer goods industries. This is recognised in the phrase 'social capital' which, though generally applied to the whole of the physical assets of the national economy, is often used in a more limited sense to mean the essential housing and public utility equipment required by the local population of a town or district.

Further, houses differ from other durable consumer goods, such as motor-cars, in two respects: they are immobile, and their length of life is significantly greater. For both these reasons, consumers are reluctant to buy their own houses. Broadly speaking, the purchase of a new car costs less than a year's income. The purchase of a new house costs several years' income, and most houses last a lifetime or more. Houses are therefore bought and sold, even by owner-occupiers, as a form of investment rather than as a form of consumer expenditure.

Thus, house-room is the only essential consumer good which is normally hired rather than bought, and the only essential consumer good of which the existing stock provides the bulk of the supply—new building adds only about 2 per cent to the total stock of houses each year. All this makes for considerable inelasticity on both the demand side and the supply side of the housing market.

Demand is inelastic for three interconnected reasons. First, since housing is essential, the demand would seem to be entirely a function of the size of the population, or, more precisely, the number of families. Every family needs a house and hardly any have two. Secondly, moving house is an expensive and laborious business. Changing one's landlord is not like changing one's butcher, and consuming less house-room is not like consuming less meat. Thirdly, rent is usually regarded as the first and most rigid charge against income, partly because it is a contractual payment, partly again because any adjustment to change means moving house. If rent rises or falls, a family will continue to pay the rent and regulate other items of expenditure, including food and clothing, accordingly. The same occurs if earnings rise or fall temporarily; which means that the *income* elasticity of demand for housing, as well as the *price* elasticity, is low.

Supply also is inelastic, firstly because houses are immobile, so that local shortages cannot be relieved by transporting supplies from elsewhere. Secondly, once they are built, houses last for half a century or more, so that, however much prices fall, the existing stock of houses will continue to be supplied. Thirdly, new production is small in relation to the total supply. Fourthly, new production depends much less on price changes than on the availability of the resources of the building industry. The last point is important, not only because building is a constructional industry, subject to wide fluctuations of total demand (for factories as well as houses) between periods of prosperity and depression, but also because in wartime new building of houses virtually ceased in Great Britain and arrears of repair and maintenance were allowed to accumulate. For all these reasons, therefore, an increase or decrease in demand does not bring about corresponding changes in supply, but places the owners of house property in a position of peculiar advantage, or peculiar vulnerability, as the case may be.

It is possible, however, to push the arguments about in-elasticities too far, and to conclude that price plays no part in regulating the supply of, and the demand for, housing. Post-war housing experience in Great Britain provides two out-standing examples which serve to show the limitations of this type of reasoning. One relates to building policy, the other to rent policy.

It is customary, in the discussion of housing programmes, to accept the slogan 'every family needs a house' and compare the number of separate dwellings with the number of separate families. The gap between them indicates the number of additional houses required. The initial figures may be obtained from the Census of Population and more or less elaborate adjustments made for new building, demolition and

conversion of property, marriages and new applications for
council houses, since the date of the Census.   The fallacy lies
in assuming that the number of houses and the number of
families may be determined irrespective of the *price* of housing.
In fact, in that part of the market which is active, price may
be the controlling influence on both the number of separate
dwellings supplied and the number of separate families
demanding them.   The owner of a large house who is deciding
whether or not to convert it into flats; the elderly parents who
are deciding whether or not to live with their married children;
the single or widowed person who is deciding whether to run
a flat or live in lodgings; all these are in a position to increase
or decrease the gap between demand and supply, and for some
of them, price will be the deciding factor.   The point of this
illustration is not the desirability or otherwise of providing
separate accommodation for everyone who would like to
enjoy it.   It is that the inelasticities of supply and demand in
the housing market are not so great as to prevent a low rent
policy from aggravating the housing shortage or a high rent
policy from relieving it.

The other example concerns the distribution of house-room
rather than the total demand and supply.   Many families,
especially parents whose children have married and gone away,
find themselves in houses that are too big for them.   Many
others, especially young couples with small children, live in
flats or lodgings which they acquired before the children
arrived and which are now too small for them.   The Rent
Restriction Acts have worked in such a way that it is a matter
of historical accident whether or not large houses have higher
rents than small houses.   Those living in houses that are too
big for them are often unwilling to move out because the small
houses cost more.   Again, the point of the illustration is not
the desirability or otherwise of forcing people to pay an
'economic price' for their accommodation.   It is that, even
if the total numbers of dwellings and families are in balance,
the inelasticities of demand and supply in the market for each
type and size of accommodation are not so great as to prevent

a better correlation between size of house and size of family if appropriate prices were charged.

To turn now from the 'intrinsic' peculiarities of housing to its special social characteristics. The first is that the social problems resulting from bad housing are of a different kind from those that arise out of insufficiency or poor quality of any other commodity. Lack of food or clothing may give rise to conditions of ill-health and poverty, but the effects are largely confined to the particular persons and families. Bad housing affects others as well. If living space is cramped, if buildings are poorly constructed or allowed to fall into disrepair, if the occupants are overcrowded, if conditions of filth and squalor develop, there emerge problems of public safety, sanitation and morality which affect the whole neighbourhood. Housing has therefore become the subject of considerable control by public authorities. Town-planning has sought to ensure that the arrangement and spacing of houses and the provision of public utility services will be such as to avoid some of the evils that accompany the growth of towns. Regulations about the construction and repair of houses have been enforced in an attempt to establish certain standards of building. Local authorities have carried out slum-clearance schemes and built houses on their own account.

Secondly, the effect of two world wars on the housing market has been more lasting than, perhaps, on any other part of the economic system. One reason is that housing is both a consumer good and, because of its durability, a form of capital. Housing suffered a double punishment because the resources required for war were obtained partly by reducing private consumption and partly by living off capital. Housing conditions were allowed to become more cramped and uncomfortable, just as other consumer goods were cut down in quantity and quality; but many of the other goods, such as food, could not be much reduced, and where consumption was postponed, as in the case of clothes, it was soon made good after the war. House repair was neglected, just as other capital was run down; but much of the other capital was needed for war purposes and could not be allowed to deteriorate. Only in the case of housing did both processes occur, and arrears of consumption and capital maintenance accumulate until after the war. Hence the severity and persistence of the post-war housing shortage.

But this is not all. The circumstances of wartime placed the owners of house property in an exceptionally strong position and tenants in an exceptionally weak one. Rents were therefore strictly controlled, both in 1914 and in 1939, and by 1956 the controls were still in force. No other commodity has been subject to price control for so long and with such chaotic results.

The third of the special social characteristics, as we have called them, is that during this century events have conspired to create an artificial set of values in regard to housing. Each thread in this tangled web can be explained and defended, but together it amounts to a sort of 'housing illusion'. It begins with the well-established fact that rent is the most prominent single item, and also the most inflexible, in the budgets of most working-class families. In order to reduce the tyranny of rent, families often choose to live in inadequate accommodation. This is especially likely if they are near the poverty line and a spell of unemployment or an increase in the family may land them in debt, but it may also occur because they do not know the advantages of better housing or value them too lightly in comparison with other ways of spending their money. In these circumstances housing subsidies may be the means of avoiding poverty, of educating the people in the acceptance of better standards, and of reducing the likelihood that overcrowding and slums, with their attendant social evils, will develop. The provision of housing by non-profit-making bodies goes back a century or more, but direct subsidies out of public funds began after the first world war and have been in operation for about thirty-five years.

The campaign against poverty has therefore been responsible for one form of cheap housing: the subsidised house. The circumstances of war have been responsible for another:

the rent-restricted house. Over the whole period since rent restriction began in 1914 there has been a housing shortage, with the result that any permitted increase in rent has appeared to be an unjustifiable concession to the landlord and an unfair penalty on the tenant. Of course there are arguments on both sides in this matter, but it is reasonable to say that the general effect of public policy has been to accustom the majority of tenants to the idea of cheap housing. Mental attitudes and patterns of family expenditure have both adjusted themselves accordingly.

§ **2. Housing Standards.** In discussing living conditions it is useful to distinguish, first, the quality and amenities of the houses in which people live; secondly, the environment, in terms of access to fresh air and light, conditions of the streets and public health and utility services; and thirdly, the quantity of house-room available to each family. A slum is probably deficient in all three aspects, but it is clearly possible for over-crowding, defined as too many persons per room on the average, to exist in property which is otherwise adequate. Similarly, house-room which is poor in quality, made of inferior materials or in a state of disrepair, or lacking in amenities, may be adequate in quantity and not overcrowded. In this section we shall try to get a glimpse of housing standards in the first of the three senses distinguished above. Instead of attempting any statistical analysis we shall take a series of snapshots to show how housing standards have changed over the past century.

In the 1951 Census, householders were asked, for the first time, 'whether the household has exclusive or shared use of a piped water supply within the house, a kitchen sink, a cooking stove or range, a watercloset and a fixed bath'. It was found that, out of 13 million families in England and Wales, only 7·2 million, or 55 per cent, had exclusive use of a fixed bath; 8 per cent shared a bath with another family; and 37 per cent were entirely without. Of course, this does not mean that nearly 5 million families never enjoy complete immersion. A great deal can be done with mobile contraptions kept under the kitchen table or behind a curtain. But many readers will be surprised to know that in the mid-twentieth century two families in every five did not possess a fixed bath. They will be equally surprised to learn that 1 million families had no water closet and ¼ million no cooking stove. Nor was this lack of amenities confined to families living in the country. In Manchester, 34 per cent of the households had no fixed bath, in London 44 per cent, in Cambridge 31 per cent.

The lack of these domestic amenities occurs mainly in houses built before the first world war, of which there were several million still standing in 1951. For, fifty years ago, a bath was not an essential part of a house. To obtain a broader picture of housing standards and see them in perspective, it is useful to look at the descriptions of housing conditions in Mr. Seebohm Rowntree's social surveys of York in 1899 and 1936.[1] In his first survey he divided the working-class houses of York, which he claimed to be no better in general than those of London and other cities, into three classes: (1) the comfortable houses of the well-to-do artisans; (2) houses, for the most part four-roomed, principally occupied by families in receipt of moderate but regular wages; (3) houses in the poorest districts, many of which are typical slum dwellings.

The first class of house, occupied in 1899 by 12 per cent of the working-class families in York, usually consisted of five rooms and a scullery; it sometimes had a little front garden and usually a small cemented back yard. It rarely had a bath, but there was a water closet in the yard. The sitting-room, or parlour, often contained a piano and an overmantel in addition to the usual furniture, but this room was chiefly used on Sunday or as a receiving room for visitors not on terms sufficiently intimate to be asked into the kitchen, which was the real living-room. Floors were covered with linoleum. There was a kitchen sink, fireplaces in most rooms, and an abundance of china ornaments on most mantelpieces.

[1] B. S. Rowntree: *Poverty—A Study of Town Life*, 1901, Chapter VI; *Poverty and Progress*, 1941, Chapter IX.

The class two house, occupied by 62 per cent of the working-class families, often had only two bedrooms, no scullery and no water closet. The street door opened straight into the living-room. There was linoleum on the floor and the walls were papered and decorated with coloured almanacs and pictures. There was a kitchen sink but never a bath. The whole accommodation was more cramped, and the houses often built of inferior materials.

The third class of house, occupied by 26 per cent of the working-class families, had usually only two or three rooms. A few were clean and tidy, but most were dirty and over-crowded, situated in narrow alleys paved with cobbles or in confined courts which admitted little sunlight and air. One water tap was often the sole supply for a large number of houses. Ashpits overflowed, midden privies were in many cases shared by several houses, floors were of brick, uneven, dirty and damp. A general appearance of dilapidation and carelessness revealed the condition and character of the tenants.

Forty years later, housing conditions in York were im-mensely better, an improvement which Rowntree attributed to subsidies, building by local authorities and slum-clearance schemes. By 1936, 29 per cent of the working-class population lived in houses better than those of the first class of 1899. Some were semi-detached houses, built since 1920 by specula-tive builders, having front and back gardens, bathrooms, and hot and cold water. They were well furnished, and had carpets as well as linoleum, a wireless set in addition to the piano, and bookcases and flowers in the 'lounge', which was more lived-in than its predecessor the 'parlour'. Others were council houses, also built since 1920, semi-detached and with similar amenities, but displaying less imagination in lay-out and furnishing.

The first class house of 1899 was occupied in 1936 by 8 per cent of the working-class population of York, the second class by 53 per cent and the third by 10 per cent. Most of those in the last class were demolished between 1936 and 1939, but some of the second class had in turn become slums.

Throughout the country, the second world war put a brake on progress in housing standards as in many other affairs. Slum clearance was held up (except by enemy action), repairs were neglected, and the post-war decade, while it witnessed the building of many excellent new houses, did little to improve the amenities of the old. Rent restriction often deprived the landlord of the means to effect repairs and improvements. But when all this is allowed for, we may generalise from the picture of York to the extent of saying that in the first half of this century housing standards have improved greatly in regard to layout, quality of construction, amenities and furnishing. Facilities which our grandparents regarded as sheer luxuries, if they dreamed of them at all, are now taken for granted and demanded as necessities. Legislation and subsidies and planning have played their part in bringing about this improvement, but the principal cause has been economic progress: higher standards of housing are part of a higher standard of living.

There is a lesson here which is worth remembering in relation to an earlier period of economic history. History books abound with accounts of the appalling conditions in which many people lived in the industrial towns of Britain in the early part of the nineteenth century, and there is no lack of evidence that in the worst slums of, particularly, Manchester, Liverpool and London, conditions were truly horrible. Many houses were built back-to-back, with no through ventilation, and of inferior materials. Whole families lived in single rooms, often in cellars, in unbelievable squalor. Refuse accumulated and the whole insanitary environment intensified the poverty, ill health and moral degradation of the inhabitants.

All this is true, and no student of social history can neglect it. But it is not true, as is sometimes suggested, that this was a consequence of the Industrial Revolution so serious and so widespread as almost to offset its benefits to the working-classes. These were the black spots, and very black they were. But they were the consequence, not of the Industrial Revolution itself, but of the extremely rapid growth of towns that accompanied it. It is significant that the worst conditions developed in those parts where a large influx of labour, especially Irish labour, had to be housed as quickly as possible with whatever materials were available. Builders and landlords may have exploited their opportunities; authorities may have been slow to take the necessary measures to improve public health and sanitation; timber duties, window taxes and rising local rates may have played their part in making building expensive and retarding improvements in the quality and amenities of housing. But it seems likely that, at least from 1830 onwards, when the effects of the Napoleonic Wars had worked themselves out, the rising standards of living which the Industrial Revolution brought to a rising population included, in general, better standards of housing than had previously been known. Even in regard to the particular evils resulting from the rapid growth of towns, Dr. George, the authority on eighteenth-century London, says: 'Appalling as was the state of things revealed by the nineteenth-century reports (1840–45) on the sanitary state of towns it can hardly be doubted that the state of London was far worse in the eighteenth century.'[1]

The point of this digression is not to prove or disprove any particular theories about the Industrial Revolution but to suggest, as it is often necessary to do in the study of social conditions, that the improvement of standards, and the acceptance of improved standards as a matter of course, tend to go hand in hand. Would-be reformers are always dissatisfied with the conditions of their time, and it is right that they should be, for their dissatisfaction is one of the spurs to social improvement and progress. It is frequently true, however, that the conditions condemned in one age would have been regarded with envy by the reformers of an earlier age. The longevity of housing, the fact that the good houses of one generation survive to become the bad houses of the next, should make it easier to see things in perspective. But

[1] M. Dorothy George: *London Life in the Eighteenth Century* (1925), Chapter II.

6

perhaps it makes it more difficult, because houses deteriorate, and public attention is concentrated on the black spots.

§ 3. Overcrowding.

The description of amenities and surroundings is one way of assessing housing standards. The calculation of the average number of rooms per person is another. Of course, the distribution of rooms among families, like the distribution of incomes, is the matter of most concern; but the average number of rooms per person, like the average real income per head, can at least show changes in the available standard of living, assuming no change in distribution. The Census of Population provides regular information on this subject. If we take the total population, irrespective of age and sex, living in private families, and divide it into the total number of rooms (living-rooms, kitchens and bedrooms) in occupied dwellings, we find that in England and Wales the average number of rooms per person in 1911 was 1·05, in 1931 1·21, and in 1951 1·36. Thus in 1931 each person had on the average 15 per cent more rooms than in 1911, and in 1951 12 per cent more rooms than in 1931.

To some extent, this improvement has been brought about by the fall in the average size of the family; that is, leaving aside the new houses and the new families that have come into being since the previous census, the occupants of the old houses would have more rooms per head. If in fact large houses had become progressively under-occupied, the average figures might conceal a most unequal redistribution of house-room. If, on the other hand, the improvement were spread over all types of houses, whether it arose from a fall in the average size of family or from new building at a faster rate than the creation of new families, it would represent a reduction in overcrowding.

To find the answer, it is necessary to bring together the distribution of houses by size and the distribution of families by size. This is done by the Census authorities, who then adopt the simple definition that overcrowding exists in houses that contain more than two persons per room. On this definition 6·9 per cent of the persons living in private families in England and Wales appeared to be in overcrowded conditions in 1931, but only 2·2 per cent in 1951. In Scotland the problem is much more serious, and the improvement over twenty years, though substantial, has not been on the same scale as in England and Wales. Overcrowding in Scotland affected 35·0 per cent of the population living in private families in 1931 and 15·5 per cent in 1951. Needless to say, there are also wide variations in different parts of England and Wales. In general there is more overcrowding in the towns than in the country districts; in some towns it is still an urgent social problem, in others it has almost disappeared —in terms of the Census definition.

Here again there arises the difficulty of changing standards. The Census definition is not only too simple, because it takes no account of how big the persons are and how big the rooms are. It is also likely to become less acceptable as housing standards in general improve. A further complication, which will recur in the discussion of poverty in Chapter VI, is the existence of a large number of families living only slightly above the standard adopted for the measurement of overcrowding. Consequently a slight raising of the standard reveals a disproportionate increase in the number of people living below the standard.

Some evidence on the matter is provided by the *Report on the Overcrowding Survey in England and Wales*, 1936. It arose out of the Housing Act of 1935 and was the most thorough investigation of its kind in this country. The standards adopted were more precise than those of the Census and in some cases more severe. They took account of the size of rooms as well as the size of families; and also the composition of families in regard to age and the need for separation of the sexes. Out of 8,925,000 working-class dwellings inspected, 342,000 were overcrowded. This gives 3·8 per cent of the families living in overcrowded conditions in 1936 compared with 6·9 per cent of the population in 1931 and according to Census standards. The worst areas, in which between 10 and 20 per cent of the families were overcrowded in 1936, were the East End of London and the towns of the North-east Coast.

The Survey showed that if the standard had been adjusted to increase the permitted number of persons per room by about 10 per cent, the number of overcrowded families would have fallen by 52,000 and the extent of overcrowding been reduced from 3·8 per cent to 3·2 per cent. On the other hand, a raising of the standard to *reduce* the permitted number of persons per room by about 10 per cent would have raised the number of overcrowded families by 380,000 and more than doubled the extent of overcrowding—from 3·8 per cent to 8·2 per cent.

It is only fair to add that the brighter side of the Survey showed that 4,185,000 families, or 46 per cent of all working-class families, had at least twice as much accommodation as was required by the standard. If the Survey had covered all families it would certainly have shown that the majority of the population was adequately housed.

There is, however, a difference between adequate accommodation and more than adequate accommodation. Returning to the Census: the incidence of overcrowding in England and Wales was reduced by two-thirds between 1931 and 1951; but this did not mean that all the families not living in overcrowded conditions were in the right size of house. The 1951 Census enumerated 12 million separate dwellings and 13·1 million separate families. Of these, 6·8 million dwellings had 5 or more rooms, but only 2·3 million families comprised 5 or more persons and only 4·8 million families 4 or more persons. On the other hand, there were 5·2 million dwellings with 4 rooms or less, and 8·3 million families of 3 persons or less. The general improvement in standards (average number of rooms per person) did not, therefore, alter the fact that there were too many large houses and too few small houses in 1951. Even if all the large families were in the large houses (which was far from being the case) there was still a need for more small houses either by sub-division of the large, or by new building.

§ **4. Slums.** Slums are houses unfit for human habitation. No further definition is required. But even slums are not what they were. To describe slums at their worst it would be necessary to quote at length from the *Reports of the Commissioners for inquiring into the State of Large Towns and Populous Districts, 1844–1845*, or from Friedrich Engels' *Condition of the Working Class in England in 1844*, or from the *Reports of the Commissioners for Inquiry into the Housing of the Working Classes, 1884–1885*. Compared with these, the descriptions of the slums of London and York at the end of the nineteenth century in Charles Booth's *Life and Labour of the People in London* and Seebohm Rowntree's *Poverty—A Study of Town Life* make almost pleasant reading. And to see slums at their best, it would be necessary to perambulate the back streets of Liverpool, Manchester or Birmingham, each of which had in November 1955 more than 50,000 houses 'deemed unfit for human habitation'.

What causes houses to become slums? Broadly speaking neglect by somebody or other. But it is not easy to apportion the blame because at various times neglect by the four parties responsible for housing conditions—the builder, the owner, the tenant and the local authority—can be explained, if not condoned, by the circumstances of the time. Take, for example, three of the principal causes: age, war and lack of sanitation. There comes a time when a house is no longer repairable and has to be demolished. But demolition is costly and it is not always the owner's fault that he cannot afford it, or that he neglects to repair it in the period before its condemnation or, in the case of leasehold property, in the few years before the expiry of the lease. The connection between wars and slums needs particular emphasis. The worst houses of the nineteenth century were probably those built in the two decades following the Napoleonic Wars when the shortage of materials, the pressure of population, and the opportunities for jerry-building were greater than at any other time. And the two world wars of this century, as was noticed on page 59, had the double effect of holding up slum clearance for ten years and promoting new slums through the diversion of building materials and labour to war purposes. Lack of sanitation, in all its aspects, was the outstanding feature of the slums of the nineteenth century. But it is not entirely fair, though it has long been fashionable, to condemn the public authorities for not planning the towns or the builders and landlords for not providing sanitary amenities. People flocked into the towns and sought accommodation near their work too fast for any-one to plan the growth of towns or to anticipate the problems that would arise. Builders and landlords were under too much pressure to provide accommodation as quickly and cheaply as possible to bother about sanitary amenities which, in the country, would have been dispensable. Undoubtedly many of those responsible for public policy did not believe in State intervention in the social sphere and had to be stung into action by the powerful persuasion of a Shaftesbury or a Chadwick. But one can understand their bewilderment at the size of the problem. One of its most baffling aspects, for example, was the enormous migrant population in every town, moving about irresponsibly from tenement to tenement.

When all this has been said, however, it was often possible to find local authorities who were dilatory, builders who neglected elementary rules in regard to structure and materials, landlords who were unscrupulous, and tenants who would turn any house into a slum—though Shaftesbury, in his evidence before the 1884 Commission, answered the question 'Is it the pig that makes the sty or the sty that makes the pig?' by saying that in most cases it was the latter.

In modern times the principal reason why houses are con-demned as unfit for human habitation is sheer age and dis-repair, a condition hastened in many cases by rent restriction, for it is the oldest houses that most need repair and the oldest houses whose rents have been held down longest while the costs of repair multiplied. Lack of sanitation is still a cause, but the words do not mean what they did a hundred years ago. The worst evils have been overcome by public health legisla-tion; by a general improvement in building standards, whether under official regulation or independently; by the private efforts of social reformers; by town planning; and by slum clearance schemes. Let us look briefly at some of the landmarks in this history.

The Public Health Act of 1848 is rightly regarded as the beginning of modern housing and health legislation. It was promoted by Edwin Chadwick and followed the findings of the Commission of 1845, which insisted that the disastrous outbreaks of cholera since 1831 had been facilitated by defective water supply and inadequate drainage. A second Public Health Act in 1875 compelled local authorities to appoint a Public Officer of Health, and promoted local bye-laws relating to drainage and sanitation. Much of the legislation was permissive and was only gradually carried out by local authorities, but by the end of the century clean water and improved sanitation had become general and removed some of the worst features of the slums.

Meanwhile the 'Shaftesbury' Act of 1851 inaugurated the inspection of common lodging-houses and empowered local authorities to borrow money for the purchase of houses. These were to be run by municipalities on the lines of the model lodging-houses that Shaftesbury himself had set up during the 1840's. The powers of local authorities were further extended by the 'Torrens' Act of 1869 and the 'Cross' Act of 1875, which permitted the demolition of insanitary houses and the clearance of slum districts. Birmingham, in particular, carried out an enormous slum clearance scheme in the 1880's through the reforming zeal of Joseph Chamberlain. The whole of this legislation was consolidated and further recommendations of the Commission of 1884 were embodied in the Housing of the Working-Classes Act of 1890.

Public regulation of the construction of new buildings and streets dates from the Public Health Act of 1875, but in this respect also the Act was permissive, and some local authorities made use of the power to issue bye-laws more promptly than others. The Housing, Town Planning, etc., Act of 1909 went further. Local authorities acquired powers of compulsory purchase for the purposes of the Housing of the Working-Classes Act and were permitted for the first time to make town-planning schemes. The Act of 1909 also prohibited the erection of back-to-back houses.

Voluntary action also played its part in tackling the slum problem in the late nineteenth century. In fact, as so often happens, philanthropic organisations carried out the pioneer work which gave confidence to the promoters of legislation. Two of these organisations deserve special mention: the housing societies and the schemes run by Octavia Hill. We noticed that Shaftesbury had acquired, by voluntary subscription, a number of lodging houses which were to be run on model lines. His action not only inspired the Act of 1851 but also stimulated the formation of a number of housing trusts, under which blocks of flats were built and the income from rents devoted entirely to repair and maintenance or to further building. The most famous was Peabody's Trust, formed in 1862, whose label can be seen on various buildings in London. Similar blocks were erected by quasi-philanthropic organisations, such as the Artisans' Dwelling Co., or Waterlow's, whose most monstrous exhibit is ·familiar to travellers from Liverpool Street Station. The success of this type of housing depended entirely on the efficiency of the caretaker in charge of the block. Evidence collected by Charles Booth included the comments 'dull and dismal', 'not very nice; one stumbles on people sleeping on the stairs' but, on the other side, 'much better than tenement houses; the restrictions make people decent', 'owners who put in strong caretakers do more than all the churches and missions'.

Octavia Hill developed a new system of house property management based on her conviction that what mattered most was the personal relationship between landlord and tenant. The collection of rents, she maintained, should be neither formal, nor unpleasant, nor impersonal, but should provide a regular opportunity for the landlord to get to know his tenants better, to discuss their personal problems, and to establish mutual friendship and respect through the strict performance of duty on either side. The landlord's duty was to visit regularly, to take a close personal interest in his tenants, to maintain the property in good repair, to ensure good sanitation and complete cleanliness of the structure and the staircases. The tenant's duty was to pay the rent without fail, to keep the rooms in decent condition, and not to make the landlord's task more difficult, e.g. by using the banisters for firewood, or wilfully damaging the structure.

The success of Octavia Hill and those who were trained by her in the art of house property management was astonishing. By personal friendship, infinite patience and a shrewd combination of moral and practical common sense, she converted the roughest and most feckless of tenants into self-respecting householders. There was nothing woolly-minded about her methods: she allowed no arrears of rent, she insisted that the duties of landlord and tenant were reciprocal, and she shamed her tenants into realising that the less she spent on repairs and replacements, the more she could spend on improvements. 'It is no use to have the right spirit,' she wrote, 'if the technical matters, all the sanitary and financial arrangements, are in a mess. . . . Have your drainage and your clean stairs and your distempering and your accounts all as perfect as possible.' Her biographer adds: 'With a characteristic twinkle she would relate how a tenant had greeted her with the remark, "Them drains are a feather in your cap!"'[1] She exemplified social case-work at its best. 'Dealing with poverty through each individual, treating each case as a man, is a slow business. To Octavia it was the only way. . . .'[2]

But public opinion was more impatient. She would probably have approved of the town-planning schemes and, with some reservations about the use of compulsory powers and the need for eliciting the voluntary co-operation of each tenant, of the slum-clearance schemes authorised by the Act of 1909. The war, however, prevented the Act from becoming effective, and by the 1920's slum clearance was not only a much bigger

---

[1] E. Moberly Bell: *Octavia Hill*, 1942, p. 123.
[2] *Ibid.*, p. 206.

problem, but was accompanied by subsidies and rent restriction, of which she would not have approved.

Up to 1914 the housing problem in Britain was almost entirely a slum problem. After 1919 it was a supply problem: the replacement of slum dwellings became part of the broader issue of how to increase the total supply of houses. The reasons for this, and the development of housing policy in general, will be discussed in the next section. We may conclude this section with an account of the extent of the slum problem and the measures specifically concerned with it, since 1919.

The years 1919 to 1930 witnessed the development of subsidised housing, but, although the legislation of that period applied to slum clearance as well as to ordinary building, only a negligible amount of demolition and replacement of slum property was undertaken. Only about 11,000 slum houses were pulled down and replaced between 1919 and 1929, while total new building by local authorities and private enterprise (including replacements) amounted to 1,275,000 houses. The urgent need to increase the total amount of accommodation and the arrangement of the subsidies encouraged ordinary building and repair rather than slum clearance. In 1930 there was a clear change of policy. The Housing Act of that year, promoted by Mr. Greenwood as Minister of Health, regulated the subsidies in such a way as to encourage the rehousing, at rents which tenants could reasonably be expected to pay, of occupants of slum property. At first, conditions were still not favourable enough to promote slum-clearance on a large scale, but by 1933 the price of building materials, wage rates in the building industry and interest rates had all fallen significantly and the stage was set for a new drive. The Ministry of Health instructed all local authorities to produce plans for clearing their slums within five years. The original programmes, which came into operation early in 1934, proposed the replacement of between 250,000 and 300,000 houses and the rehousing of about 1,250,000 persons. These figures represented 2·7 per cent of the houses and 3·1 per cent of the population of England and Wales at the time of the 1931

Census. As a result of the Housing Act of 1935 and the
Overcrowding Survey of the following year, additional slum
clearance programmes were inaugurated, and by March 1939
the total clearance programme, including the original estimates
of 1934, covered 472,000 houses.

The demolition and replacement of slums actually achieved
between 1934 and 1939 was about 250,000, and in addition
459,000 houses had been rendered fit for occupation by repair.
By the outbreak of the second world war, therefore, about half
the slum-clearance programme had been carried out and
'de-crowding' of overcrowded dwellings had just begun.
Many of the 225,000 houses destroyed by enemy action during
the war were slum property, but replacements virtually ceased,
and neglect and damage created new slums on an unprecedented scale. Once again, after the war, the slum problem
was swallowed up in the supply problem, and it was not until
1954 that slum-clearance as such became a separate item in
housing policy. The Housing Repairs and Rents Act of 1954
required every local authority to submit proposals for dealing
with houses 'unfit for human habitation'. The definition had
not changed, but the guidance given to local authorities suggested higher standards than those applicable in 1890, 1909 or
1930. 'In determining whether a house is unfit,' says the Act,
'regard shall be had to its condition in respect of repair;
stability; freedom from damp; natural lighting; ventilation;
water supply; drainage and sanitary conveniences; and facilities for storage, preparation and cooking of food and for the
disposal of waste water.' The returns showed[1] that out of a
total of 12,935,000 permanent houses, 847,000, or 6½ per cent,
were unfit. Of these, 375,000 were to be demolished in the
five years 1956–1960. Of the provincial towns, Liverpool
had the largest total, with 88,000 unfit out of a total of 204,000;
Manchester had 68,000 unfit out of 208,000; and Birmingham
50,000 out of 312,000. The standards applied by different
local authorities probably cover a very wide range. But there

[1] Ministry of Housing and Local Government: *Slum Clearance*, Cmd.
9593, November 1955.

seems to be no doubt that by average post-war standards the abolition of the slums is yet a long way off.

§ 5. Building Policy and Subsidies.

§ 5. **Building Policy and Subsidies.** It was explained in the last section that before the first world war Government policy on housing consisted almost entirely of attempts to deal with the social problems of the slums. It had achieved most success in regard to water supply and drainage. Clean water had become generally available, typhus had been banished, and in most parts of most towns drainage and sanitation had improved enormously. Some local authorities had made use of their powers to demolish slum districts. A beginning had been made with the regulation of the construction of new buildings and streets. In a few cases local authorities had purchased or built houses to show, as Shaftesbury and others had shown earlier, that by improvement and good management potential slums could be made into property fit for human habitation. But up to 1910, 99 per cent of all housing was provided by private enterprise, and between 1910 and 1914, 95 per cent.

From 1919 Government policy was mainly concerned with the total supply of housing and with rents. Slum clearance became a secondary issue. The reason for the change was not simply that neglect of repair and the cessation of new building created a post-war housing shortage. There were several contributory factors. The price of house-room, like other prices, had been controlled during the war, and an Act of 1915 prohibited, with certain exceptions, any increase in rents above the level of August 1914. The relaxation of price control would clearly have had more awkward consequences, economically and politically, in this field than in any other; but as long as rents were held down, demand exceeded supply and the Government had to assume some responsibility for increasing supply.

A second contributory factor was the increase in the cost of house-building. The price of building materials had trebled since 1913, building wage rates had more than doubled, and the working week had been reduced. Even in the inflationary conditions of 1919–1920, building costs were exceptionally high and it was impossible to build houses to 1914 standards and let them at rents equivalent in real terms to those of 1914. In any case the public were demanding standards higher than those of 1914. Two of the most popular election slogans: 'Homes fit for heroes' and 'No profiteering' promised better houses at lower rents which, in the circumstances of the time, was economic nonsense.

And so, while rent restriction took care of the price (if not the maintenance) of the old houses, a policy of subsidised house building was developed for the new. Perhaps it is only fair to add that if the average wage-earner had been offered the choice between inferior housing and higher rents he would most probably have chosen the former and thereby increased the danger of a new and bigger slum problem in the mid-twentieth century.

In her excellent study of housing policy in the inter-war period, Dr. Marian Bowley distinguished three experiments in State intervention: the first from 1919 to 1923, the second from 1923 to 1933/4, and the third from 1933/4 to 1939.[1] The first period saw the working out of the short-lived but extremely bold 'Addison' Scheme incorporated in the Housing and Town Planning, etc., Act, 1919. Under this scheme local authorities were called upon to draw up and carry out programmes for the construction of new working-class houses, without any reference to slum clearance. This in itself was a big advance on pre-war policy. But bolder still was the authorisation to let such houses at rents which the tenants could afford and to receive a State subsidy to cover most of the resulting loss. The local authorities were to subsidise to the extent of a penny rate, but no more. Further, the rents could be determined not only in relation to the general level of rents, which was heavily depressed by the Rent Restriction Act, but also in relation to the circumstances of each family. The only

[1] The author is greatly indebted to Dr. Bowley's book *Housing and the State* (1945) for much of the material used in this chapter.

condition of receiving the subsidy was that the building programmes and the rent scales must be approved by the Ministry
of Health, which succeeded the Local Government Board as the
department responsible for housing policy. The scheme was
flexible and, as Dr. Bowley points out, could have been so
administered by the Ministry of Health as to combine flexibility with strict control over the total amount of the State
subsidy. As it turned out the local authorities, having nothing
to lose, went ahead with commendable speed, and the Government took fright and discontinued the scheme in July 1921.
The completion of programmes already approved kept the
industry fairly busy in 1922, when prices and costs were falling
and unsubsidised private enterprise building was almost at a
standstill. The only other relief to the housing shortage, and
to the mounting unemployment in the building industry,
came from a small amount of subsidised private enterprise
building under the Housing (Additional Powers) Act of 1919,
which provided a small lump-sum subsidy for each house that
conformed to certain conditions as to size.

The history of this brief period is of special interest because
under the Addison Scheme housing came nearer to being a
social service than at any other time. We shall see later (in
Chapters VIII and X) that housing subsidies and the cost of
building 'council houses' may reasonably be classed as social
service expenditure. But the Addison Scheme, in providing
virtually unlimited State subsidies and restricting them to
local authority building, while at the same time permitting
wide variations of rents in accordance with tenants' incomes
and needs, had the makings of a national housing service comparable with the national health service of thirty years later.

The second period of the inter-war history was marked by
the Chamberlain (1923) and Wheatley (1924) Schemes and by
a revival, from 1924 onwards, of unsubsidised private enterprise building. The Housing, etc., Act of 1923, promoted by
Neville Chamberlain, maintained the principle that working-
class housing should be subsidised, but was otherwise in sharp
contrast to the Addison Scheme. First, the subsidy was

granted primarily for houses built by private enterprise; local authorities were only to build if private building was shown to be inadequate. Secondly, the amount of the State subsidy was fixed at £6 per annum per house for twenty years, and there was no compulsory supplement from local rates, though local authorities could add to the subsidy if they wished. Thirdly, the scheme was to apply only to houses built by October 1925; by which time it was assumed that the housing shortage would be over. Fourthly, although landlords could let at any rent they desired, the fixed subsidy clearly prevented any concessions to poorer tenants unless the local authority provided an additional subsidy out of rates.

The Wheatley scheme, embodied in the Housing (Financial Provisions) Act of 1924, was a compromise between Chamberlain and Addison. Local authorities could now build and claim subsidies on an equal footing with private enterprise. The State subsidies were raised from £6 to £9, with a special subsidy of £12 10s. in rural parishes, and were to be payable for forty years instead of twenty; and local authorities were to fix rents of houses built by them at levels comparable *on the average* with those of 1914 provided this did not involve an additional subsidy from rates equivalent to more than £4 10s. per house per annum. Discrimination among tenants was therefore possible, but the total loss which local authorities were obliged to incur on their housing schemes was limited. Finally, the Chamberlain scheme was extended to houses built by 1939 (instead of 1925) and for both schemes a long-term building programme was introduced.

The two schemes ran side by side until 1930, private enterprise using the Chamberlain subsidies and local authorities, for the most part, the Wheatley subsidies. In 1930 the Chamberlain scheme was discontinued. In the same year the Greenwood scheme, concerned mainly with slum clearance, came into operation to supplement the Wheatley scheme, and in 1933 the Wheatley scheme was repealed.

The third period is described by Dr. Bowley as 'the return to a sanitary policy'. It was assumed that the general housing shortage, if it still existed, could be taken care of by unsubsidised building both by local authorities and by private enterprise. Subsidies were to be concentrated on slum clearance and replacement and, after the Housing Act of 1935, the abatement of overcrowding. The doctrine that housing subsidies should be confined to these fields of housing policy was supported by the economy campaigns of the depression years and in particular by the *Report on Local Expenditure* of 1932.

Under the Greenwood slum clearance scheme, the local authority subsidy was fixed at £3 15s. per house for forty years, but the Treasury subsidy varied in amount according to the number of people rehoused. It therefore assisted large families. Also, it was higher in agricultural than in urban parishes, and there was a special addition in the case of flats erected on expensive town sites. Under the 1935 Act, however, the payment of any Treasury subsidy at all for the rehousing of overcrowded families was limited to the special cases of agricultural dwellings and town flats, unless the burden on the local rates could be shown to be unreasonable. Discrimination among tenants in the fixing of rents for local authority houses had thus become less and less feasible. Under the Addison Act full discrimination was possible; the Wheatley Act restricted discrimination by limiting the total subsidy; the Greenwood and 1935 Acts confined it to certain special classes. Some flexibility was restored by the Housing Act of 1936, which allowed local authorities to merge all their housing subsidies, under the various schemes, in one account, the only proviso being that total rents plus total subsidies must cover total costs.

Between 1920 and 1939 nearly 4 million houses were built in England and Wales. The average annual rate of building was 67,000 up to 1924; 199,000 between 1925 and 1934; and 334,000 between 1935 and 1939. Only twice did local authority building contribute more than 100,000 houses in one year; in 1928, at the height of the Wheatley programme, and in 1939, when slum clearance and de-crowding got well under way. Subsidised private enterprise building rose to a peak in 1927, when nearly 80,000 Chamberlain houses were built. Unsubsidised private enterprise contributed more than 100,000 a year from 1931 and more than 200,000 from 1934. Altogether local authorities built 1·1 million and private enterprise 2·9 million, of which 2·5 million carried no subsidy. It should be added that the fall in building costs and interest rates reduced the 'economic rent' of new houses continuously from 1925 to 1935. The economic rent of an ordinary working-class house was 12s. a week in 1925 and less than 8s. in 1935. The various subsidies would reduce the rent by anything up to 4s. 8d. a week. For example, in 1934, the net rent of a new Wheatley or Greenwood house was less than 4s. a week. On the other hand the majority of the houses built by private enterprise were not of ordinary working-class type and carried correspondingly higher rents.

Whatever the position on rents and subsidies, however (not forgetting that the majority of pre-1914 houses were still rent restricted), the total supply of housing by 1939 seemed to be more than adequate. Four million houses had been built since 1919. The initial shortage, plus replacement of houses demolished, plus the increase in the number of families, amounted to a total requirement of about 3·4 million. With a total surplus of over half a million houses, the solution of the rent, slum and overcrowding problems was less formidable.

The war put the clock back, and in 1945 the supply problem again dominated housing policy. The need for a Government post-war housing programme was recognised even before the end of the war, and the first statement of policy[1] set out a requirement for 1¼ million new houses. Of these, 300,000 were needed to make up for the small amount of building during the war; 200,000 to replace houses totally destroyed, and 250,000 to replace those made uninhabitable by enemy action; and 500,000 to replace houses which had become unfit through age and neglect. It was expected that building costs would be abnormally high while the building industry was recovering its pre-war capacity, and during this period subsidies

[1] Ministry of Reconstruction: *Housing*, Cmd. 6609, March 1945.

7

would, it was said, be provided both to local authorities and to private enterprise. The programme was to include about 150,000 temporary houses of the prefabricated type, costing about £1,000 each and financed entirely by the Exchequer.

By the end of 1951, 1,016,000 new permanent houses and 157,000 temporary houses had been built in Great Britain. The average annual rate of building had been about 200,000 since 1948. Mr. Bevan's Housing Act of 1946 had confined subsidies to houses built by local authorities, the normal annual subsidy being £22, of which the Treasury contributed £16 10s. and the local authority £5 10s. The special rates of subsidy for agricultural dwellings and town flats built on expensive sites had continued. A licensing system had restricted private enterprise building to one house for every four built by the local authority.

This period also saw some interesting developments in town planning. First, the Town and Country Planning Act of 1947 was used to control the location and expansion of factories. Secondly, it became fashionable for local authorities to publish long-term Plans, drawn up by distinguished architects, showing the shape of things to come, and requiring future construction of streets and buildings to conform to the Plan. Thirdly, under the New Towns Act of 1946, the Government appointed Development Corporations to supervise the expansion of certain areas in which the 'overspill' population of existing towns, especially Greater London, would be housed. In some cases, the New Towns would also develop their own industries and continue the encouragement of the setting up of new industries which before the war had been the main function of the Industrial Trading Estates. Within four years fourteen New Towns were designated, eight around London, and six in other parts of the country.[1]

In 1952 a new Government came into power, having committed itself to a building policy of 300,000 houses a year. The

[1] The London 'Ring' consists of: Basildon, Bracknell, Crawley, Harlow, Hatfield, Hemel Hempstead, Stevenage and Welwyn. The others: Corby, Cwmbrun, East Kilbride, Glenrother, Newton Aycliffe and Peterlee.

first statement of policy issued by the new Ministry of Housing and Local Government[1] did not suggest what the total building programme should be, but the Census figures of 1951 had pointed to a deficiency of between 1 and 2 million. The Census recorded 13·3 million occupied dwellings in Great Britain and 14·5 million actual 'households'. The apparent need for 1·2 million additional dwellings could easily become 2 million or more if many families living together in one household at the time of the Census were to divide and demand separate accommodation. The problem, as we noticed in section 1, was very much a matter of definition and of price. But clearly the housing shortage was not over, and so the new Minister of Housing, Mr. Macmillan, set about achieving his target. In the Housing Act of 1952, the normal annual subsidy was increased to £35 12s. (Exchequer share £26 14s.; rate subsidy £8 18s.). The restrictions on private building were gradually relaxed and licensing ended in November 1954.

From 1952 to 1955, 1,223,000 new houses were built in Great Britain, making a total of 2,240,000 since the war. From 1953 onwards, the annual rate was well above 300,000. In England and Wales local authority building fell rapidly as private enterprise expanded; in Scotland more than 90 per cent of the building was still by local authorities.

Important changes were introduced in 1955. Although the housing shortage was still serious in some places, the general position was much easier, and policy was diverted, as we saw on page 75, to slum clearance. The Housing Subsidies Act of 1956 first reduced subsidies and then (from November 1956) abolished them for all new building other than one-bedroom houses for elderly people, replacement of slum dwellings, and buildings in the New Towns. Local authorities were urged to review their rents in order to use the existing pool of subsidies for the benefit of tenants who most needed them. Government lending to local authorities through the Public Works Loans Board was checked in October 1955, when authorities were

[1] *Houses—The Next Step*, Cmd. 8996, Nov. 1953.

instructed to borrow in the open market wherever possible and the interest rates charged by the Board were raised accordingly.

There were, of course, important differences between the inter-war and the post-war histories of housing policy, but the similarities were remarkable: post-war shortage, high costs, subsidies, the drive for expansion, the shift to private enterprise, the 'return to a sanitary policy'. All this, however, related to new building. There was also a remarkable similarity in policy as it related to old houses: in neither period was any serious attempt made to deal with the intractable problems resulting from the Rent Restriction Acts. To these problems we now turn.

§ **6. Rent Restriction.** The responsibility for rent restriction is sometimes laid at the doors of the citizens of Glasgow, whose outcry against rising rents in 1915 was the immediate cause of the Increase of Rent and Mortgate Interest (War Restrictions) Act of that year. But they were merely spokesmen for the general popular resentment against rising prices and the profits that accrue, at such times, to those who hold stocks of scarce commodities. Ordinarily, and for most commodities, such profits play a significant part in the functioning of the economic system: demand is choked off by higher prices while profits attract more resources and encourage an increase in supply. In wartime, and especially in the case of housing, the system does not work in this way. Demand is made less elastic by rising incomes, supply by the cessation of building. In these circumstances the case for rent restriction is strong.

The Act of 1915 made it illegal to charge higher rents than those charged in August 1914 for all unfurnished houses or rooms of an annual value (net rateable value or actual rent) up to £35 in London and £26 elsewhere. Increases in rent would be permitted only when improvements were made or rates increased. It also became illegal for building societies and other lenders to call in mortgages or raise interest rates. Finally, tenants were not to be ejected from controlled property without good cause.

Subsequent legislation did not alter the principles of this first Act. In 1920 an increase of 40 per cent in controlled rents was permitted and the scope of the Act was extended to unfurnished houses and rooms of an annual value up to £105 in London and £78 elsewhere. From 1923 control was removed if the landlord obtained vacant possession. In 1933 all houses with an annual value (net rateable value *and* actual rent) above £45 in London and £35 elsewhere were released from control. Those of £20–£45 in London and £13–35 elsewhere were decontrollable on vacant possession. The rest ceased to be decontrollable. In 1938 all houses above £35 in London and £20 elsewhere were released; controlled houses below these values were to remain permanently controlled.

In 1939 a new Act fixed the rents of all unfurnished houses and rooms of an annual value up to £100 in London and £75 elsewhere at the level of September 1939, if they were not still subject to control under earlier legislation. Moreover, new houses and houses let for the first time after September 1939 were to remain at their initial rent. In 1946 Rent Tribunals were set up to review the rents of *furnished* accommodation; and in 1949 they were empowered to fix the rents of unfurnished accommodation let for the first time. No relaxation took place until 1954, when the Housing Repairs and Rents Act allowed increases in controlled rents up to not more than twice the rateable value of the house, provided the additional rent was spent on repairs.

The scope of rent restriction in 1939, twenty years after the war conditions which justified its introduction, is shown in the following estimates, published by the Ridley Committee:[1]

Dwellings in Great Britain in 1939

	millions
Owner-occupied . . .	3·0
Publicly owned . . .	1·5
Rented from private landlords:	
Not controlled . . .	4·5
Controlled . . .	4·0
Total . .	13·0

[1] *Report of the Inter-Departmental Committee on Rent Control*, Cmd. 6621, April 1945.

In 1956, eleven years after the second world war, an official statement[1] showed the position as follows:

Dwellings in Great Britain in 1956

	millions
Owner-occupied below Rent Act limits	4·65
Privately owned above Rent Act limits	0·1
Publicly owned . . .	3·5
Let furnished; let at low rents; tied cottages; etc. . . .	1·05
Let unfurnished at controlled rents	5·7
Total . .	15·0

Thus, in 1956, 5·7 million, or more than one-third of the total houses in Great Britain, were directly controlled, and these would include, allowing for demolitions, many of the 4 million which had been controlled since 1914. A further million were let furnished at rents subject to review by the Rent Tribunals. Any of the 4½ million owner-occupiers who attempted to let houses or rooms, furnished or unfurnished, would be subject to the approval of the Rent Tribunals. Most of the 3½ million owned by local authorities were subsidised. Only these are normally classed as part of the social services, but the fact remains that all the pressures worked in the direction of cheap housing, except for those who in desperation had bought their own houses at inflated prices.

The first consequence of rent restriction is the deterioration of property. The White Paper of 1953[2] estimated that, of the 7¼ million houses rented from private landlords, 2¼ million were a hundred years old or more; a further 1¾ million were more than seventy-five years old; and a further ¾ million more

[1] Ministry of Housing and Local Government: *Rent Control—Statistical Information*, Cmd. 17, November 1956.

[2] *Houses—The Next Step*. Comparison with the 1956 figures suggests that the number of rented houses was overestimated and the number of owner-occupied houses underestimated in this document.

than sixty-five years old.   Before the 1954 Act, most of these
houses were controlled at 1939 rents.   Many were controlled
at 1914 rents, plus the 40 per cent increase allowed in 1920.
Repairs costing £100 in 1939 cost £316 in 1953,[1] quite apart
from any allowance on account of increased age and the effects
of war.   Many landlords had therefore to forgo any return
on their capital and devote the whole of the rent to maintenance.   Some chose to maintain their property out of other
income.   Others were forced to neglect all but the most urgent
repairs, or sold out, usually to less conscientious landlords
who made no attempt to maintain the property.   Some even
attempted to give their property away, or donated it to the
local authority, who refused to accept it.   The last resort was
to execute a conveyance to a man of straw, who, when the
local authority sought to take action under the Public Health
Acts, because the property was becoming a public nuisance,
could not be found.[2]   Of course, not all these consequences are
attributable to rent restriction alone.   Higher rents would not
necessarily have prevented the progressive deterioration of old
property.   But rent restriction undoubtedly hastened it, and
no owner of property, old or new, can maintain it adequately
if revenue remains stable while the costs of maintenance
increase threefold.

The second consequence of rent restriction is to reduce the
mobility of labour.   The tenant of a rent-restricted house is
in effect being subsidised at the expense of the landlord.   He
becomes accustomed to spending a lower proportion of his
income on rent.   Any change of employment which necessi-
tates moving house means forfeiting the subsidy and adjusting
his standard of living accordingly.   He is hardly likely to find
another rent-restricted house, for most landlords, on obtaining
vacant possession, tend to sell, furnish, or convert their property in some way which enables them to escape from the

[1] Report of the (Girdwood) Committee on *The Cost of House Maintenance*, 1953.
[2] For a fascinating account of this and many other housing problems
in Salford, see Barbara N. Stancliffe and Mary S. Muray: *Till We Build
Again*, Social Welfare, October 1948.

unprofitable market for unfurnished accommodation. Indeed the tenant may forfeit not only the subsidy but the right to similar accommodation at any price. He will not want to store his furniture and take a furnished house. Local authority houses tend to be allocated by reference to long waiting lists and certain social priorities. Mobility of labour is heavily discouraged unless the new employer can provide accommodation or the worker is willing to wait his chance in the lottery of the housing market.

The third result of rent restriction is the maldistribution of housing by size. The owner-occupier of a large house, who finds it too big for him, is discouraged from converting it into flats at current building prices if the rent may be 'reviewed' by reference to the price of similar accommodation built many years earlier. The tenant of a large house, who finds it too big for him, may be paying a controlled rent much lower than that of any smaller house which he is likely to acquire. There is thus no price- or other mechanism by which the small family in the large house and the large family in the small house can change places.

Fourthly, rent restriction creates anomalies and inequities which are not justifiable on any grounds whatever. The longer rent restriction continues, the more rents become the reflection of nothing other than historical accident. There may be three identical houses in the same street, one of which is let at a 1914 rent (plus 40 per cent), another at a 1939 rent and another at a 1954 rent. In general, rent restriction penalises the landlord class and benefits the tenant class, and in wartime such a policy is defensible on the ground that landlords are in an exceptionally strong position. In peacetime it is sometimes defended on the grounds of redistribution of income from rich to poor, but it has long ceased to be true that all landlords are rich and all tenants poor. As for equity between one class of tenant and another, rent restriction does nothing to ensure that the poorest tenants occupy the cheapest houses.

Finally, rent restriction has the same result as any other price

control: it establishes an excess of demand over supply; supplies are allocated by rationing, queueing or luck; and the excess
demand is diverted into the uncontrolled sector of the market, in this case the sector in which houses are bought and sold.

Whatever its justification in the circumstances of war, rent
restriction has little to be said in its favour in peacetime. It
is not surprising, however, that politicians have been reluctant
to tackle the problem. The difficulties in the way of relaxation
are plain enough: how to ensure that increases in rent will be
devoted, to a reasonable extent, to maintenance and repair of
property; how to avoid the hardship of a sudden and substantial increase in rent for all tenants who have become accustomed to a standard of living based on exceptionally cheap
housing; how to avoid special hardship for tenants with very
low incomes, in particular pensioners, who are only kept above
the poverty line by the good fortune of having rent-restricted
accommodation; above all, how to overcome the attitudes
engendered by a forty years' campaign for protecting the tenant
against the landlord.

To some extent, the difficulties have been eased by the continued high rate of house building, and with the passing of the
Rent Act of 1957 there is a prospect of bringing the housing
market into balance by a combination of increased supply and
gradual relaxation of rent restriction.

The Act of 1957 removes control from (a) all houses with
a rateable value on 6 November 1956 of more than £40 a
year in London and £30 a year elsewhere in England and
Wales; (b) all owner-occupied houses; (c) all new lettings
after 6 June 1957 of houses of any value which become vacant.
Unfurnished houses below the value limits remain controlled
but may have their rents increased to between $1\frac{1}{3}$ and $2\frac{1}{3}$ times
their gross value,[1] depending on whether the landlord or the
tenant is responsible for repair and decoration. Furnished
houses below the value limits remain subject to supervision by
the Rent Tribunals.

[1] In most cases the gross value is between 30 and 50 per cent higher
than the rateable value.

To protect the tenants of houses which are decontrolled, no increase in rent or notice to quit is allowed before October 1958, unless the landlord and tenant negotiate a new agreement before that date.   Such an agreement must be for at least three years; it may provide for a higher rent to be paid before October 1958, but it cannot provide for notice to quit before October 1958, and even then six months' notice must be given. To protect the tenants of houses which remain controlled, three months' notice of rent increase must be given, and for the first six months during which increased rent is payable, the increase must not exceed 7s. 6d. per week.

In the case of furnished accommodation which remains under supervision, three months' notice to quit must be given until July 1958; thereafter four weeks' notice is necessary.

As for repairs, the tenant of a controlled house may make a list of necessary repairs and obtain a certificate from the local authority requiring the landlord to carry them out.   If he does not, deductions may be made from the increased rents.   Disagreement on this or any other matter may be resolved by appeal to the county courts.

Finally, the Act provides for a minimum of four weeks' notice, by landlord or tenant, for the conclusion of *any* tenancy. This replaces the one week's notice previously in force and applies to housing of any kind, including local authority housing.

CHAPTER IV

WORKING CONDITIONS

§ **1. Wages and Net Advantages.** Just as living conditions are not simply a matter of housing but depend largely on personal relationships in the household and the family, so working conditions do not merely consist in the physical environment of factory or office or shop but are similarly influenced by personal relationships. Few people work in isolation, and few would want to, but many a job which is otherwise congenial is marred by a difficult workmate, an awkward subordinate, a tiresome boss or a general atmosphere of tension between management and workers. Personnel problems, and the whole complex of industrial relations have, however, been excluded from this book, and in this chapter we are concerned with the description of the physical environment in which people work and the changes that have come about through the initiative of employers, the pressure of workers and, especially, State regulation through the Factories Acts. It will be convenient to concentrate on four aspects of working conditions, corresponding to the four principal fields of activity of the Factory Inspectorate: health, safety, welfare and the employment of women and young persons.

It is useful, however, to begin by examining the relationship between working conditions and wages. There is obviously a certain amount of interplay between the two, in the sense that workers may be willing to accept attractive working conditions as a compensation for low wages, or high wages as a compensation for unattractive working conditions. But we need to analyse this problem more carefully if we are to find the answer to such questions as: Why are the most unpleasant jobs not the highest paid? To what extent do working conditions affect the supply price of labour? How much in the way of 'welfare' facilities should the employer provide?

From time to time it is suggested, usually by engineers or members of that awe-inspiring profession, the industrial consultant, that the present 'chaotic' structure of wages should be replaced by a new system under which every job would be assessed and given a 'points' value. Points would be allotted for skill, accuracy, judgment, nervous strain, disagreeableness of the work and so on. The points would then be translated into money terms, the scheme would be agreed with the trade unions, wages policy would be rationalised and bargaining would no longer be necessary. The objections to such schemes are obvious: the vast difference between the grading of work in an engineering shop and the evaluation of wages in the labour market as a whole; the nice question as to who would decide the points; the fact that bargaining would not cease but merely shift from wage-rates to points; the difficulty of selling the scheme to any worker whose wages would be reduced; above all, the fact that wages are determined not only by technical considerations but by supply and demand.

Nevertheless, though these proposals ignore the fundamental element of scarcity, they have the merit of drawing attention to those advantages and disadvantages which explain many existing wage differences. They provide a useful introduction to the doctrine of equality of net advantages which partly governs the supply of labour to different occupations. 'Every occupation,' said Marshall, 'involves other disadvantages besides the fatigue of the work required in it, and every occupation offers other advantages besides the receipt of money wages. The true reward which an occupation offers to labour has to be calculated by deducting the money value of all its disadvantages from that of all its advantages; and we may describe this true reward as the net advantages of the occupation.'[1] We must now consider what these advantages and disadvantages are, and then ask to what extent competition will bring about a wage structure that equalises net advantages.

[1] *Principles*, p. 73.

One important consideration is the period of work: how many hours per week and how many weeks per year. Of two occupations, similar in all other respects, the one which has a longer normal working week or a shorter annual holiday (assuming holidays with pay) will not attract labour unless it offers higher wages. Then, there is the agreeableness of the work itself. Scientists of equal skill and ability may be attracted into academic work at a lower salary than they would require in the business world because, amongst other reasons, the work is said to be more congenial and the pressure less great. Again, the environment is important: workers may move from a dirty and dismal factory to a bright and clean one in the same trade and locality, unless there is an appropriate difference in wages. Social prestige also counts: given the choice between lower-paid clerical work and higher-paid manual work, many will choose the former, because of prejudices about the inferiority of manual work.

Another significant consideration is security and regularity of employment. Other things being equal, workers will accept lower wages in an occupation which provides regular work all the year round than in one subject to interruption. Work on the railways provides an example of the first, building work of the second. Closely allied to this is the matter of stability of income: a job that brings in a steady income of £10 a week will be preferred to one that brings in £14 in one week and £6 in another, even though the average income may be £10 a week. The average must be higher to compensate for the element of uncertainty. But there are exceptions to this principle in occupations providing occasional large prizes, because the disadvantage of uncertainty is more than offset by the lure of the lottery. Already in Adam Smith's day the legal profession was overcrowded and 'in point of pecuniary gain, evidently under-recompenced' because of 'the desire of the reputation which attends upon superior excellence . . . and . . . the natural confidence which every man has more or less, not only in his own abilities, but in his own good fortune.'[1]

[1] *Wealth of Nations*, Cannan Edition, Vol. I, p. 108.

And dock labour is a special case where higher rates of pay, to compensate for the irregularity of the work, attract a disproportionate supply of workers who overestimate their chances of employment.

Another advantage may be the opportunity to supplement normal earnings. Workers may accept lower wages in an occupation which provides gratuities. They may prefer a job in which there is, up to a point, 'guaranteed overtime', or a recognised opportunity for doing other remunerative work 'on the side'.

Finally, wages will be lower if commodities or services which the worker would normally purchase out of his income are provided in kind; and higher if the worker has to meet, out of his income, expenses that he would not otherwise incur. In the one case housing, or meals, or products of the firm may be supplied free or at less than their market prices. In the other case tools, or travelling expenses, or special clothing may be necessary, but the worker is responsible for providing them.

These last situations are of peculiar interest for two reasons. First, they are the only advantages and disadvantages in our long list (apart from supplementary earnings) which are recognised and taken account of by the Inland Revenue authorities. Secondly, in attempting to calculate their value, in the manner suggested by Marshall, several complications may arise. One is that the cost to the employer of providing free goods or services of a given quality may be higher or lower than the cost to the worker of providing them for himself. Products of the firm, for example, may be supplied to employees without incurring marketing costs. The value to the employee is greater than the cost to the employer. On the other hand, the canteen may be run on a scale which, compared with domestic or commercial catering, is uneconomical. The value to the employee is less than the cost to the employer. Another complication is that the employer may supply free goods or services of a better or worse quality than those which the employee would choose for himself. The traveller may be supplied with a bigger car than he needs because it enhances the reputation of the firm. On the other hand, the free meals which the worker gets in the canteen may be of a kind that he would not otherwise consume at any price. In each case the value to the employee is less than the cost to the employer. A third point is that where goods and services are provided, not free of charge, but at a price which the worker has to pay out of his money income, the price may be higher or lower than the open market price. If the firm's products are sold at wholesale prices, the employee's money income is supplemented by the difference between the wholesale and the retail price. But if, as under the truck system, the worker is compelled to buy inferior goods at prices appropriate to goods of better quality, his money income is thereby discounted.

We can now turn to the question of how far competition is likely to bring about equality of net advantages. We are not concerned with the whole theory of wages, but simply with the extent to which the *supply* of labour will adjust itself among occupations and localities in such a way as to equalise net advantages. If labour were homogeneous and completely mobile, we should expect a movement from the unpleasant to the pleasant occupations until the relative scarcity of labour in the first and the relative abundance of labour in the second brought about appropriate adjustments in their relative wages. But, of course, labour is not homogeneous. Even if there were equality of opportunity, relatively few people have the ability to become doctors or film stars or highly skilled technicians, and wages in these occupations reflect a natural scarcity as well as relative advantages. Nor is labour completely mobile. There are 'non-competing groups' among the different grades of labour, such that mobility within the groups tends to be much greater than between the groups. The groups commonly distinguished are the unskilled; the semi-skilled; the skilled; the clerical; and the professional. Moreover, mobility is a function of time. At any one time the existing labour may only be mobile between firms in the same industry and the same locality. Over a period, the flow of new recruits permits mobility between occupations and localities. Even within groups, mobility over time may be hampered by ignorance, family tradition, restriction of entry, lack of opportunity or the simple fact that demand is changing more rapidly than supply. Between groups, mobility is further impeded by inequality of natural ability and inequality of opportunity. Lastly, there tends to be a residuum of low-grade labour which is mobile within the unskilled group but rarely rises above it and depresses earnings in the group as a whole.

Thus, net advantages play some part in regulating the supply of labour, and in certain cases, e.g. where a worker will not accept a job unless he is promised a house, they are all-important; but, in many cases, their influence is secondary; and in some situations, though the outside observer may imagine them to be important, they do not in fact affect labour supply at all.

§ 2. Working Conditions in the Nineteenth Century.

One of the most difficult tasks of the social historian, or any other sort of historian, is to decide how much weight to attach to contemporary documents. He must ask not only whether they give a true picture, but also why they were written and by whom, in order to place them in their proper setting against the broader background of social conditions. In no field is this exercise in perspective more important than in the study of working conditions in the early nineteenth century. The most striking and the most accessible documents for this period are the reports of various Royal Commissions and Select Committees on the conditions of work of women and children in factories and mines, and the employment of boys in the sweeping of chimneys. These were the major evils of their time; these were the things about which the social reformers of the day felt most strongly; these were the facts which cried out to be publicised in order that something should be done.

The student of social problems should look at some of these reports, and especially at the arguments put forward in defence of conditions which are now considered indefensible; for, in so doing, he will learn that social progress requires not only legislation, not only the removal of ignorance and prejudice, but also the persuasion of minds often dominated by high motives and sincerely held doctrines. He will also realise that these conditions did not exist in every firm in the industries concerned, and that those industries and occupations comprised a quite small part of the whole economy. He will further discover that the employment of women and children for long hours of arduous work was not in itself new. It applied under the 'domestic system' of the eighteenth century. It had long been, and continued to be, customary in agriculture, which was the principal occupation in Britain throughout the nineteenth century. The new features were: in regard to health, the employment of men, women and children in the physically and morally unhealthy conditions of certain types of factory work; in regard to safety, the danger of accident and injury from new and unfenced machinery; in regard to hours of work, the likelihood of inadequate periods for meals and rest, and any sort of education of the children, on account of the tyranny of mechanised production; in regard to the age of the children, the employment of extremely young children for particular tasks to which they seemed to be specially suited.

These are the impressions that emerge from a critical assessment of the reports of the early nineteenth century. Later there were reports on a much wider range of industries and occupations, and though they were still mainly concerned with the employment of children, they served to emphasise the contrast between the bad conditions in certain firms, industries and occupations, and the less onerous conditions that prevailed over a large part of the economy, and so gave a more complete account of working conditions as a whole. Other contemporary literature fills out the picture to some extent, but the social survey, which sets out to describe social conditions, good and bad, impartially, and to measure them statistically, was unknown until the end of the century.

Before we turn to a descriptive account, three further general points are worth making in relation to the history of the early

8

part of the century. First, it seems improbable, though it has often been suggested, that employers as a class had changed their character and become grasping, brutal and callous as a result of the pressures of capitalist factory production. The reports throw up some shocking examples of this type of employer, but they may only represent the minority of bad employers that exist under any system, and there are also outstanding examples of good employers. In this connection the argument that employers cannot afford to spend money on the welfare of their employees unless their competitors are forced to do the same is most frequently found where market conditions are exceptionally tight on account of growing foreign competition or falling prices. Nevertheless, it is clear that where sub-contracting took place, e.g. a foreman had to pay his assistants out of a fixed gross wage, there was unusual scope for exploitation.

Secondly, there was a noticeable improvement, quite apart from the consequence of the Factories Acts, as the exceptional circumstances of the period following the Napoleonic Wars worked themselves out. Much of the misery of the 1820's was the consequence of war, of the high price of bread, of the extraordinary growth in population, of the bad administration of the Poor Law (which permitted pauper children to be drafted into factories), and of the influx, for a period, of an inferior type of employer and a low grade of labour. These circumstances did not last, and in the course of time the rising productivity of male labour and the use of more and heavier machinery facilitated the increase of money and real wages, the release of women and children, and the provision of 'welfare' services on a more generous scale.

Thirdly, a word must be put in for the economists. It is widely believed, and stands imprinted in many history books, that opposition to the Factory Acts was based on a doctrine known as *laissez-faire* and propounded by contemporary economists. In the first place, it is worth mentioning that the words *laissez-faire*, coined in France in the mid-eighteenth century, were only put into currency in this country by John

Stuart Mill in 1848. In the second place, it was not the economists, but politicians and publicists, who opposed factory legislation in the name of 'the great principle of Political Economy that labour ought to be free'. Further, of the economists of the time, Adam Smith and Bentham were too early to express an opinion but would probably have supported the Factory Acts; Ricardo made no reference to them; Malthus, McCulloch, Tooke and Newmarch supported them; Senior at first opposed them but later supported them. And Senior's early opposition was not based on '*laissez-faire*', but on a curiously simple idea that if profits were, say, 10 per cent of total revenue, and legislation reduced the total hours worked by 10 per cent, there would be no profits, trade would decline and the last state of the workers would be worse than the first. He later found the answer to this problem, and he did not at any time oppose intervention on behalf of children.

§ 3. **Nineteenth-Century Legislation.**   With all this in mind, we may now attempt to survey some of the campaigns that were carried on during the nineteenth century, often simultaneously and by the same people, for the improvement of working conditions.

The most extraordinary of these, since it lasted more than a century and seems, in retrospect, to have been obvious from the start, was the campaign for the climbing boys.

'In 1773 Jonas Hanway, traveller, philanthropist, and inventor of the umbrella, drew attention to the miserable condition of climbing boys, as the children employed in the sweeping of chimneys were generally called.   In 1873 Lord Shaftesbury, after a long life spent in public service, drew attention in the House of Lords to an inquest on a climbing boy, aged seven and a half years, who had been suffocated in a flue in the County of Durham.'[1]

The first Chimney Sweeps Act was passed in 1788.   It said that no boy should be apprenticed before the age of 8 and that

[1] J. L. and Barbara Hammond: *Lord Shaftesbury*, Chapter XV.

certain precautions should be taken.   The final effective Act
was passed in 1875, when the police took over the licensing of
sweeps and the enforcement of earlier Acts which had forbidden
climbing under the age of 21 (in 1840), apprenticeship under
16 (also in 1840), and employment for any purpose under 10
(in 1864), but had been extensively evaded.   During this
period four Commissions, the first in 1818[1], had shown the
practice to be not only dangerous and inhuman, but unnecessary, since nearly all chimneys could be adequately swept by
other means.   At least half a dozen Bills, the first in 1817, had
been promoted, several of them by Shaftesbury, and failed
to win a majority in Parliament.   Two societies, the London
Society for Superseding Climbing Boys, sponsored in 1803 by
the economist Tooke, and the Climbing Boys Society, formed
under Shaftesbury in 1847, had published case after case to
show that the law was being evaded.   Dickens' *Oliver Twist*
and Kingsley's *Water Babies* had brought home the facts to
those who did not read official documents.   But in spite of all
this, householders and housekeepers, master-sweeps and magistrates, conspired to continue the practice because it had always
been done, because the boys (those who survived) got used to
it, because with care the danger of injury, deformity and
disease would be lessened, and so on.   The opposition to other
pieces of social legislation can at least be explained and understood, even if it is thought to be unreasonable.   In this case
it is barely comprehensible.

The case for intervention on behalf of children in coal mines
was equally strong, but the history took a different course.
The facts only came to light round about 1840, and by 1842 an
Act had been passed which dealt effectively, if not entirely
adequately, with the problem.   There was a Select Committee
on Accidents in Mines in 1835, and some of its findings
prompted the inclusion of the coal mines in the terms of reference of the *Children's Employment Commission* of 1842.   This
was the Commission whose report exposed the scandal of

---

[1] *Report from the Committee on Employment of Boys in Sweeping of
Chimnies.*

young children aged 7 and 8 working long hours underground as 'trappers', 'fillers' and 'hurriers'. The trappers opened and shut the doors that regulated the flow of air through the underground passages; the fillers helped to fill the tubs of coal; and the hurriers pushed, or pulled with a harness, the tubs along the rails between the coal face and the pit shaft. They were often in complete darkness, accidents were frequent, and they sometimes suffered unbelievable cruelty. In a few areas women and girls as well as boys were employed in the mines. The revelation of these conditions so shocked the House of Commons that they passed Lord Ashley's Bill with hardly any opposition. The Lords took more persuading, and some concessions had to be made, but by the end of the same year the Mines and Collieries Act had excluded all women and girls, and boys under 10, from the pits. Government inspectors were to ensure that the legislation was effective and to enforce new regulations for the prevention of accidents.

The climbing boys and the children in the mines were, so to speak, self-contained issues. When we turn to the case of children in cotton factories, the story becomes more complicated. For the legislation that was first applied to children in cotton mills was gradually expanded into the network of factory law which, by the end of the century, covered factories and workshops in all industries; regulated the hours of women as well as 'young persons'; included health, safety and welfare provisions that affected all workers; and was administered by a Government inspectorate whose work was as varied and as valuable as that of any agent in the whole field of social services. Moreover, although the early factory legislation was inspired by the discovery of conditions as shocking as those of the coal-miners and chimney-sweepers, it did not aim at excluding children from factories altogether, but at regulating their conditions of employment to ensure, in the circumstances of the time, reasonable hours of work at different ages and adequate periods for rest and instruction. It may still be true that development in this fashion was partly the result of concessions to the opponents of factory legislation.

The first Factory Act is usually said to be the Act of 1802 'for the Preservation of the Health and Morals of Apprentices, and others, employed in Cotton and other Mills and Cotton and other Factories'. It resulted from the rapid growth in the practice of apprenticing pauper children, at a very early age, in the cotton and woollen mills of Lancashire and Yorkshire. Apprenticeships had to be licensed by magistrates, and when Dr. Percival, a Manchester surgeon, drew attention to the long hours, the hardship, the cruelty and the deformities suffered by many of these children, some of the magistrates refused to grant licences. Sir Robert Peel, himself a large manufacturer and employer of children, responded laudably to the pricking of his conscience by promoting the Bill in Parliament, and it passed with little opposition. The hours of apprentices were to be limited to 12 a day and they were not to work at night; they were to have suitable sleeping accommodation and a new suit of clothing once a year; they were to be taught 'the three R's' and to attend church once a month; factories were to have proper ventilation, and to be whitewashed twice a year; and joint visits by a magistrate and clergyman were to ensure that the Act was complied with.

Hours of work; education and welfare; healthy surroundings; inspection: here, except for any reference to the age of employment, was the embryonic outline of all subsequent factory legislation. But it was nothing more than that. The arrangements for inspection proved inadequate, and, in any case, the problem itself was changing. More and more 'free' children were being employed without any formal apprenticeship. Some were pauper children, many were from the towns, where the new mills driven by steam power were superseding the earlier ones which depended on water power.

The next stage is associated with the name of Robert Owen, who by 1815 had achieved astonishing success in a model factory at New Lanark, where no children under 10 were employed, well-organised education was provided, and the hours of all workers were limited to 12 a day, including 1¼ for meals. His evidence before the Select Committee of 1818 on

The State of Children employed in the Manufactories of the United Kingdom is the first convincing account of a pheno-menon that has been rediscovered time and again from that day to this: that, up to a point, shorter hours and better working conditions may lead to a compensatory increase in productivity.

The second Factory Act, passed in 1819, was a much watered-down version of what Owen, in the hope of extending the conditions of his experiment to the whole textile industry, had proposed. The Act applied only to cotton mills; it pro-hibited the employment of any children under 9 years of age; and those under 16 were not to work more than 12 hours a day, excluding meal times. But inspection was no more satisfactory than under the 1802 Act, and the next outburst of enquiry and publicity, beginning in 1830, revealed little im-provement in working conditions even in the limited field covered by the Acts.

Whatever the output of the factories may have been, the output of literature on the subject of factories was probably higher in the years 1830–1833 than at any other time in the century. The most prominent names in the campaign were those of Oastler, Sadler and Ashley. Richard Oastler, church-man, Tory and an advocate of the abolition of slavery in the West Indies, published a series of letters on 'Yorkshire Slavery' in the *Leeds Mercury*. He claimed that the con-dition of the children in the woollen factories was no better than that of the slaves in the West Indies; and since Yorkshire was a centre of the evangelical anti-slavery campaign, his comparison was as provocative as it could be. He demanded a 10-hour day for all factory workers under 21 years of age, and in 1832 Michael Sadler introduced a Bill on these lines. Sadler presided over the resultant *Committee on the Bill to Regulate the Labour of Children in the Mills and Factories of the United Kingdom* and produced devastating evidence that intervention was necessary. But his witnesses represented only one side of the case, and the session closed before the other side could be heard. Action was postponed, and in the first election after the Reform Act, Sadler lost his seat. Lord

Ashley (later Lord Shaftesbury, but at that time a Member of the House of Commons) took up the cause, and introduced another Bill, whereupon a Royal Commission, the *Factories Inquiry Commission*, was appointed to collect information. The Commission was extremely well organised, and its two main reports came out the same year, in 1833. It covered wool, linen, cotton and silk mills, and found in all these trades evidence of children being overworked at a tender age. On the whole, the woollen trade was better than the others; in the West of England both woollen and silk mills received much higher marks than elsewhere; small mills were in much greater need of supervision than large; and in any mill an unscrupulous manager or foreman could make the work unbearably hard for those under him. The damp of the flax mills, the dust of the cotton mills, and the necessity of standing for long hours and of stooping, especially in worsted spinning, entailed unusual hardship; and the evidence showed that the health of many children was permanently affected.

The reports were signed by Thomas Tooke, the economist, Edwin Chadwick, the administrator, and Thomas Southwood Smith, the authority on public health, probably the three most influential members of the Commission. They recommended legislation, and stressed the necessity for appointing full-time inspectors with full powers of entry. The Government accepted the reports, and in 1833 'An Act to Regulate the Labour of Children and Young Persons in Mills and Factories', the first effective Factory Act, was passed. It covered all the main textile trades but specifically excluded lace-making. In respect of age, it forbade employment of any child under 9, except in silk mills. In regard to hours, no child under 11 (to be raised to 13 in 1835) was to work more than 9 hours a day or 48 hours a week, with a variation in silk mills, where no child under 13 was to work more than 10 hours a day. No one under 18 was to work more than 12 hours a day, or at night. In regard to education, children under 13 were to attend school for 12 hours a week. The whitewashing of factory walls and ceilings was continued. Most important of all, four

Government inspectors were given all the necessary powers to enforce the regulations and were required to make regular reports.

From 1833 onwards it is more convenient to take, in turn, each of the separate aspects of factory legislation that we have distinguished, than to try to cover the whole field chronologically. We shall see how subsequent Acts extended the scope of the legislation, how they affected the age of employment, the hours of work, the education and welfare provisions, and the protection of the health and safety of workers. But first, two other reports, published in 1842 and 1863–7, should be mentioned. The *Children's Employment Commission* of 1842 is best known for its First Report on the mines. But a Second Report dealt with a number of other industries, including paper mills, potteries and lace-making, in the last of which it found children employed at an excessively early age, and night work taking place on a scale which apparently injured the health of the women and children employed. This was still largely a domestic industry and exceedingly difficult to regulate. Another *Children's Employment Commission* reported between 1863 and 1867 on a wide range of industries not already covered by the Factory Acts. It found, for example, that in the potteries children were still being employed at the age of 6, in hosiery at 4; that older children worked more than 14 hours a day; and that night work for children was common.

These enquiries were partly responsible for the extension of the scope of the Factory Acts during the 1860's. From 1833 until 1860 they applied only to the main textile trades. By 1861 lace-making in factories was taken in, so was textile finishing: the bleaching, dyeing and printing of yarn and cloth. In 1864 factories making pottery, matches, cartridges and percussion caps, and the trades of paper-staining and fustian-cutting, were included. The fustian cutters were the first home industry to come under the Factory Acts. In 1867 the field was extended to all factories, in all industries not already covered by legislation, employing 50 persons or more; and the first Workshops Act was passed, to regulate working conditions where less than 50 people were employed.   But, in covering the greater part of industry in this way, the two Acts included an enormous list of modifications and exceptions. The regulations for workshops were extremely varied and complicated, and inspection of workshops was, until 1871, placed not under the Home Office inspectors, but under the local authorities.   It remains only to mention the consolidating Act of 1878, when the distinction between factories and workshops was newly defined and, instead of depending on numbers employed, was based on the use or non-use of mechanical power.

We now turn to the age of employment.   In the 1833 Act the minimum age was 9.   Strange to relate, it was reduced to 8 in 1844, and there it remained for thirty years.   From 1874 no child under 10 was to be employed in any industry, from 1891 no child under 11, and from 1901 no child under 12. It was raised to 14 in 1920.   Throughout, persons under these ages were classed as 'children', but a new category, called 'young persons', was recognised from 1847 onwards.   These were persons who had ceased to be children but were still under 18.   Already in 1833 they were prohibited from doing night work, and in course of time regulations which applied to women of 18 and over were also applied to young persons of both sexes.

Developments in regard to hours of work for children became part of the wider political campaign known as the Ten Hours Movement.   The aim of the movement was to limit work to 10 hours a day for all workers.   Owen claimed it for children in 1817, Sadler for all under 21 in 1830; and the agitation grew to a climax with the Ten Hours Act of 1847 and continued into the 1850's.   But the tactics changed with the political climate.   Some of the thunder was stolen when the Government limited the hours of children to no more than 9 a day under the 1833 Act but left the hours of other workers uncontrolled, the argument being that the children were most in need of protection and that 10 hours a day for all would not discriminate sufficiently in their favour.   The movement was further embarrassed when Robert Owen decided that all the world's work could be done in an 8-hour day and set up a rival organisation to achieve this aim. By 1840 the 10-hour enthusiasts had decided to fight for women and children only, assuming that they were more likely to succeed on this basis and that in most factories the proportion of female and child labour was such that the men could not work when the women and children were not there. In 1844 the hours of children only were reduced to 6½ hours. The Act of 1847, which applied only to textile factories, established a 10-hour day for women and young persons, and there the matter stood until 1937, except for wartime regulations which permitted a temporary increase in hours. For non-textile factories and workshops, however, to which the legislation was extended in the 1860's, the normal hours of work for women and young persons were 10½.

Meanwhile, soon after the 1847 Act came into effect, it became clear that the times of work, as well as the total hours, would have to be regulated. The agitators, finding that men were still working long hours, came out openly in favour of 10 hours a day for adult male workers. The inspectors, for their part, found it impossible to administer the Act when different workers were stopping and starting work at different times. And so a normal working day began to be defined. An Act of 1850 laid down that women and young persons must not be *employed*—working, eating or resting—outside the hours of 6 a.m. to 6 p.m. or 7 a.m. to 7 p.m. Later Acts stipulated time limits for children, went into more detail about meal and rest periods, and in some cases varied the hours to allow for shift working and the special conditions of workshops.

The development of education was to some extent linked to the Factory Acts. When, in 1833, factory children were required to have instruction for 12 hours a week, they attended either a factory school or one of the schools maintained by charitable organisations and Churches. The Sunday schools, also, did not confine themselves to religious knowledge, but taught reading, writing and arithmetic.   The first Parliamentary Grant for education was made in 1833, but for a time the only grants received by factory schools were allocations which the factory inspectors were allowed to make out of the fines exacted for breaches of the Factory Acts.   In due course other bodies started schools and a regular grant system from public funds was established.   The quality of the teaching and the regularity of attendance varied greatly, but the growth of the 'half-time system', whereby children could work their $6\frac{1}{2}$ hours in the mornings and be free for instruction in the afternoons, or *vice-versa*, provided an opportunity for improving the arrangements.   The system would have been regularised in the Factory Act of 1844, but in drafting the Bill, the Government made the mistake of placing the direction of the education of factory children in the hands of Anglican clergymen, and the education clauses were thrown out by the Nonconformist opposition.   But the main obstacle to the efficient education of factory children was the lack of an efficient Education Act, and a big improvement took place from 1870 onwards, when the Elementary Education Act came into force.

Lastly, the health and safety of workers received increasing attention during the century.   Cleanliness, sanitation, temperature, ventilation, were all made subject to regulation and inspection; the fencing of machinery and the reporting of accidents was enforced; and towards the end of the century certain trades were designated as 'dangerous' and special precautions were introduced.   By 1901, when a new consolidating Act of 81 pages was passed, the inspectorate had grown from 4 to 137, including 8 lady inspectors, and their intervention, so far from being resented, was welcomed throughout industry. Inspection was only a part of their activities; they advised on all matters concerning the health, safety and welfare of workers; they reported on accidents; they collected and published valuable statistics, including, incidentally, a mass of figures on the number, capacity and employment of factories in the textile industries half a century before the first Census of Production.

§ **4. The Factory Acts Today.** The regulation of working conditions at the present day is mainly governed by the Factories Act of 1937, which repealed the Act of 1901 and consolidated the legislation passed since that date. In 1940 the administration of the Act was transferred from the Home Secretary to the Minister of Labour and National Service. By 1955 the staff consisted of 381 inspectors and their territory included 214,000 factories with mechanical power and 18,000 without mechanical power. During the last half-century, however, various other 'premises' have been gathered in. The Act applies, for example, to dry docks and wharves, to building sites (27,000 in 1955), to railway sidings ancillary to a factory, to film studios, and to places where theatrical costumes and properties are made, adapted or repaired. But the stage and dressing-rooms are specifically excluded, and in this industry as in all others, the Act applies only where 'work is carried on by way of trade or for purposes of gain'. The amateur dramatic enthusiasts need not fear a visit from the inspector.

The minimum age of employment is still 14, but in practice it is 15 or 16, because the Education Act of 1944 has raised the school-leaving age to 15 and proposes to raise it to 16 as soon as possible. The health, safety and welfare clauses of the Factories Act apply to all workers, but the conditions as to hours of employment apply only to women and to young persons under 18. Children have risen in status and become 'young persons under sixteen', or juveniles. Their hours of work are limited to 9 a day and 44 a week, while women and young persons over 16 may work 48 hours a week; and in all cases the times of work and the periods for meals and rest are specified. Overtime work is permitted in special circumstances, but Sunday work is forbidden. The campaigners of last century would, however, not be disappointed to find that the hours of men are still uncontrolled by the Factory Acts, for the men have achieved a much more satisfactory and flexible system through collective agreements between trade unions and employers' associations. It is the women who now complain, in the name of equality of the sexes, that they suffer restrictions which do not apply to the men; but whether they would like the men to be restricted, or themselves to be unrestricted, is not clear.

The health clauses specify certain minimum standards for every factory room: how often it must be swept, washed and painted, how many cubic feet of space each worker must have, the temperature for sitting workers, the temperature for standing workers, the ventilation, the lighting and the sanitary arrangements. The safety clauses provide for the fencing of machinery, the control of lifts and cranes and hoisting tackle, and the taking of special precautions with dangerous material or equipment. The welfare clauses provide for drinking water, washing facilities, accommodation for clothing, and first aid. Accidents and industrial diseases must be notified, and a considerable part of the inspectors' work consists of investigating accidents. In 1955, 703 fatal accidents and 187,700 non-fatal accidents were reported, the most dangerous trades being apparently building, shipbuilding, iron and steel manufacture, electrical engineering and motor vehicles.

It must not be thought, however, that the elaborate detail of some of the clauses of the Factories Act implies standards that are either rigid, costly to the employer, or difficult of achievement. There is ample provision for the Minister or the inspectors to impose different standards where special circumstances require them. As for the cost, many employers made provision for their workers on a more generous scale than that required by the Factory Acts, before the Acts came into operation. The standards are minimum standards, and are designed to ensure satisfactory working conditions in a minority of backward firms, not to make everyone conform to average standards or to emulate the higher standards of the progressive firms. Nevertheless, technical progress has the dual effect of permitting the minimum standards to be raised and of introducing new processes, new dangers and new diseases which call for special attention. The recent reports of the Chief Inspector of Factories deal with the precautions necessary for protecting the health and safety of the workers where, for example, automation is introduced, new techniques in chemical engineering are developed, and radioactive materials are used.

§ 5. Working Conditions in Full Employment. The detailed account of the development of the Factory Acts may have given the impression that the improvement of working conditions is entirely the fruit of legislation. All that is needed is an energetic group in Parliament to carry the laws through, and an efficient inspectorate to see that they are enforced. But it was suggested on page 98 that technical progress, by lowering costs of production, facilitated an improvement in working conditions which the Factory Acts merely endorsed. And, since the end of the second world war, there have been substantial improvements unaccompanied by legislation, largely as a consequence of a high level of demand and employment. Is it possible to assess the respective roles of legislation, technical progress and prosperity in promoting better conditions of work? What of Robert Owen's contention that better working conditions are the *cause* of higher output? Were the manufacturers of the Victorian Age entirely misguided in saying they couldn't afford it? Was Dickens's sarcasm justified when he wrote in *Hard Times* of the millers of Coketown?

'They were ruined when they were required to send labouring children to school; they were ruined when inspectors were appointed to look into their works; they were ruined when such inspectors considered it doubtful whether they were quite justified in chopping people up with their machinery; they were utterly undone when it was hinted that perhaps they need not always make quite so much smoke.'[1]

In trying to sort out these issues, let us assume that weekly wage rates do not change, whatever happens to hours of work and output. Then the *initial* effect of providing better working

[1] Quoted by Mrs. C. D. Rackham in her useful little book on *Factory Law* (1938).

conditions is to increase the average costs of production: if hours of work are reduced, the same total cost is spread over few units of output; if more amenities are provided, higher total costs are spread over the same amount of output. The *further* consequences depend on the health and morale of the worker, the efficiency of the other factors of production, and the state of the market for the product. Let us take the workers first. Robert Owen's contention applies only where the worker's effort has been so weakened by bad working conditions that he now increases his output to an extent that compensates for the additional cost of providing better conditions. If long hours of work have sapped his energy by depriving him of rest and leisure, shorter hours may enable him to produce more per hour and the same amount per day; so that, if wages remain the same, total and average costs are back where they were. If the improvement consists, not of shorter hours, but of pleasanter surroundings or better welfare facilities, the worker may become less fatigued or depressed and produce more output per day than before. Total costs are higher, but so is output and revenue, and average costs may be unchanged. Owen was certainly right in saying that long hours and bad conditions affected the health and output of the workers. He was probably right in maintaining that in many cases a combination of shorter hours and better conditions, wisely administered, would have the same results as in his factory at New Lanark. But he may have been wrong in contending that the results could be achieved by legislation. All of which applies equally to more recent experiments in increasing the enthusiasm of workers in factories.[1]

We turn now to the other factors of production. We assume that the improvement in conditions does not lead to a compensatory increase in output, and we assume for the moment that the price of the product does not change. Average costs are increased, and the average rate of profit reduced. If profits have been more than adequate, the result at this

[1] See, for example, the famous Hawthorne Experiment, described in Elton Mayo: *The Social Problems of an Industrial Civilisation*, 1949, ch. IV.

stage is a redistribution of rewards between capital and labour, without any effect on employment or enterprise. If profits become less than adequate, the entrepreneur may either increase the efficiency, and so reduce the average costs, of management; or he may substitute capital for labour in a way which reduces the average cost of the two together; or, if neither is possible, he may close down. In different industries and at different times all these possibilities arise. The political problem is that employers are too ready to argue that they will be ruined and workers are too ready to assume that profits are more than adequate. The historical problem is that better conditions, whether enforced by legislation or introduced voluntarily, often coincided with improved mechanisation and a lowering of average capital costs, and it is dangerous to generalise about which came first, or whether one could have taken place without the other.[1]

Finally, we consider the market for the product. We suppose that the improvement in conditions raises costs and that the price of the product may vary. The result now depends on the elasticity of demand. But it is important to distinguish between the firm and the industry. If there are differences of efficiency, the efficient firms can afford to provide better conditions without raising their price, and the general enforcement of better conditions by legislation may drive some inefficient firms out of the market. If the firms are of equal efficiency,

---

[1] In this connection, see the copy of G. H. Wood's scholarly *History of Wages in the Cotton Trade* (1910) in the Marshall Library in Cambridge, which contains some interesting pencil comments in Marshall's handwriting. On page 135, Wood says: 'We thus arrive at the negative conclusion that reductions in the hours of labour have not prevented wages from rising. We may, therefore, ignore the question which is naturally raised in considering the causes of the advance, namely, "How much higher would wages have been if the old hours had been continued?" We have no evidence that they would have been any higher. The operatives have soon earned as much in the short week as in the previous long one, because they have drawn on their "reserves of personal efficiency" and the organisation of the work has been improved and the machines speeded'. Marshall comments: 'Yes, but a fallacy of the first order is involved in assuming that this improvement is *caused* by the reduction of hours. . . .'

9

a single competitive firm which incurred higher costs by improving working conditions would be at a disadvantage. There is then a case for enforcing a general improvement by legislation if the demand for the product in the market as a whole is inelastic. Higher costs and higher prices can be passed on to the consumer without much reduction in demand. If, however, the market demand is elastic, the enforcement of better conditions will intensify the pressure to reduce costs in other directions or, if this is not possible, raise prices and bring about a substantial fall in demand. Many of the arguments used in connection with nineteenth-century legislation turned on different interpretations of the market situation. Thus, as between firms, some employers could claim that they had introduced better conditions without any legislative interference; others argued that they could not afford better conditions unless their competitors were forced to do likewise; others maintained that they would be ruined. As between industries, employers in highly competitive export markets could complain that the increase in costs would drive them out of the market and throw their workers out of employment, while reformers, with an eye on the home market, argued that lower output and higher prices would both be for the benefit of the workers in the industry in question.

Nothing that has been said alters the fact that in certain cases working conditions were so bad, especially as they affected the health of children, that they needed to be improved on humanitarian grounds, by legislation or otherwise, whatever the economic consequences. But all work becomes exhausting at some point, and the further one goes beyond the obvious cases of hardship, the more the economic considerations become relevant. Political discussion on the reform of social conditions is bedevilled by exaggeration of one aspect or another.

We have been discussing the improvement of working conditions in market situations in which demand conditions were stable: price elasticity might be high or low, but at any given price, demand was fixed. We may now consider what happens when demand is expanding, either because consumers' expenditure on some products is growing, while on others it is declining, or because aggregate incomes are increasing, and expenditure on nearly all products seems to be on the up-grade. In the first case, in the expanding markets, prices will rise through the pressure of demand, producers will get higher profits and will attempt to expand output. They will try to attract labour by offering higher wages, and in these circum-stances an improvement in working conditions is highly probable. Demands by the existing labour force for better amenities will be more readily met, and from the point of view of recruitment, good conditions may prove as strong an attractive force as high wages. As between firms, also, competition for additional labour may result in a general improvement in working conditions. But the improvement is not likely to take the form of shorter hours; on the contrary overtime work will be encouraged and made more acceptable in various ways.

The second case, in which aggregate incomes are increasing faster than aggregate output, is the situation in Great Britain since the end of the war. Prices rise generally. A very high proportion of firms and industries want to expand and com-plain of labour shortage. The level of employment is very high; there are no reserves of unemployed labour and no declining industries throwing up labour. For the improve-ment of working conditions, this is a field day; it goes beyond anything achieved by legislation, by social progress or by the pressure of expanding industries in a stable economy; and to some extent better working conditions may even take pre-cedence over higher wages. How does this come about?

In the first place, an economy with a very high level of employment soon develops wage-inflation. Employers com-pete for labour; wages rise; costs of production increase; prices are raised; demand is not reduced because incomes are rising; incomes are rising because employers compete for labour. Official policy attempts to break the circle by dis-couraging increases in wages. Employers respond, if at all, by offering other inducements to labour.   Some of them, such as rent-free houses and generous pension schemes, would not normally come under the heading of better working conditions. But that is what they amount to.

In the second place, employers may intensify this practice, not because increases in wages are officially frowned upon, but because they are ineffective in redistributing labour between industries.   This also encourages the practice of offering inducements in kind which could be broadly described as improvements in working conditions.

Thirdly, although mobility of labour in a fully employed economy tends to be low between industries and areas, it is high between local firms.   This explains the apparent contradiction between official complaints that workers are not moving into the so-called under-manned industries and simultaneous complaints by employers that they cannot keep their labour. Attempts to reduce local mobility, and even to 'hoard' labour, again take the form of offering attractions in kind: canteens, music-while-you-work, sports facilities and what not.

Fourthly, special inducements, ·in addition to high wages, tend to be offered to the only two groups in the labour market which are, so to speak, floating: the new recruits from schools and universities, and the married women.   The one is offered training schemes, grants for further education and promises of excellent conditions; the other is offered day-nurseries, baby clinics and rest-rooms.

Fifthly, an overloaded economy, as it has been called, has interesting results in relation to the 'non-competing groups' described at the beginning of this chapter.   The general shortage of labour leads to the employment, wherever possible, of semi-skilled workers to do skilled work, and of unskilled workers to do semi-skilled work.   Workers at the top of each group have an exceptional opportunity of moving up to the bottom of the next group.   The lowest group is depleted, unskilled labour becomes scarce, and, in so far as unskilled work is also unpleasant work, 'net advantages' come into their own and the worst jobs become relatively well paid.

As for hours of work, the effect of full employment is not to reduce them, but to encourage a shorter normal working week, combined with longer periods of overtime at higher rates of pay. Here, in conclusion, are some of the comments of the Chief Inspector of Factories in his Annual Report for 1955:

'Serious manpower shortages, consequent on full employment, were experienced by all industries, except the cotton industry, where as the result of some recession there was short-time working and some redundancy; workers affected were, however, quickly absorbed into other industries.'

'The basic week remained one of 44–45 hours worked in five days, but considerable overtime beyond the basic week was worked. Sunday work by men was widespread, and some illegal employment of women and young persons on Sundays took place. On the whole, workers are not disposed to work on Saturdays, being quite prepared to substitute Sunday for Saturday, which they claim is their only free day for shopping, sport and most forms of entertainment.'

'Part-time work by married women is now an integral and indispensable feature of factory life. The hours favoured by married women on day-work are from 9 a.m. to 4 p.m., which permit them to see the children off to school and to be back at home for their return. . . . The most popular system of all is the part-time evening shift between 5 p.m. and 10 p.m.'

'The actual hours of work continued to be determined by the wishes and convenience of the workpeople available. In consequence, in many factories, several schemes of hours operated simultaneously. . . . Many of the schemes, being outside the provisions of the Factories Acts, were allowed by relaxations . . . under the Defence Regulations.'

'. . . children of compulsory school age have been employed in factories after school hours, on Saturdays and

during vacations, particularly during the summer holidays.
. . . Employers are only too glad to avail themselves of the
services of these children, not only to meet immediate production requirements, but in the hope that they will take up
permanent employment with them on leaving school.'

'. . . a large firm . . . introduced a special scheme of employment for their old-age pensioners . . . they start half an
hour later and finish an hour earlier than the rest of the
factory . . . and are provided with a small rest-room for
their private use.'

CHAPTER V

UNEMPLOYMENT

§ 1. Unemployment Statistics. The most serious aspect of unemployment is the personal aspect. The man who is out of a job may go through several stages of personal distress. He suffers, first, loss of income, and whatever may be done to assist him, his whole outlook on life, and his decisions from day to day, tend to be dominated by financial insecurity. In time he may also suffer loss of self-respect, with the growing conviction that he is unwanted and useless. Eventually, he may suffer loss of hope, and cease to care about finding a job, or, for that matter, about anything else. In a few cases of mental or emotional instability unemployment is entirely a personal problem requiring personal treatment. But in general it is an economic and social problem; a question of finding out why the economic system does not provide regular employment for everyone and how far social policy can provide satisfactory remedies.

From the point of view of the entrepreneur, unemployment has more than a personal aspect. He may or may not be able to concern himself about the welfare of those whom he has dismissed. But he is vitally interested in the efficiency of his firm, and this will suffer just as much if he can only employ half his normal complement of workers as it will if he employs them all but they are not doing suitable and continuous work.

From the point of view of the economy as a whole, unemployed resources are wasted resources. But this does not mean that if every employable person had a job there would be no waste. For one thing, it frequently happens that people are in the wrong job. Their contribution to the national product would be higher elsewhere, but for some reason they do not move, or, through some fault in organisation, they are doing work that is unnecessary or producing things that nobody wants. Or, they may be working short-time because demand is slack, when they could be released for other work and leave behind a smaller labour force working full time. More important, however, is the fact that the pattern of consumers' demand is constantly changing, the structure of industry is constantly adapting itself to change, and some workers are consequently moving about from one job to another. This mobile labour force is not wasted; on the contrary, it provides the necessary margin for adjustment to change, and if there were not this elbow-room, the waste would probably be far greater. It would mean that workers were being held back in jobs of declining importance instead of moving to new and expanding trades.

Thus, on the one hand, some workers who are not actually unemployed may constitute wasted labour, while, on the other hand, some who are unemployed may not be wasted, but contribute to the more efficient functioning of the economic system. In part, the difficulty is a statistical one: the only simple way to measure unemployment is to record the numbers of people who report themselves as being out of work. In Great Britain since 1948, the whole working population have become contributors to the compulsory National Insurance Scheme, and anyone who has been unemployed for three days must lodge his contribution card with the nearest Labour Exchange in order to draw unemployment benefit. These cards are counted once a month, and the level of unemployment can then be expressed as a percentage of the insured population. But the limitations of these figures must be borne in mind. They do not include, for example, those who did half a week's work, or those who did not report to the Labour Exchange; nor do they include the self-employed, who are not entitled to unemployment benefit; and a large number of married women, who may choose whether or not to participate in the insurance scheme.

Unemployment statistics have been based on the insured population since 1926, but from 1926 to 1948 the insured population was not co-extensive with the working population: it consisted of all manual workers, and non-manual workers earning less than £250 a year (raised to £420 in 1942). For earlier years, there are figures going back to 1856, based on returns made by certain trade unions. Comparisons over long periods must therefore be made with caution. In the trade union period, unemployment was probably lower among the unions which reported than in the working population as a whole; in the 1930's it was probably higher among the insured population than in the working population as a whole.

The statistics now published by the Ministry of Labour make a useful distinction between the 'wholly unemployed' and the 'temporarily stopped'. The first category are out of a job and looking for a new one. The second are out of work but expect to be taken back in their old job as soon as possible. The wholly unemployed are further analysed according to the duration of their unemployment, and it is therefore possible to make a rough division between the 'hard core' who have endured a long period of unemployment and the others who, though unemployed, may not be suffering great hardship. The distinction is, of course, important: a small percentage of long-period unemployed may constitute a much more serious social problem than a larger percentage of short-term unemployed.

With some reservations, the statistics tell us all we want to know about how many men, women and young persons are unemployed; how long they have been so; where they are; and to what industries they belong. But they do not tell us *why*; and this is precisely the information needed to devise an effective employment policy. The cure of the disease depends on the cause. The first step is therefore to set out the possible causes of unemployment.

§ 2. Types and Causes of Unemployment.

§ **2. Types and Causes of Unemployment.** Some unemployment may be called *voluntary*. There are those, probably very few, who do not want to work and can afford a life of leisure.

There are others, especially those whose earning power is very low, who find it possible to survive on unemployment benefits and charitable donations, and who make no effort to obtain regular work. In earlier centuries, as will be seen in Chapter VIII, this group was a major concern of the Poor Law authorities; and when the wages of unskilled labour provided a bare subsistence, and vagrancy was common, the likelihood of voluntary unemployment was considerable. Today it is negligible.

Then, there are the *unemployable*. In a working population of 24 million there will inevitably be some who, through chronic sickness, mental instability or some other cause, are unable to find any suitable job or, having found it, to keep it for long. In addition, there are a number of elderly people who are fit for work, but whom no employer will engage because of difficulties associated with their age.

Casual unemployment arises in trades where the demand is irregular from day to day and from week to week. Dock labour, for example, is hired for the loading or unloading of a particular ship. Dockers report at the dock gates each morning and their employment depends on the arrival and departure of ships, which is obviously much more erratic than that of road and rail transport. What is more, the prospect of short spells of fairly remunerative work tends to attract more labour into these industries than is justified by the average level of demand. Unless recruitment is regulated in some way, therefore, casual unemployment becomes inflated, and if there is unemployment in other industries, some of their labour force may join the ranks of the casuals. In addition to work in the docks, certain kinds of repair work, and work which is affected by the weather, also give rise to casual unemployment.

Seasonal unemployment occurs when demand fluctuates, not erratically from day to day, but fairly regularly according to the time of the year. The hotel and catering trades, for example, reach their peak in the holiday season, building work tends to be brisker in the summer, agricultural work at harvest time; and the fashion trades also have their seasons.

Frictional unemployment is a term generally used in connection with all industries subject to short-period changes in demand, including casual and seasonal trades. It is useful, however, to reserve the word frictional for that unemployment which exists at any time simply because people are changing jobs. Such changes cannot always take place between Friday night and Monday morning, and, if there is a gap of a week or more, the worker is registered as unemployed. The question of replacement may determine the dates of relinquishing and resuming employment. The worker may decide to take a holiday. He may have to move house. He may have left one job, voluntarily or by dismissal, without the prospect of another, but in the knowledge that something suitable will soon turn up. Frictional unemployment in this sense may be reducible, but it does not usually involve hardship, and it indicates a degree of flexibility in the economy.

Another brand commonly distinguished is *technological* unemployment. Improvements in organisation, and the introduction of new machines, often throw men out of employment. This is an aspect of industrial efficiency, which, says Professor Robinson, 'consists in trying to do with eight men what we have hitherto been doing with ten men. It consists in creating unemployment . . . (it) has led to the release of workers, to the setting free of time and effort for the making of other things. We ought to regard every man added to the unemployment figures as a success, as an achievement, provided that we still get as much as we did before. It is only because the second half of our industrial organisation, the re-employment of the unemployed has broken down, that we do not so regard it.'[1] This sort of technical change is continually taking place, and for the individual worker who loses a skilled job and cannot get another at the same rate of pay it means serious personal hardship. Often, re-absorption of the unemployed is soon possible. But technical change sometimes occurs at too rapid a pace or on too big a scale and

[1] E. A. G. Robinson: *The Structure of Competitive Industry*, Cambridge Economic Handbooks, 1931, pp. 2–3.

becomes a significant cause of unemployment and distress. The growth of factory production in the nineteenth century was frequently the cause of technological unemployment, not merely because the machines themselves became more efficient, but because the organisation of production in power-driven factories required less labour. More recently, it has been associated with the reorganisation of particular large firms, rather than with technical developments in industry as a whole. 'When Ford reorganised his works in 1921, he succeeded in reducing the number of workers employed for every car built daily from sixteen to nine.'[1] Between 1926 and 1929 Cadbury's large-scale mechanisation of the Bournville factory displaced about 27 per cent of their labour force of 10,000.[2] At the present time, the various techniques that go under the heading of 'automation' threaten to create patches of technological unemployment as they are introduced in particular firms, industries and areas.

Export unemployment is worth mentioning as a separate category because fluctuations in the demand for exports have certain peculiar characteristics. Some industries produce mainly for export, they become exceptionally dependent on overseas markets, and a fall in demand may create localised unemployment when the remainder of the economy is very fully employed. The demand may drop suddenly, and sometimes only temporarily, because of political disturbances, changes in international trade policy, currency restrictions, crop failures and so on. Or, the setting up of a new manufacturing industry overseas may bring a gradual and permanent fall in demand. Whatever the cause, it is likely to be outside the control of the home Government, and it presents a different sort of problem from those consequent upon changes in the home market. The cotton industry is an outstanding example.

[1] E. A. G. Robinson: *op. cit.*
[2] Cadbury Bros.: *Industrial Record 1919–1939*, p. 60. The book contains an interesting account of the measures taken by Cadbury's to prevent hardship among the displaced workers, many of whom were re-employed by the firm as output expanded during the 1930's.

Structural unemployment results from long-term changes in the structure of industry. Invention and discovery provide new products, such as plastics, which replace the existing products and employ different processes and skills. Rising standards of living provide a new and varied demand for products and services previously enjoyed by only a small minority. The expanding industries employ more capital and labour, the declining industries less. But, as a rule, labour does not move from one industry and occupation to another. It is rather that the flow of labour into and out of industry changes its course. In the declining industries the rate of retirement exceeds the rate of recruitment, and the opposite occurs in the expanding industries. Where the structural change requires a more rapid adjustment than can be absorbed by this method, structural unemployment arises in the declining industries. This is more than a matter of allowing time for workers to move to another job, as in the case of frictional unemployment. It is different from export unemployment, caused by a fall in demand with no compensating rise elsewhere. Structural unemployment is a consequence of specialisation. There are, we assume, unfilled jobs in the new industries and unemployed workers in the old, but they lack the skill, or the adaptability, or the opportunity to move.

Finally, there is *cyclical* unemployment, associated with the movements of the trade cycle. The succession of boom and slump, prosperity and depression, which is discernible in the history of, at least, the 1830's to the 1930's, has been characterised by alternating periods of high and low unemployment in nearly all industries. Cyclical unemployment, therefore, is not confined to declining industries, or export industries, or seasonal trades; it is spread over the whole economy.

The trade cycle is not only an employment cycle. It is also an income cycle, a spending cycle, and, particularly, an investment cycle. Cyclical fluctuations in employment are much greater in the industries making investment or capital goods than in those making consumer goods. The demand for new consumer goods will rise and fall as incomes rise and fall, but people take time to adjust their level of consumption. If incomes rise, the increase will at first be saved rather than spent; if incomes fall, saving rather than spending takes the first cut; and there is a basic standard of consumption which must be satisfied. The demand for new capital goods, or investment, is much more erratic. In the first place, since they are much more durable, the existing stock of capital goods can provide a continuing flow of consumer goods for a long period without replacement or addition to the stock. There is not necessarily any urgency about investment: it can be postponed. In the second place, investment depends on how investors expect the level of consumption to behave over a period of years. If they expect it to rise, new investment will be undertaken, if they expect it to fall, even replacement may be neglected. In the third place, investment depends on an assessment of prices and costs during the lifetime of the equipment. The best time to invest would seem to be when the cost of capital and the rate of interest are low, but this is likely to be during the slump, when the price of the product and the prospect of profit are also low. Investors are pessimistic, and their pessimism prolongs the slump. Conversely, during the boom, capital costs and interest rates are high, but the expectation of rising prices and profits is higher. Investors are optimistic, and their optimism intensifies the boom. When it breaks, new investment is abandoned.

Fourthly, there is a peculiar relationship between the demand for consumer goods and the demand for capital goods. Let us suppose that the shipping industry has a fleet of 100 ships and that the ships last twenty years. The capacity and employment of the shipbuilding industry will normally be such as to supply a replacement demand of five ships per year. If the demand for shipping now increases by 5 per cent, five new ships will be required and the demand for ships is increased by 100 per cent. The shipbuilding industry will double its capacity and employment, but this level of employment in shipbuilding will not be maintained unless the demand for shipping *continues to increase* by 5 per cent every year. Of course, the expansion will not take place as simply and suddenly as this example suggests. But the principle of acceleration which it illustrates provides a further reason why employment in the capital goods industries is much more unstable than in the consumer goods industries.

Investment, then, is of special importance in the analysis of cyclical unemployment. New investment will increase the incomes of those newly employed, and that part of their income which was not saved will be spent, and so increase the incomes of others. These in turn will save part of their income and pass on the remainder. The process will continue, and the eventual increase in income and employment will depend on how much is saved at each stage. If the initial investment amounts to one million pounds, and each recipient of new income saves one-fifth and spends four-fifths, increases in income will accumulate until one million pounds has been saved and five million has been spent. This is the principle of the multiplier. Like the accelerator, it will not operate as simply and as thoroughly as this example suggests. But the part which it plays in spreading the effects of an increase, or a decrease, in investment is generally recognised.

The types and causes of unemployment have been separated out with a certain sharpness in order to prepare the ground for the discussion of employment policy in section 4. But it must not be imagined that they can be so clearly identified in practice. It may be possible to attach a label to a group of workers dismissed from a car factory in Birmingham or a pocket of unemployed in a Lancashire weaving town, but the unemployment statistics as a whole are not divisible into seasonal, structural and so forth. Nor can any particular unemployed man be consoled with the information that he is frictionally or cyclically unemployed. A man whose skill and experience make him particularly suited for a certain seasonal trade may, if there is general prosperity, easily find employment, in the off-season, in some other seasonal trade or in some industry which has no seasonal fluctuation at all. And, conversely, in a general depression, he may be out of work in the off-season, not because it is the off-season but because it is a declining trade or because there is a shortage of work everywhere.

One of the reasons for the severity of the depression of the 1930's was that we had all these types of unemployment together, and, in particular, a combination of cyclical, structural and export unemployment more intense than ever before. Before turning to employment policy in general, we must say a little about the social aspects of this period of unemployment.

§ 3. **The Social Aspects of Unemployment.** At this time of day (in 1956), after seventeen years of full employment, it might seem hardly necessary to devote much space to the social aspects of unemployment in the 1930's. For one thing, full employment has its own economic and social problems, scarcely dreamed of until after the war, but now far more interesting and urgent. For another, a depression on the scale of that experienced in the inter-war years is unlikely ever to be repeated. Slumps and unemployment in some measure there may be, but 'That disaster', as Professor Robertson says, 'was produced by a constellation of causes which may never recur, and aggravated by mistakes which *need* never recur.'[1] Far too many people continue to discuss the current economic situation as though the major problem were still mass unemployment; as though every little jump in the percentage of unemployed heralded a new era of misery and despair for one in every four of the population.

But this is precisely the reason why a study of unemployment in the 1930's is important and relevant. The student reader may not remember it, but the older wage-earner does, and those in authority do; and much of their thinking is dominated by the unforgettable experience of those years.

Let us first look at the extent of unemployment over the inter-war period. Following the very high level of employment in the first world war, there was some dislocation in 1919, a short-lived boom in 1920, and then a sudden slump, with

[1] Sir Dennis Robertson: *Britain in the World Economy* (1954), p. 60. The context actually refers to the years 1929 to 1932 in the United States.

unemployment soaring from 2 per cent to 17 per cent of the insured population, in 1921. Conditions improved up to 1923, when 11½ per cent were unemployed, and, apart from the coal strike in 1926, the percentage remained in the region of 10–11 until 1929. The severe depression then set in, and in 1931 and 1932 over 20 per cent were unemployed. The figure dropped continuously to just over 10 per cent in 1937. A new rise in 1938 was thought by many to mark the onset of another slump, but the rearmament programme introduced in that year prevented them from ever knowing whether it would in fact have come.

It is difficult to say whether the worst year was 1932, when the total number of unemployed in Great Britain was 2,750,000, including 350,000 long-term unemployed, who had been out of work for more than a year; or 1933, when the total was 2,480,000 but the number of long-term unemployed had risen to 460,000. For Great Britain as a whole, the unemployment rate in 1932 was 22 per cent, but it was higher in the North and Wales (28 per cent) than in the South (16 per cent). London had 13½ per cent and Wales 36 per cent unemployed in that year. The particular black spots were South Wales, Tyneside, Lancashire, Glasgow and Barrow-in-Furness. The coal and textile industries, especially cotton, were the first to suffer, followed by the metal trades, especially iron and steel; then engineering, shipbuilding and vehicles; and, quite soon afterwards, the building and constructional trades. Unemployment in coal and textiles could probably be labelled 'export' and 'structural' in our list of causes; the rest 'structural' and 'cyclical'; they included all the main capital goods industries. At the end of 1932, 60 per cent of all workers in shipbuilding were unemployed, 40 per cent of all workers in iron and steel.

It is not possible in a few pages to give an account of what all this meant in terms of economic, financial, social and personal dislocation. No other social problem has been studied and written about from so many angles. Lord Beveridge gives a concise analysis of the incidence of unemployment in Part II of his book *Full Employment in a Free Society*. On the

10

question of labour mobility, Mr. S. R. Dennison, in *The Location of Industry and the Depressed Areas*, shows how, in spite of the existence of some unemployment in all parts of the country, there was a noticeable 'drift to the South', where industry was relatively prosperous, year by year from 1923 to 1936. The proportion of insured workers in the South increased from less than 47 per cent in 1923 to 51½ per cent in 1936; the proportion of employed workers in the South increased from 47½ to 55 per cent. On the financial problems of unemployment relief, Miss Polly Hill, in a Fabian Society Report, *The Unemployment Services*, describes how various systems of relief, operating on different principles, under separate authorities, and drawing funds from different sources, attempted to provide at least a subsistence income for two million unemployed and their families. We shall return to this subject in Chapter IX. On the part played by the voluntary social services, a report made to the Pilgrim Trust, *Men Without Work*, gives a penetrating account of the attempts to prevent the isolation of the unemployed from the rest of society by providing clubs and other means of recreation and education. The personal attitudes and reactions of the unemployed are vividly portrayed in *The Unemployed Man* by Dr. E. W. Bakke, who went to live among them in Greenwich in order to find out what the world looked like from their point of view. The tragedy of concentrated unemployment in an area specialised on two industries that were particularly hard hit is passionately described in Miss Ellen Wilkinson's story of Jarrow: *The Town that was Murdered*.

Some of the clearest impressions come from the first part of the Pilgrim Trust Report, in which the circumstances of the long-term unemployed were surveyed by interviewing a representative sample in six different towns in 1936. These were men and women who had not had more than three days' continuous work for a year or longer and who were receiving benefits from the Unemployment Assistance Board. The survey left no doubt that the 'long unemployed' presented special problems that persisted long after the forces of recovery and mobility had eased the situation in regard to short-term unemployment.

In 1929, out of a total of $1\frac{1}{4}$ million unemployed, only 53,000, or less than 5 per cent, had been unemployed for more than a year; and 38,000 of these were miners, many of whom had not been employed since the strike of 1926. At that time, therefore, the long unemployed were a limited group mainly in one industry. In an average community, say a town of 40,000 inhabitants, only 50 families would be affected by long unemployment; in a non-mining community, only 15 families. This was the size of problem that the social services, voluntary and public, could be expected to deal with.

By the end of 1932, the situation was quite different. Total unemployment had more than doubled, to 2,750,000, but the long unemployed had been multiplied by seven: there were now 400,000, or 15 per cent of the total. In the autumn of 1933, when total unemployment was declining, the long unemployed were still increasing. They numbered 460,000, or 25 per cent of the total; which means that in our average community of 40,000 inhabitants, 480 families would be affected by long unemployment; a much bigger proposition for the welfare services. Three years later, in the autumn of 1936, there were still 300,000 long unemployed, and they accounted for 26 per cent of total unemployment.

Here in fact was the hard core of the pre-war unemployed. They did not share in the general recovery of 1933–1937. Nearly half of them were in four basic and, at that time, declining industries: coal, shipbuilding, iron and steel, and textiles. Since these industries are also geographically concentrated, the depression of the depressed areas was, measured by the proportion of long unemployed, greatly intensified. The industries which are more evenly spread over the country, such as distribution, public utilities and building, continued to be depressed in the depressed areas although they had fully recovered in the prosperous areas.

These men were not, for the most part, skilled workers, men whose specialisation suited them only for a particular trade and who could not qualify for work in a new industry. Nor were they, necessarily, immobile in the geographical sense: many of them had toured the country in search of work and returned to their home town disappointed. The major obstacles to their re-employment seemed to be, first, their age, and, secondly, the very fact that they had been unemployed for a long time. The survey found that the risk of long unemployment increased very sharply after the age of 40; a discovery repeated sixteen years later in the Report of the Watkinson Committee.[1] The Survey also found that within the hard core of long unemployed was a still harder core of very long unemployed whose numbers continued to increase year by year up to 1936. The very long unemployed had been out of work for five years or more, and it was clear that as the period of unemployment lengthened, the chances of re-employment declined, and declined for that reason, quite apart from any loss of skill or enterprise.

The income and economic welfare of the long-term unemployed was not always adversely affected. The results varied according to whether they had dependants, whether they had other sources of income, and what they had been earning when in work. The significant fact was that unemployment benefits, miserable though they might be, had two advantages over wages as a form of income: they were regular and predictable, and they varied according to the size of family. Thus the casual worker was at least 'decasualised', and in place of irregular wages, received a regular benefit. The unskilled labourer, whose earnings had been barely sufficient to keep him above the poverty line, sometimes found that the allowances for wife and children brought him a total benefit higher than his normal wages. Moreover, the 'life cycle of income' first elucidated by Rowntree in his survey of poverty in York, was to some extent counterbalanced by unemployment benefits. Here is Rowntree's account of the cycle:

'The life of a labourer is marked by five alternating periods

[1] See p. 53.

of want and comparative plenty. During early childhood, unless his father is a skilled worker, he will probably be in poverty; this will last until he, or some of his brothers or sisters, begin to earn money and thus augment their father's wage sufficiently to raise the family above the poverty line. Then follows the period during which he is earning money and living under his parents' roof; for some portion of this period he will be earning more money than is required for lodging, food and clothes. This is his chance to save money. If he has saved enough to pay for furnishing a cottage, this period of comparative prosperity may continue after marriage until he has two or three children, when poverty will again overtake him. This period of poverty will last perhaps for ten years, i.e. until the first child is fourteen years old and begins to earn wages; but if there are more than three children it may last longer. While the children are earning, and before they leave home to marry, the man enjoys another period of prosperity—possibly, however, only to sink back again into poverty when his children have married and left him, and he himself is too old for work, for his income has never permitted his saving enough for him and his wife to live upon for more than a very short time.'[1]

This was written in 1899, when the principal cause of poverty was not unemployment, but low wages, and before old age pensions and insurance benefits had been instituted. But the point in 1936 was that unemployment benefits which included family allowances would reduce the likelihood of poverty if the chief wage-earner was unemployed at the first and third of Rowntree's five periods; and would reduce the likelihood of 'prosperity' at the second and fourth periods. Benefits which varied in this way had a considerable levelling effect; they provided equality of income according to needs, even though it might be equality of misery. Nevertheless, the number of people who found themselves better off when out of work was comparatively small.

[1] B. S. Rowntree: *Poverty—A Study of Town Life*, p. 136.

The Pilgrim Trust survey showed that 55 per cent of the long unemployed were entirely dependent on unemployment benefits. The rest had some other income, from Friendly Societies, small savings, charitable gifts, the earnings of children, payments by lodgers and so on. This, of course, did not determine whether or not they were in poverty, which was a question of the relationship between total income and total needs of the family. But it did mean that most of the unemployed were fairly near the poverty line. The survey established that at the end of 1936 30 per cent of the long unemployed were suffering moderate or severe poverty, and a further 14 per cent were just about subsisting. The remaining 56 per cent were living, in spite of unemployment, above the poverty line, though that was not much consolation to those whose standard of living, when in work, would have been considerably higher.

Turning from family income to family expenditure, the effect of long unemployment on housekeeping varied according to how far the family, especially the housewife, was able and willing to make do in straitened circumstances. Some managed, by skilful paring of the cheese, to avoid an adverse domestic balance of payments, though this often meant withdrawing almost entirely from the social life of the pub, the cinema and the club. Others gave up the struggle and made no attempt to establish rigid priorities of family expenditure. Some made extensive use of credit facilities, postponed payments as long and as often as possible, and popped their valuables in and out of the pawnshop. Others took to betting, wherein the diminishing hope of employment was replaced by the expanding hope of a capital gain. Small economies in expenditure became very important and had a disproportionate influence on habits and timetable. Long distances were walked to buy in a slightly cheaper market. Oil was burnt instead of gas. People went to bed early to avoid using lights and got up late to avoid having breakfast.

The effect of long unemployment on health was most noticeable in the larger families, but it was not the health of the children that suffered. Most parents made extreme sacrifices for the sake of their children. Many parents suffered from shortage of food, and even where there was enough to go round, mothers would go short in order that children could have more. Neglect of medical attention, and especially of dental treatment, was a frequent cause of ill-health. It was difficult to say whether the men suffered more from malnutrition or from the nervous and psychological effects of being out of work. The two combined to decrease their suitability for employment should the opportunity come. Poverty became not only a consequence but also a cause of unemployment.

Finally, long unemployment had strange effects on morale. At one stage men thought of nothing else, day or night, than how to find work. They took no interest in ordinary daily events and surroundings. They became insensitive to the needs even of their own families. At another stage they would begin to accept unemployment as the normal thing and make only desultory efforts to find work. In time they became resigned to a life of unemployment and made no effort to find work. Domestic relationships became strained as insensitiveness gave place to irritation. If the wife went out to earn money, the financial position became easier but the personal problems became worse and tension was increased. Deciding how to occupy his time became a time-absorbing occupation. Pride showed itself in curious ways: in continuous efforts to persuade himself and the world that something called respectability was being maintained; in unnecessary and even lavish expenditure on items of household furnishing and clothing which were thought to keep up appearances; in resentment against the institutions that provided benefits; in unwillingness to accept employment at a lower wage or status than he had once enjoyed.

Two groups in particular seemed to the investigators of the Pilgrim Trust survey to represent the most tragic results of long-term unemployment: those of employable age whose adjustment to a condition of unemployment was so complete that they could not be roused to work; and those above employable age who could not be made to accept their situation.

§ 4. Employment Policy.

If unemployment is a social problem, that is, if it occurs on a scale that causes social distress, and if a free enterprise system seems to give rise to such unemployment, there is a case for some degree of State intervention in order to avoid it. This is the purpose of employment policy in its widest sense. But in a narrower sense it is concerned with cyclical unemployment: with the attempt to regulate aggregate demand, and especially investment, in such a way as to avoid large-scale unemployment in the slump and large-scale inflation, which also causes social distress, in the boom.

But we must bear in mind that not all unemployment is a social problem. Of the types enumerated in section 2, some were merely part of the mechanism of a dynamic economy and did not cause personal distress or economic waste. It follows that the aim of employment policy is not to achieve 100 per cent employment. The nearer the approach to 100 per cent employment, the more the possibility of adjustment to changing conditions is likely to be reduced. For this reason the phrase 'a high and stable level of employment' is sometimes preferred to 'full employment', which may suggest a 100 per cent target.

Further, if we believe in freedom, it is clearly desirable that the intervention of the State should consist of trying to regulate the economic climate rather than telling every individual where to go and what to do. It is significant that the only 'industry' in which full employment is guaranteed, in principle if not in practice, is the armed forces, and that in a recent United Nations Report no figures of unemployment were available for Soviet Russia because 'In the fully controlled State economies of Eastern Europe and the U.S.S.R., full employment is not only guaranteed by law but in fact the State, in complete control of manpower policy, is in a position to direct all those capable of working to employment according to the production targets established by the national economic plans.'[1]

The first task of employment policy is diagnosis of the type of unemployment. Often this is not possible, but it needs to be attempted in order to apply the right treatment, or to decide if any treatment at all is required.

In the case of voluntary unemployment, the remedy might seem to be to stop relief. But this would have to be done on an individual basis, rather than by limiting the period of payment for unemployment benefit or applying general deterrent measures. Past experience is instructive here. One of the regrettable features of pre-war unemployment insurance was that benefits ceased after a period and, in some cases, just at the time when an unemployed man had exhausted his savings and his capital and was becoming wholly dependent on them. One of the misfortunes of the Poor Law administration was that in its anxiety to prevent abuse by some they made the system deterrent for all. Under the present system there is still a time limit for the payment of unemployment benefit but voluntary unemployment is more likely to be disclosed earlier through the repeated refusal of a worker to accept suitable jobs offered him by the Labour Exchange; and in this case the National Assistance Board would take over the task of getting him to work and supporting him meanwhile.

The National Assistance Board is also doing valuable case-work in connection with those who are unemployable on account of physical or mental instability, and this is clearly the most suitable remedy. The elderly unemployed are a different and larger problem. At the end of 1952, out of 350,000 unemployed, 30,000 had been out of work for more than a year, and of these 25,000 were over 40 and 13,000 over 55 years of age. This is the most serious aspect, perhaps the only serious aspect of unemployment in the post-war decade. The two Reports of the Watkinson Committee on *The Employment of Older Men and Women* have done little more than

[1] *Preliminary Report on the World Social Situation* (1952), p. 109.

suggest that the remedy lies in a change of attitude on the part of employers.

In the case of casual unemployment, it is hardly possible to stabilise demand, but attempts have been made to stabilise the income and the supply of casual workers. Since the war, the Dock Labour Scheme has 'decasualised' dock workers to the extent of guaranteeing a minimum weekly income to all registered workers who report for work daily. If there is work available and their earnings exceed the minimum, no further payment is made; but if they fall short, earnings are made up from a fund subscribed by the dock employers. Clearly the efficiency of the scheme depends on the method adopted for registering workers in the first place, and for engaging them when they subsequently report at the dock gates. Since little skill is required,[1] demand is uncertain, and the attraction of a guaranteed income is considerable, the Dock Labour Board has to exercise discretion in registering applicants. So have the foremen who choose their gangs for each day's work, especially as some cargoes are more highly paid than others and some workers are more enthusiastic than others about working on any particular day. But if the register does not become inflated, this is probably a satisfactory cure for casual unemployment.

Seasonal unemployment may, in certain trades, be unavoidable, but it does not necessarily involve hardship, and if the general level of employment is high it may be, so to speak, swallowed up. There are several possibilities. Earnings during the season may be sufficient for the whole year: this is the case with many proprietors of seaside and holiday establishments. Workers may find a complementary activity during the off-season; as when ice-cream vendors turn to distributing firewood during the winter, or waiters and entertainers alternate between seaside resorts and inland towns; and the Labour Exchanges can facilitate this sort of migration. If there is a general shortage of labour, employers may make

---

[1] Except in the case of stevedores. A docker simply loads and unloads ships. A stevedore is skilled in the storage of cargo in the holds.

special efforts to keep a basic labour force busy all the year round, finding work for them in the off-season and supplementing them in the on-season by part-time workers who would not otherwise count among the unemployed. Thus Cambridge colleges, which used to dismiss their staffs during the vacations, are now so anxious not to lose them that they invite conferences and summer schools to enjoy the pleasures of college residence when the undergraduates are away. The undergraduates, having reduced the demand for labour in one seasonal trade, increase the supply in another by doing harvest work or running holiday camps.

Frictional unemployment, as has already been suggested, does not call for any active policy, except that an efficient system of Labour Exchanges can help to reduce the period between the end of one job and the beginning of another in certain cases.

Technological unemployment may work itself out in various ways. A mechanisation scheme, which replaces workers by machines, is presumably introduced because it reduces costs. The price of the product will be reduced, and, if the demand is elastic, output will be expanded and some workers will be re-employed in association with the new machines. If the demand is not elastic, consumers will spend more on other products, and more labour will be required in those industries. On the other hand, the unemployed workers will spend less money, and may in some degree spread unemployment locally. The eventual outcome will depend on the scale of the operation, on the mobility of labour, and on the general level of employment. The firm which initiates the change may take special steps to retrain workers or to assist them in finding other employment, or to pay them full wages for a considerable period after their release. The important thing is that changes of this kind are the essence of economic progress and that policy should be concerned with easing the process of adjustment, and not with retarding the change. If automatic cranes reduce employment of dockers; recordings, of musicians; and carbon papers, of typists; the solution is to find them other employment, not to abolish the cranes, the recordings and the carbon papers.

The problem with export unemployment is to decide whether it is the result of a temporary recession in demand or a permanent change. If, for example, it arises out of political disturbance, or overstocking by merchants in an overseas country, the object of policy should be to give temporary assistance until normal trading conditions are restored. The familiar prescription of short-time working is, in these circumstances, the right one. The labour force is kept in being and earnings may be supplemented by social security benefits. Or it may be possible for Government Departments to place larger orders and build up their own stocks of certain commodities. If, on the other hand, the overseas customer is developing his own industry, or the market is clearly being lost to some powerful competitor, short-time working and 'bolstering-up' may only hinder the release of workers to other industries where there is a shortage of labour. The difficulty is, of course, that employers cannot and will not easily recognise a permanent decline in demand and persist in the belief that it is temporary or that they can easily find other markets. The Government will be under pressure to provide temporary support and will find it increasingly difficult to withdraw such support. The recession in the cotton industry in 1952 was resolved by a combination of all these forces. Some Government orders were placed, some revival of export demand occurred, and some transfer of labour to aircraft and other factories in Lancashire took place.

Structural unemployment, as has been seen, is largely a question of mobility; and the obvious remedy seems to lie in measures that facilitate both the occupational and the geographical mobility of labour. A well-organised system of Labour Exchanges is one such measure. The State may further encourage occupational mobility by financing retraining schemes for displaced workers, if the firms in the expanding industries do not undertake this. Similarly, geographical mobility may be assisted by the provision of cheap housing, the payment of removal costs and so on. In the past, occupational mobility has been eased by the fact that many of the expanding industries were assembly trades using a high proportion of semi-skilled workers who required only a short period of training. Geographical mobility, on the other hand, has been made more difficult by the attachment of the declining industries to the ports and coalfields of the North and West, while the location of the expanding industries was more influenced by the magnetic force of the London market.

Measures designed to 'take the workers to the work', however, do not solve all the problems of the declining areas. Even if there is no longer a surplus of unemployed workers, there is a surplus of unemployed capital, not merely in the principal declining industry, where it ought to be scrapped, but in many other trades, where it could still be used if the consumers had not migrated. All the trades supplying consumer goods and services, as well as housing and other social capital, come into this category. Partly for this reason, partly to deal with other problems of the 'Development Areas' which we cannot discuss here, attempts have been made to 'take the work to the workers' and devote less attention to the encouragement of geographical mobility of labour. These have taken the form, first, of offering inducements to entrepreneurs to set up new factories in the Development Areas, and secondly, of controlling all new factory building in order to diversify the pattern of industry: to mingle the old industries with the new, the light industries with the heavy, and so on. The theoretical basis of this policy is the balancing of private and social costs. From the point of view of the entrepreneur, the costs of production may be the same, or they may be higher, if he is persuaded to set up his factory in a Development Area and refused permission to set up in another area of his own choosing. From the point of view of the economy as a whole the disadvantage of the higher costs of production in the Development Area may be reckoned to be more than offset by the advantage of using existing unemployed labour and social capital, rather than attracting new labour and constructing additional social capital in another area. Of course, social costs are not easily calculated, entrepreneurs are not easily persuaded, and expanding and declining industries are not easily identified and labelled. But, if unemployment can be imputed to structural change, a policy designed to speed the movement of the workers to the work, or the work to the workers, is logical and appropriate.

It is now generally accepted that the cure for cyclical unemployment is to attempt to regulate aggregate demand: to ensure that the total demand for consumer goods and capital goods is such as to keep a high proportion of the community's resources continuously employed. Employment policy therefore consists in avoiding, on the one hand, a general deficiency of demand and large-scale unemployment; and, on the other hand, a general excess of demand and large-scale inflation. In particular, it is concerned with the aggregate demand for capital goods, or investment, which, as we have seen, is liable to wider fluctuation than the demand for consumer goods.

We may therefore follow the Government's White Paper of 1944 on *Employment Policy* in analysing the components of aggregate demand, examining how amenable they may be to regulation, and what form of regulation may be appropriate.

Consumer goods and capital goods are demanded not only by private consumers and investors but also by Government agencies. Thus, we may distinguish four components of aggregate demand: first, private demand for consumer goods; secondly, public demand for consumer goods; thirdly, private investment; fourthly, public investment; and, since some demand comes from abroad and some income is spent abroad, we may add, fifthly, the foreign balance, as a separate component.

The two items of public demand are, by definition, under Government control. The State may decide, as a matter of policy, to spend more or less on investment in nationalised industries, on building schools and hospitals, on carrying out public works, on purchasing equipment and stores, on employing teachers and nurses and civil servants.

Private consumption, on the other hand, results from the independent decisions of millions of income earners. But their decisions will depend partly on their total income, which may be influenced by public spending and State benefits; partly on the distribution of income, on which the economic and social policies of the State have some effect; partly on its disposability, which will be more or less according to the level of taxation; and partly on the propensity to consume, which may be affected by policies that make the holding or lending of money more or less attractive in comparison with the spending of it.

Private investment is more intractable: it may be influenced by changes in interest rates and control of credit, but when the outlook is bright, private investors will persist even at quite high rates of interest; and when it is gloomy, they may not be tempted even if the rate of interest falls to zero.

The foreign balance may be disturbed by changes in international trade conditions quite outside the control of the home Government. The most serious danger is that another country, faced with a slump, may try to increase employment by banning imports and pushing exports, both of which actions would adversely affect the foreign balance in this country and transfer some of the slump conditions here. If the other country is as large as the United States, even a slight recession may have a shattering effect on smaller suppliers and competitors. What is a sneeze to Gulliver may be a hurricane to the Lilliputians. This danger can only be reduced if other countries aim at maintaining a high level of employment, as many of them, including the United States, are now trying to do. Other disturbances to the foreign balance may sometimes be removed by the negotiation of trade agreements and the general liberalisation of international trade. And, of course, the level of employment at home may be a cause, as well as a consequence, of changes in the foreign balance. Deflation, relatively to what is happening abroad, reduces incomes and imports in this country; it also reduces prices and makes exports easier to sell. Inflation has the opposite effect.

To sum up: the key to employment policy seems to be in the control of investment. If private investment is deficient and there is unemployment in the capital goods industries, an increase in public investment may increase employment and incomes and spending to an extent that encourages a revival in private investment. Once the revival is under way, low interest rates, easy credit facilities and low rates of taxation will assist the process. If private investment is high, a cut in public investment may remove inflationary pressure, and high interest rates, restriction of credit and high taxation will assist the process in this direction.

The relationship between budgetary policy (the Government's decision to spend more or less than it receives in taxes) and monetary policy (the regulation of interest rates and credit) will be determined partly by political considerations. The Government may, for example, wish to maintain a high level of public investment and spending even when unemployment has been diminished, and so concentrate on those branches of policy which regulate private investment, or private consumption, or both. Or it may wish to promote a high level of investment, public and private, at the expense of consumption, and adopt a more severe policy in relation to spending than to investment. There was a particularly important difference of view in regard to the respective roles of public and private investment between the official policy enunciated in the White Paper of 1944 and the policy propounded by Lord Beveridge in his book *Full Employment in a Free Society* published the same year. The White Paper policy, while admitting the need for some regulation of private investment, tended to regard some degree of fluctuation as inevitable and sought to influence it only by monetary policy and persuasion. The scale of public investment would, as far as possible, be accommodated to the swings in private investment. Beveridge was in favour of controlling all investment directly through a National Investment Board. Every investment project, public or private, would be considered in relation to other social criteria as well as the needs of employment policy, and sanctioned or prohibited accordingly.

Both documents stressed the need for an economic general staff to study national income statistics and watch the movement of the various components of aggregate demand in order to detect any signs of an approaching slump and take appropriate measures in good time. Much importance was attached to the variation of national insurance contributions as a quick and easy method of influencing one of the components: the private demand for consumer goods.

§ 5. Unemployment since the War.

The whole tenor of wartime discussion of employment policy was influenced by the expected danger of a post-war slump. For those who had lived through the inter-war period, the possibility of a repetition of the events of 1919–21 was very real, and in the longer term, an average rate of unemployment of between 5 and 10 per cent of the working population did not seem unreasonable. The need for quick action to offset an incipient decline in aggregate demand was stressed both in the White Paper and by Beveridge, and it was hoped that by this means the dislocation of the transition period would be minimised and the mass unemployment of the 1930's avoided. Beveridge himself, having advised the Government Actuary in 1942 to assume, for the social insurance scheme, an average rate of unemployment of $8\frac{1}{2}$ per cent, decided in 1944 that it might be kept down to 3 per cent.[1]

For most of the period from 1945 to 1955 unemployment was at a rate of less than 2 per cent, and, except for a few

[1] 'I have assumed, after consultation with Sir William Beveridge, that under normal peacetime conditions the enlarged population insured against unemployment will experience an average rate of $8\frac{1}{2}$ per cent unemployment.'—Appendix A (Memorandum by the Government Actuary) to the *Report on Social Insurance and Allied Services*, Cmd. 6404, 1942, para. 14.
'Three per cent appears as a conservative, rather than an unduly hopeful, aim to set for the average unemployment rate of the future under conditions of full employment.'—*Full Employment in a Free Society*, 1944, para. 169.

11

weeks in 1947, it never exceeded 3 per cent. But it could hardly be said that this was the consequence of successful employment policy. Aggregate demand was maintained by a combination of policies which had very beneficial effects on employment but were chiefly pursued for other reasons. The re-equipment of private industry, coupled with ambitious programmes for the development of the newly nationalised industries; a defence programme larger than had previously been envisaged in peacetime; a vigorous promotion of exports to offset the deterioration in the foreign trade balance; extensive Government spending on social services; redistribution of incomes and the discouragement of voluntary saving through high rates of progressive taxation: all these contributed to an overloaded economy in which unemployment was lower than the most optimistic had hoped it might be.

The result was an almost continuous rise in prices. The retail price index increased by about 50 per cent between 1946 and 1955. Some of this rise was attributable to changes in subsidies and indirect taxes. Some was the consequence of increases in the prices of imports. But the greater part was the outcome of rising incomes and costs at home; and this was a signal of over-full employment. Up to a certain point, increases in aggregate demand enable additional resources to be employed and additional output to be produced at current prices. Beyond that point, increases in aggregate demand lead to competition for resources already employed, and result, not in higher output, but in higher incomes for the suppliers of those resources. From the point of view of the employer, the higher incomes are an increase in cost, which he passes on to the consumer in higher prices. Other income earners demand higher income because the cost of living has risen, or in order to maintain traditional relationships between wages in one industry and another, and so the process of wage-inflation develops.

The most serious social consequence of rising prices is that it threatens the security of incomes. There is a continual fear that the inflation will get out of hand: that prices will begin to rise at a rate that makes all money balances insecure, and people try to spend money as fast as they receive it. But even if social security is not completely destroyed by hyper-inflation, as it is sometimes called, all those whose real incomes depend on stability in the value of money find their security impaired. Pensioners, clergy, recipients of fixed incomes, all who cannot climb on to the escalator of rising incomes, suffer in this way.

Thus, too little demand and too much demand for the employable resources of the community give rise to social problems which are not dissimilar. In both cases certain groups, through no fault of their own, are afflicted by economic insecurity: in one case those whose livelihood depends on the availability of work, in the other case those whose livelihood depends on the stability of prices.

CHAPTER VI

POVERTY

§ 1. The Problem of Definition. For many economists the existence of poverty has provided both the subject-matter and the inspiration of their studies. It has provided the subject-matter in the broad sense that any economic problem is a problem of scarce resources, of means which are not abundant enough to satisfy all our wants, so that we have to choose between alternative ways of using them. It has provided the inspiration and the challenge to economic study in the narrower sense that not only the wants but the *needs* of many people go unsatisfied; and that there would seem to be, if we could find it, an eventual solution to this *social* problem, because needs are definable and limited, while wants are not.

'. . . the question,' says Marshall, 'whether it is really impossible that all should start in the world with a fair chance of leading a cultured life, free from the pain of poverty and the stagnating influences of mechanical toil . . . cannot be fully answered by economic science . . . But the answer depends in a great measure upon facts and inferences which are within the province of economics; and this it is which gives to economic studies their chief and highest interest.'[1]

And Professor Pigou follows in the same tradition when he says:

'It is . . . the social enthusiasm which revolts from the sordidness of mean streets and the joylessness of withered lives, that is the beginning of economic science. Here, if in no other field, Comte's great phrase holds good: "It is for the heart to suggest our problems; it is for the intellect to solve them . . . The only position for which the intellect is

[1] *Principles of Economics*, 8th Edition, 1920, p. 4.

primarily adapted is to be the servant of the social sym-
pathies".' [1]

Poverty in this narrower sense has been at the centre of the
special field of study of the social economist since the end of
last century.   This chapter deals with the extent and causes of
poverty as they have been revealed by successive social surveys;
with the way in which economic and social legislation has been
directed to the removal of those causes; and with the question
whether or not the problem of poverty has been solved in
Great Britain.

First, however, some attention must be given to the problem
of definition.   Poverty can be defined from either a subjective
or an objective standpoint.   The individual has his own view
of what constitutes poverty at any time.   His standard depends on the width, or the narrowness, of his experience and
judgment; the narrower it is, the more it reflects his own
personal circumstances and psychology.   Similarly, society
seems to develop an attitude to poverty which reflects the state
of the public conscience at any time or place.   This social
standard tends to work on averages: those whose incomes are
above the average feel an obligation to those whose incomes
are below, though this charitable feeling will not normally
bear the test of arithmetic.   One writer has claimed that, if
anyone with a lively conscience is asked what he regards as
the minimum level of income below which no one should fall
and the maximum above which excess income should be con-
fiscated and re-distributed, the income available above the
maximum will always be found to be insufficient to provide
the minimum.   All this is mere guesswork; but these subjective
standards, vague and unrealistic though they may be, have
political significance.   It is these standards which will determine whether proposals and schemes for dealing with poverty
will meet with public support or opposition.   Rowntree, for
example, in his investigations into the incidence of poverty
in York, was able to adopt a more generous standard in 1936

---

[1] *Economics of Welfare*, 4th Edition, 1932, p. 5.

than in 1899, not because he himself had mellowed, or simply because the general standard of living had increased, but because the climate of social opinion had become more temperate in the matter of what was a tolerable level of subsistence for the poorest members of society.

The objective standards are of three kinds: physical, social and economic. The physical standard is that which is sufficient, but no more than sufficient for physical efficiency. 'We must ascertain,' wrote Rowntree in 1899, 'what income is required to provide the minimum of food, clothing and shelter needful for the maintenance of merely physical health.'[1] Marshall's definition was more picturesque, but related to a similarly severe physical standard:

> '. . . the necessaries for the efficiency of an ordinary agricultural or of an unskilled town labourer and his family, in England, in this generation . . . may be said to consist of a well-drained dwelling with several rooms, warm clothing, with some changes of underclothing, pure water, a plentiful supply of cereal food, with a moderate allowance of meat and milk, and a little tea, etc., some education and some recreation, and lastly sufficient freedom for his wife from other work to enable her to perform properly her maternal and her household duties. If in any district unskilled labour is deprived of any of these things, its efficiency will suffer in the same way as that of a horse that is not properly tended, or a steam engine that has an inadequate supply of coals. All consumption up to this limit is strictly productive consumption: any stinting of this consumption is not economical, but wasteful.'[2]

The social standard allows not only for physical necessities but also for some 'conventional' necessities. Adam Smith recognised this when he wrote:

> 'By necessaries, I understand, not only the commodities which are indispensably necessary for the support of

[1] B. S. Rowntree: *Poverty—A Study of Town Life*, p. 87.
[2] Marshall: *op. cit.*, pp. 69–70.

life, but whatever the custom of the country renders it indecent for creditable people, even of the lowest order, to be without. A linen shirt, for example, is, strictly speaking, not a necessary of life. The Greeks and Romans lived, I suppose, very comfortably, though they had no linen. But in the present times, through the greater part of Europe, a creditable day-labourer would be ashamed to appear in public without a linen shirt, the want of which would be supposed to denote that disgraceful degree of poverty, which, it is presumed, nobody can well fall into without extreme bad conduct.'[1]

But Adam Smith would not include beer and ale, because 'Nature does not render them necessary for the support of life; and custom nowhere renders it indecent to live without them.' Marshall, on the other hand, writing a century later, says '. . . some consumption of alcohol and tobacco, and some indulgence in fashionable dress, are in many places so habitual, that they may be said to be conventionally necessary, since in order to obtain them the average man and woman will sacrifice some things which are necessary for efficiency.'[2]

The economic standard is that level of income which is necessary for economic efficiency: the physical and social standards adjusted according to occupation. Thus, in order to do their jobs properly, the heavy worker needs extra food, the dirty worker needs extra soap, the doctor needs a car, the professor needs books; and their incomes must be sufficient to provide for these 'occupational necessities'.

These objective standards are of great value to the social economist because they can be determined, not only with impartiality, but also with tolerable precision. The 'necessities' of a family, however defined, can be expressed in terms of a definite amount of money expenditure and compared with the family's money income in order to establish whether or not the family is in poverty. Basically, this is the method of most

[1] Adam Smith: *The Wealth of Nations*, Cannan Edition, Vol. II, p. 354.
[2] Marshall: *op. cit.*, p. 70.

social surveys. But even these standards, though precise, are not as simple as they appear to be. In the case of the physical standard, people's needs in the matter of diet vary enormously according to their physical make-up. The diet which would keep one person in good health would be insufficient or unsuitable for another. This variety of individual needs would not invalidate the results of a survey based on a standard diet. The deviations would cancel out. But it would be significant, for example, in a scheme for assisting undernourished children by providing a standard ration of free milk. Further, some allowance must be made, in translating the physical standard into money expenditure, for the fact that people cannot always buy in the cheapest market or distribute their expenditure as wisely and efficiently as they would like to do.

The social standard also has its complications. It is one thing to include such 'conventional necessities' as, in Adam Smith's phrase, 'custom renders it indecent to live without'. It is quite another matter to include commodities to obtain which, as Marshall puts it, 'the average man and woman will sacrifice some things which are necessary for efficiency'. The first standard has a downward bias: people must not be allowed to become so poor that they offend society. The second standard has an upward bias: people must not be allowed to become so poor that they cannot take part in society and have to live, as one modern writer expresses it, 'in a social vacuum'. Are families to be classified as 'above the poverty line' if they have the means of subsistence but cannot afford a few cigarettes, an occasional glass of beer, or any entertainment or recreation that costs money?—if they cannot afford subscriptions to church or club or trade Union?—if they cannot have toys and sweets for the children, or any sort of holiday, unless these are provided by some benefactor?

Here is the crucial point in the determination of standards for the measurement of poverty. It is crucial because, in the first place, there tends to be a large number of families living not very far above the poverty line as defined by physical standards; so that the inclusion of a few more commodities as 'conventional necessities' tends to increase disproportionately the incidence of poverty as revealed by this type of survey. Secondly, public opinion regarding a tolerable level of subsistence tends to become more generous as the average standard of living rises, not by extending the physical standard, but by including more of those conventional necessities which form such a flexible element in the social standard. Thirdly, Marshall's dictum that allowance must be made for some conventional necessities to obtain which people would 'sacrifice some things which are necessary for efficiency', crosses the borderline between what Rowntree has called 'primary' poverty and 'secondary' poverty. Primary poverty is the situation in which 'earnings are insufficient to obtain the minimum necessaries for the maintenance of merely physical efficiency'. Secondary poverty is that in which 'earnings would be sufficient for the maintenance of merely physical efficiency were it not that some portion is absorbed by other expenditure either useful or wasteful'.[1] Secondary poverty cannot be measured by the method of comparing actual income with standard physical needs. But it is a concession in this direction to allow, in the evaluation of needs, for a certain margin of inefficient or ignorant expenditure. It is a further concession to admit that some conventional necessities are regarded as being so important that people will go short of the physical necessities in order to obtain them. And the point at which convention ends and improvidence begins is obviously difficult to define.

This is no mere quibble about definitions, but is of considerable practical importance. It is often found, for instance, that in time of unemployment people will go short of food rather than give up entirely their amusements and indulgences. How far should allowance be made for such practices in the determination of a standard which can be used not only in the measurement, but also in the relief, of poverty?

The economic standard is similarly complicated. To say that there is poverty when income is insufficient for economic

[1] Rowntree: *op. cit.*, pp. 86-7.

efficiency, is to include in the assessment of needs not only the physical and conventional necessities but also the occupational. For the ordinary workman, this may mean the cost of providing and maintaining his tools, and the cost of transport to and from his place of work. At a somewhat different level, but on the same principles, it could include those highly variable amounts which can be declared to the Income Tax authorities under the heading of 'business expenses'. And we soon find ourselves arguing that, if people will not take on more skilled and more responsible jobs unless they are paid accordingly, the whole of everybody's income is essential for economic efficiency! Marshall went a long way in this direction. He first defined his economic standard by saying that 'the income of any class in the ranks of industry is below its *necessary* level, when any increase in their income would in the course of time produce a more than proportionate increase in their efficiency'.[1] He then added a footnote to say that for an individual of exceptional abilities, 'all his consumption is strictly productive and necessary, so long as by cutting off any part of it he would diminish his efficiency by an amount that is of more real value to him or the rest of the world than he saved from his consumption'.

Finally, all standards for the measurement of poverty are relative to time and place. The minimum standard now tolerated in Great Britain is much higher than that of fifty years ago, though physical needs have not changed. The minimum standard in the country is probably lower than in the towns. And the minimum standards for Britain would be regarded as sheer luxury in some European countries and most Middle Eastern and Far Eastern countries.

§ **2. Social Surveys.** If poverty, by any definition, is so widespread that virtually the whole community is poor, there would not seem to be much point in analysing its extent and its causes by means of social surveys. There is only one cause, namely that the national income, however it is distributed, is too small;

[1] *Principles*, p. 69.

and only one remedy, namely to increase the national income by every possible means. This is the situation in the so-called underdeveloped countries. But if poverty afflicts only a section of the community, it is useful to analyse its extent and its causes, because economic and social policy can then be directed, both through the redistribution of incomes and by other means, to removing those causes according to their relative importance.

Social investigators were enquiring into and writing about poverty in Britain long before the social surveys that are associated with the names of Booth, Rowntree and Bowley from about 1890 onwards. From very early times private sympathy, public concern and sheer curiosity had stimulated the publication of more or less accurate statistics and more or less coloured accounts of the number of paupers and the causes of their distress. There were Gregory King's remarkable estimates, made at the end of the seventeenth century when he held the posts of Lancaster Herald and Secretary of the Commissioners for stating the Public Accounts. He calculated that in 1688, out of a total population of $5\frac{1}{2}$ millions, $1\frac{1}{4}$ millions were 'cottagers, paupers and vagrants' whose yearly income was two pounds per head and whose yearly cost to the community was between two pounds five shillings and three pounds per head. There were greater and lesser reports published officially from time to time in connection with the administration of the Poor Laws. Between 1776 and 1815, for example, there were no less than four complete censuses, covering every parish of England and Wales, of the amounts of money raised and expended for the maintenance of the poor, together with the numbers of paupers receiving permanent or occasional relief, in or out of the workhouse, the membership of friendly societies, and the amount of charitable donations dispensed by parish officers. Again, there was Sir Frederic Morton Eden's *The State of the Poor*, begun 'from motives both of benevolence and personal curiosity' aroused by the difficulties experienced by the labouring classes from the high prices of 1794 and 1795. He organised, in between his considerable business activities (he was Chairman of the Globe Insurance Company), the collection of information about economic and social conditions in sample parishes in nearly all the counties of England and Wales, and incorporated it in a scholarly work on the history of the labouring classes published in 1798. Then there was Henry Mayhew, a journalist of versatility and imagination (and, incidentally, the first Editor of *Punch*), whose *London Labour and the London Poor* gave a rambling and lurid account of the underworld of the Metropolis in the decade round about 1850. It is difficult to place this welter of personal anecdotes and scraps of gossip, criminal statistics and pious aspirations, in any sort of perspective, but there is no doubt that it stirred many consciences, including those of Octavia Hill and F. D. Maurice, on the question of poverty and its attendant degradation. And of course there was Engels' *Condition of the Working Class in England in 1844* (though not published in English until 1885), and Disraeli's *The Two Nations*, and the novels of Dickens.

Why did not these earlier social studies, influential though they were, become landmarks in our social history of the same outstanding kind as the great surveys of Booth and Rowntree? One reason is that many of them did not make a distinction between poverty and pauperism. Pauperism is the condition of being in receipt of poor relief. Discussion of paupers and pauperism was therefore inevitably discussion of the existing Poor Law, its merits or defects, its income and expenditure; its administration and its possible reform. Another reason is that they lacked the precision and objectivity of the later surveys. Sympathy was aroused, voluntary service stepped in, and poor relief was supplemented by a cavalcade of philanthropy and mutual aid. But public opinion, whether of the voters or the writers or the men of affairs, could not get any clear idea of the scope of the problem of poverty, or discuss dispassionately along what lines (apart from the Poor Law) the State might assist in its solution, until accurate statistical analysis revealed a convincing and comprehensive picture.

§ 3. Poverty in London and the Question of Methods. Booth's survey of poverty in London in 1889 is of special interest, not only because it was the first of its kind, but also because it was repeated, with comparable results, in 1929. Only in two other cases has there been such a repetition. Rowntree's first survey of poverty in York in 1899 was repeated in 1936 and, on a smaller scale, in 1950; and by a remarkable piece of good fortune Rowntree himself lived to conduct all three enquiries. The other case was the survey of five selected towns directed by Professor Bowley in 1912–14 and repeated in 1923–4. The different methods of enquiry and the different standards adopted for the measurement of poverty are best illustrated in the London and York surveys, so let us examine these in some detail, set out their results, and compare them with the results of the five towns' surveys and a number of others.

Charles Booth was a Liverpool shipowner, a founder and chairman of the steamship company that still bears his name. He developed a keen interest in the conditions under which people lived and worked, and began, when he was already approaching the age of fifty, a systematic study of social conditions extending over more than twenty years. Most of his researches are embodied in the seventeen volumes of *Life and Labour of the People in London*, published between 1891 and 1903, but he also wrote other books and articles and played a considerable part in public life. Amongst other things he was President of the Royal Statistical Society, a Privy Councillor and, for a time, a member of the Royal Commission on the Poor Laws.

Booth's aim was not simply to measure poverty. He wanted to describe 'the condition and occupations of the inhabitants of London . . . dividing the people by districts and again by trades, so as to show at once the manner of their life and of their work'; and the breadth and balance of his whole survey is shown by the fact that, of the seventeen volumes, four are entitled 'Poverty', five 'Industry', and seven 'Religious Influences', with a final volume of conclusions and summaries. Nevertheless, the outstanding facts that emerged were those relating to the extent and causes of poverty, and Booth himself, having throughout his enquiry 'leaned to the safe side, preferring to paint things too dark rather than too bright, not because I myself take a gloomy view, but to avoid the chance of misunderstanding the evils with which society has to deal',[1] concluded at the end of his survey: 'I undoubtedly expected that this investigation would expose exaggerations, and it did so; but the actual poverty disclosed was so great, both in mass and in degree, and so absolutely certain, that I have gradually become equally anxious not to overstate.'

The method and basis of Booth's investigations had already been fully explained in a 'pilot survey', as we should now call it, relating to a district known as *The Tower Hamlets*; the results of which were set out in a paper to the Royal Statistical Society in 1887. Booth used as his agents the School Board visitors, whose duties brought them into regular contact with households in which there were children. For the most part these people already had the knowledge and the records from which they could give to Booth the information he required, namely, the occupation of the head of each household, the number of children and other dependants, and the general 'class' of the family. For this last purpose he specified eight different classes:

A. The lowest class of occasional labourers, loafers and semi-criminals.
B. Casual earnings—'very poor'.
C. Intermittent earnings ⎫
D. Small regular earnings ⎭ together the 'poor'.
E. Regular standard earnings—above the line of poverty.
F. Higher class labour.
G. Lower middle class.
H. Upper middle class.

His definitions were not as precise as those of later investigators, but they were convincing enough:

[1] Booth: *Life and Labour*, First Series, Vol. I, p. 5.

'By the word "poor" I mean to describe those who have a sufficiently regular though bare income, such as 18s. to 21s. per week for a moderate family, and by "very poor" those who from any cause fall much below this standard. . . . My "poor" may be described as living under a struggle to obtain the necessaries of life and make both ends meet; while the "very poor" live in a state of chronic want. It may be their own fault that this is so; that is another question; my first business is simply with the numbers who, from whatever cause, do live under conditions of poverty or destitution.'[1]

Having covered East London, Central London and Battersea by this method, Booth changed his basic unit, in order to speed up the survey, from the family to the street. His visitors ascertained the number of children in each street and classified them as before. He then brought together his figures by parishes, because he had the population figures for each parish from the Census of 1881. He first assumed that the increase in the total population since 1881 had been in the same proportion as the increase in the number of children. Secondly, he assumed that, in each parish where he had carried out a household survey, the distribution of the total population among his eight classes would be proportionately the same as the distribution of that part of the population which was living in families with children. Thirdly, he assumed that, in each parish where he had carried out a street survey, the distribution of the total population among his eight classes would be proportionately the same as the distribution of the children. He felt that these assumptions were reasonable, and so he was able to classify the whole of London in 1889 as follows:

Very Poor (Classes A and B)	8·4 per cent
Poor (Classes C and D)	22·3 ,,
Comfortable (Classes E and F)	51·5 ,,
Well-to-do (Classes G and H)	17·8 ,,

[1] Booth: *op. cit.*, First Series, Vol. I, 1892, p. 33.

Thus 30·7 per cent of the people of London were in poverty at that time. Taking the working-class population only (excluding G and H), the proportion in poverty was 37·3 per cent.

The second London survey was begun in 1928 and its results published between 1930 and 1935 in the nine volumes of the *New Survey of London Life and Labour*. Its aim was similar to that of Booth: of the nine volumes two entitled 'Social Survey' were concerned with the conditions under which people lived, and three entitled 'London Industries' with the conditions under which they worked. The first volume was historical—'Forty years of change'; the last on 'Life and Leisure'; and there were two volumes of maps.

The New Survey was, however, different in its organisation, its scope and its methods. In place of a single private investigator there was a whole team of economists and statisticians, backed by a distinguished committee of advisers, centred on the London School of Economics, and using money provided by various British and American trust funds. The name of Professor Bowley is associated with this survey, because he contributed most to the solution of the many difficult statistical problems, but it was directed, and large parts of it were written, by Sir Hubert Llewellyn Smith, who had been one of Booth's collaborators, and the whole work was a fine example of joint research by a group of skilled investigators. In place of Booth's County of London, covering 74,000 acres, there was a larger County, plus a few boroughs outside the County boundary, covering 106,000 acres. In place of a population of 4¼ millions was one of 5½ millions resulting from four separate changes: the changes in boundary, the natural increase of the resident population, the substantial migration into London from other parts of the country, and, in the other direction, the growing tendency for those who worked within the County boundary to live on its fringe or just outside it.

The authors of the New Survey were careful to provide figures that would be directly comparable with those of Booth, but they also provided a great deal of new information based on the larger London and the changed circumstances of 1929. In particular they adopted two important improvements in technique which had been developed since the time of Booth, and were able to check the accuracy of Booth's methods and assumptions.

The first of these was the application of the statistical technique of sampling to the social survey. It had been used by Bowley in his survey of five towns in 1912–13 and had proved its reliability in a number of other surveys. Instead of collecting information from every single house and street in which it was possible, or convenient, to obtain it, the interviewers visited every tenth or even every fiftieth house (the sample varied according to the size of the district), in order to get a representative set of returns, from which accurate results could be derived. Once it is clear that the sample is free from 'bias', or that the bias can be measured and allowed for, this method clearly reduces the work of a social survey considerably. In order to make comparisons of method, Bowley and his colleagues carried out in 1929 both a sample survey, using trained interviewers, and a street survey, using school attendance officers.

The second improvement in technique made use of developments in the science of nutrition. It became known that, in order to maintain good health, the diet must satisfy two conditions. First, its total energy value must amount to a certain minimum number of calories. Secondly, although the three essential constituents of food—protein, fats and carbohydrates —all yielded energy, only protein could do the building and repair work of the body as well as providing the fuel, so that a certain minimum quantity of protein must be included in the diet. Since all foodstuffs can be converted into calories, and the protein content ascertained, it is possible to compile a dietary which satisfies the minimum standard for health and efficiency and is reasonably accessible to working-class families. The market cost of this dietary, allowing a certain margin for inefficient spending, is therefore an objective measure of the minimum income required to satisfy essential needs

12

in regard to food.   It will vary according to the age and sex of the different members of the family and according to the nature of their work.

This method of calculating the minimum cost of food, and combining it with estimates for rent, clothing, fuel, and household sundries in order to build up a figure of the minimum essential income for each family, was first used by Rowntree in his social survey of York in 1899.   Booth did things the other way round.   He first fixed his poverty line subjectively —'those who have a . . . bare income, such as 18s. to 21s. per week for a moderate family'—and *then* he went on to collect, as part of his survey, the family budgets which showed how people in fact spent this income.

Bowley was anxious that his poverty line in 1929 should be roughly at the same level as that of Booth, allowing only for changes in prices.   He therefore worked out, from the budgets collected by Booth, the probable pattern of expenditure of a family living just above the poverty line at that time.   The total cost came to 22s. a week (a little above Booth's 'bare income'); the food consumption yielded about 3,000 calories per day for an adult man; and the corresponding cost in 1929 was 40s. But Bowley had also used a Standard Budget, calculated objectively and yielding more than the 3,600 calories and 125 grammes of protein which the experts considered necessary, for his survey of five towns in 1924; and the 1929 cost of this was 41s. 7d.   Thus, although Booth's rather severe standard, costing 40s. a week in 1929, was used as a poverty line for the second survey, Bowley was able to show that it was roughly equivalent to the standards used in other surveys and that it could provide, if knowledgeably spent, the necessary calories and protein.

What were the results of this very thorough enquiry?   First, let us compare like with like.   The proportion of the *total population* of London in poverty, which Booth had found in 1889 to be 30·7 per cent, was, forty years later, 9·6 per cent. This means that, taking the same area of London, and using the same poverty line and the same method of enquiry, the amount of poverty had been reduced by more than two-thirds. The proportion of the *working-class population* in poverty had declined from 37·3 to 11·8 per cent, again a drop of more than two-thirds.

In the larger area of the New Survey, it was found that the proportion in poverty was slightly less than in the area of Booth's London—9·5 per cent of the total population and 11·6 per cent of the working population; the outer fringes were apparently more 'comfortable' than the inner parts of the Metropolis. If the degree of poverty was expressed in families instead of individuals, the proportions became slightly higher. The reason for this was that although a much higher *proportion* of large families were in poverty than of small families, there was a much greater *number* of small families, especially of old people living alone, below the poverty line.

This last result came from the sample survey, in which a precise comparison was made between actual earnings and objectively calculated needs in selected households; and we noted earlier the difference between this method and the looser and more subjective method of the street survey. The accuracy of the sampling method had already been tested elsewhere, but the 1929 survey was the only one in which both methods were employed, so that there was a useful check on the validity of Booth's conclusions, based entirely on the street survey. Bowley found that in nearly every district in 1929 the sample survey revealed a lower proportion of people in poverty than the street survey. Taking the working-class population only, but for the whole of the New Survey Area, the proportion in poverty, according to the street survey, was as we have already noted 11·6 per cent; according to the sample survey it was only 10·7 per cent. There seemed to be three main reasons for this divergence. First, the sample method tended to under-state the amount of poverty because it assumed a complete pooling of the family resources. It was clear, however, from the street survey, that some families were in obvious poverty, although individual members of them, earning and retaining separate incomes, were not. On the other hand, the sample method overstated the amount of poverty because it assumed that the income accruing in the week of the investigation was the only income available to meet the family needs. Obviously, there would be some carry-over from one week to another, quite apart from the possibility of drawing on savings.

Thirdly, the street survey method tended to show a higher proportion of poverty because it inevitably included some 'secondary' as well as 'primary' poverty. We have already mentioned the important distinction, first made by Rowntree, between primary poverty, arising from insufficient income; and secondary poverty, arising from the misapplication of an income which would otherwise be sufficient. In the sample survey, secondary poverty was excluded by definition; in the street survey, where assessment was made partly by appearance, the borderline between primary and secondary was somewhat fluid. 'A good many families', wrote Booth, 'have been reported as poor, who though they are poor, are so without any economic necessity. On the other hand . . . many a painful struggling life hidden under a decent exterior has passed in our books as "comfortably poor", to borrow a phrase used by one of the most sympathetic of the School Board visitors . . . In so far as there is any general error, it will I think be found on the safe side;—that is in overstating rather than understating the volume of poverty.'[1]

Finally, a check was made on Booth's important assumption that the results obtained from a survey of households where there were schoolchildren would apply to the population as a whole. Bowley found that the percentage of *families* in poverty was roughly the same, whether one took the whole population, or only that part of it living in households where there were schoolchildren. But the percentage of *individuals* in poverty was lower, by about one-fifth, in the whole population than in households with schoolchildren. The conclusion seemed to be that Booth's method of investigation tended to overstate the amount of poverty, and that if the results were expressed in terms of families this overstatement would tend

[1] Booth: *op. cit.*, First Series, Vol. II, 1892, pp. 19–20.

to be concealed by the fact of large numbers of old people living alone and in poverty, who would be counted as separate families.

§ 4. Poverty in York and the Question of Standards. It was important to go into considerable detail on the methods and results of the London Surveys, not because it makes much difference to the main conclusion—the enormous reduction in the amount of poverty between 1889 and 1929 is plain enough however the figures are qualified—but because it illustrates the sort of problem that arises in any social survey, and the sort of question that the social economist must ask when planning a survey or interpreting its results. We now turn to the York Surveys, in which very little will be said about the methods but rather more about the standards of measurement.

Seebohm Rowntree belonged to one of the Quaker families which have played such a distinctive part in British industrial and social history. His father, Joseph Rowntree, determined that the firm he had founded in the 1860's should not only be a successful business but should also set an example, in the payment of good wages and the provision of income security to its employees; in the guarantee of healthy and pleasant working and living conditions; and in the promotion of joint consultation and joint control in the factory. He created, among his workers at York, a community in which many of the ideals of the Welfare State were pursued and achieved long in advance of national legislation. When Seebohm Rowntree became Chairman of the Company in 1923 he had already had a great deal to do with the various trusts and funds established by his predecessors. He had also published a number of books on social problems, inspired by his father's concern for getting to the root of things: 'I feel that much current philanthropic effort', Joseph had said in 1904, 'is directed to remedying the more superficial manifestations of weakness or evil, while little thought or effort is directed to searching out their underlying causes.'

Poverty—A Study of Town Life was published in 1901 and embodied the results of the first social survey of York. Rowntree and Booth knew, of course, of each other's work, and they felt that their surveys were roughly comparable. But there were differences of method and standard, and it was felt too that London was a special case, and that York was probably a typical provincial town.

Rowntree's investigators called at every working-class household in York. They distinguished working-class households from others by a method which would certainly not have been reliable in more recent years: the keeping or not keeping of domestic servants! By direct enquiry they obtained information about the housing conditions, the rent, and the number, age and occupations of the people. Where possible, they also ascertained the earnings of the family, but this information could be reliably estimated from other sources, since Rowntree had access to a great deal of information from employers (himself included) about the wages paid to different classes of workers in York. Precise comparison could then be made between actual earnings and family needs calculated according to the objective standards which, we noted earlier, Rowntree was the first to adopt. His basic food standard was a diet supplying 3,500 calories per day, including 125 grams of protein, for a man doing moderate muscular work. The cost of his standard dietary, for a family of five, was 12*s.* 9*d.* a week. Including rent and household sundries, the poverty line for such a family came out at 21*s.* 8*d.* per week, compared with Booth's '18*s.* to 21*s.*' ten years earlier. In each individual case Rowntree of course adjusted his calculation of needs according to the size and composition of the family, and, since rents varied considerably, he took the *actual* rent, rather than a hypothetical minimum. He also assumed that family earnings were pooled.

The result was that 15·46 per cent of the wage-earning population of York or 9·91 per cent of the total population (assuming that the families with domestic servants, and the domestic servants themselves, and the inmates of institutions, were above the poverty line) were found to be in 'primary poverty'. Including 'secondary poverty'—the households where income was sufficient but the obvious appearance of poverty made it clear that it was being mis-spent—the figures rose to 43·4 per cent of the wage-earning population, or 27·84 per cent of the total population. The last figure was the one which Rowntree thought comparable with Booth's 30·7 per cent in London, bearing in mind the greater general prosperity in 1899, the slightly higher standards adopted by Rowntree, and the inclusion of all secondary poverty in York. 'We are faced', concluded Rowntree, 'with the startling probability that from 25 to 30 per cent of the town populations of the United Kingdom are living in poverty.'[1]

By the time of his second survey of York, in 1936, Rowntree had done a great deal of further work on the accurate calculation of a minimum standard. The results appeared in *The Human Needs of Labour* which, though entirely materialistic in its content, was published in the faith that if only basic material needs were assured, a great deal of industrial and social unrest would be avoided and men would find new vision and new energy to strive for higher ideals. Rowntree took account of substantial improvements in the science of nutrition, and especially of the work of Committees set up by the Ministry of Health in 1931, by the British Medical Association in 1933, and by the League of Nations in 1935. This last, however, was concerned with an optimum standard, such that no alteration in it could improve health, while the other committees, like Rowntree himself, were concerned with minimum standards, 'below which no one should be compelled to live'.

How had things changed since 1899? On the one hand, the experts had decided that a daily intake of food supplying 3,400 calories and 100 grams of protein (of which half must be 'animal protein') was sufficient for an adult man doing moderate work. On the other hand, the relative requirements of women and children were put higher than they had been, so that the average family's needs in terms of food were

[1] *Poverty—A Study of Town Life*, p. 301.

raised.   And in addition, Rowntree felt that his earlier standards had in general been too severe—'bare subsistence rather than living'.   His graphic description of the 1899 standard is worth quoting in full:

> 'A family living upon the scale allowed for in this estimate must never spend a penny on railway fare or omnibus. They must never go into the country unless they walk. They must never purchase a halfpenny newspaper or spend a penny to buy a ticket for a popular concert.   They must write no letters to absent children, for they cannot afford to pay the postage.   They must never contribute anything to their church or chapel, or give any help to a neighbour which costs them money.   They cannot save, nor can they join sick club or trade union, because they cannot pay the necessary subscriptions.   The children must have no pocket money for dolls, marbles or sweets.   The father must smoke no tobacco, and must drink no beer.   The mother must never buy any pretty clothes for herself or for her children, the character of the family wardrobe, as for the family diet, being governed by the regulation, "Nothing must be bought but that which is absolutely necessary for the maintenance of physical health, and what is bought must be of the plainest and most economical description."   Should a child fall ill, it must be attended by the parish doctor; should it die it must be buried by the parish.   Finally, the wage-earner must never be absent from his work for a single day.   If any of these conditions are broken, the extra expenditure involved is met, *and can only be met*, by limiting the diet; or, in other words, by sacrificing physical efficiency.'[1]

This standard, which in 1899 had cost 17*s*. 8*d*. per week (exclusive of rent) for a family of five, cost, at 1936 prices, 30*s*. 7*d*.   The Human Needs Standard cost 43*s*. 6*d*. per week, or 53*s*. inclusive of average rent.   It allowed for the dietary changes, and included 9*s*. per week for 'personal sundries',

[1] *Poverty—A Study of Town Life*, pp. 133–4.

such as insurance and trade union subscriptions, travel to and from work, stamps and stationery, a daily paper and wireless. But even this 'erred on the side of stringency rather than extravagance . . . '

'I have been increasingly impressed', wrote Rowntree, 'by the fact that to keep a family of five in health on 53s. a week, even when the income is guaranteed for 52 weeks in the year, needs constant watchfulness and a high degree of skill on the part of the housewife. Moreover, practically the whole income is absorbed in providing the absolute necessaries of physical health. After these and certain almost indispensable items are provided for, there remains scarcely anything—certainly not more than 3s. 4d. a week for "all else". Out of this must come all recreation, all luxuries, such as beer and tobacco, all travelling except that of the breadwinner to and from work, all savings for holidays —indeed almost every item of expenditure not absolutely required to maintain the family in physical health, and there is no allowance for contingencies.'[1]

The results of the 1936 survey were published in 1941 in *Poverty and Progress*, probably the most readable, for the general reader, of all the social surveys. Rowntree had decided not to use the sampling method, though he made some valuable checks on its accuracy. He collected information from every working-class household, defining such households no longer as 'not having a domestic servant' but as 'earning not more than £250 a year'.

Using the 1899 standards, the amount of primary poverty in York, which had been 9·91 per cent of the total population, was in 1936 only 3·9 per cent—a reduction of more than three-fifths. Taking the working-class population only, the proportion in primary poverty had fallen from 15·46 per cent in 1899 to 6·8 per cent in 1936—a reduction of between one-half and three-fifths. The different ways of defining the working-

[1] Rowntree: *The Human Needs of Labour*, 1937 Edition, pp. 124–5.

class population probably explain the slightly different results, but the magnitude of the reduction is remarkable either way.

Rowntree did not attempt to measure secondary poverty in 1936. He felt that its assessment depended too much on the attitude of the investigator, and that this also would have changed since 1899. Probably several changes went hand in hand: the reduction in primary poverty brought about a change in attitude not only to secondary poverty but also to the whole question of standards. It was this which enabled Rowntree to abandon his 'subsistence minimum' for the new Human Needs Standard without fear of being accused, as he would have been in 1899, of pitching his poverty line too high. The application of the new Standard, however, though it represented an advance in social attitudes, put the clock back in the sense that it increased substantially the number of people now classified as below the poverty line. By the old subsistence standard, the proportion of the total population in primary poverty in 1936 was, as we have just seen, 3·9 per cent; by the new Human Needs Standard it was 17·7 per cent. For the working-class population the percentage was 6·8 by the old standard, 31·1 by the new. Here is striking confirmation of the point mentioned on page 152 that there tends to be a large number of families not very far above the poverty line. In 1899 Rowntree had found that by raising his poverty line by about 30 per cent, he more than doubled the proportion of the wage-earning class in poverty. So in 1936 a raising of the poverty line by about 40 per cent more than quadrupled the proportion of the working-class population in poverty.

The third social survey of York, undertaken in 1950, was on a less elaborate scale than the first two, but yielded comparable results which appeared in *Poverty and the Welfare State* in 1951. For this survey the sampling method was used. The investigators called at every ninth house, hoping to get a sample of one-in-ten after allowing for the possibility that some returns might have to be discarded. Working-class households only were covered, the definition being now 'earning not more than £550 a year'. The standard was again the Human

Needs Standard, but Rowntree had not only to allow for price changes since 1936. Some foods were rationed in 1950, some were subsidised, some were provided free or cheaply to children at school, and all this was taken into account. The new poverty line, corresponding to the 1936 figure of 43s. 6d. a week (excluding rent) for a family of five, was in 1950 100s. 2d. a week. The calories provided by the new dietary were not clearly explained, but appeared to work out at less than 3,000, with 93 grams of protein, for a man doing moderate muscular work. These seemed to be lower than the standards for 1899 and 1936, but the difference is explained by the fact that the 1936 figures were calculated *gross* (i.e. without allowance for wastage) and the 1950 figures *net*.

Once again the results showed an astonishing improvement, which Rowntree thought was typical of most provincial towns, since the date of the previous survey. The proportion of the total population in poverty had fallen from 17·7 per cent to 1·66 per cent, a reduction of more than nine-tenths. For the working-class population there was a similar fall, from 31·1 per cent to 2·77 per cent.

§ 5. Poverty in Other Towns.
We can obtain some idea of the validity of Rowntree's claim that York was a typical provincial town, and some idea of the special conditions obtaining in London, by looking at the results of other surveys.

One of the earliest of the modern surveys was a small enquiry undertaken in 1889 in two working-class districts of Manchester and Salford. It was carried out by Fred Scott, who had been inspired by Booth, and the results were given in a paper to the Manchester Statistical Society, whose *Transactions*, incidentally, contain a great deal of valuable information on social conditions in the nineteenth century. Scott found that 37·4 per cent of the working-class population were 'very poor', having less than 4s. per adult per week and not having 'the means of independent subsistence'; while a further 13·1 per cent were 'poor', earning between 4s. and 6s. 3d. per adult per week and having 'the means of procuring bare necessities only'.

Bowley's survey of five towns, the first to use the sampling method, was also the first to make a comparative study of different types of urban community. The towns surveyed in 1912–14 and again in 1923–4 were Reading, Northampton, Warrington, Bolton and Stanley, all, like York, of medium size, but scattered in different parts of the country and dependent on different industries. Reading and Warrington had a mixed industrial make-up, Northampton was largely specialised on boot and shoe manufacture, Stanley on coal and Bolton on cotton.

Bowley took as his unit the household, and his investigators visited a representative sample of working-class households in each town and classified them according to how far the income of the households fell above or below his standard, which was roughly the same as Rowntree's 1899 standard, allowing of course for changes in prices. He assumed that income was pooled and that if the household as a whole fell below the standard, every member of it was in poverty. In 1912–14 he also made the important assumption that a full week's earnings were coming into the family. He did not allow, therefore, for poverty caused by unemployment or underemployment, but in 1923–4 he obtained results both for a full week's earnings and for the actual earnings in the week of the investigation.

He found that, taking the five towns together, the proportion of the working-class population in poverty in 1912–14 was 12·6 per cent. In 1923–4 it had fallen to 3·5 per cent. But these combined figures concealed substantial differences between the various towns. In the earlier period the lowest was 6·1 per cent in Stanley and the highest 29 per cent in Reading. In the later years Bolton was the lowest, with 1·6 per cent and Reading again the highest with 7·9 per cent. Since the earlier period was one of prosperity the results, Bowley thought, were 'surprising, and, in Warrington and Reading—shocking'. Equally surprising, however, is the improvement over a decade which included four years of war.

Using methods and standards similar to those of the New London Survey, the Social Science Department of the University of Liverpool made a survey of Merseyside[1] in 1929–30 and found that 16·1 per cent of the working-class families were below the poverty line. Again, in Southampton[2] in 1928, 12½ per cent of all families were found to be in poverty; in Sheffield in 1931–2 17·1 per cent.

Three broad conclusions emerge from all these surveys, and others which we have not mentioned. The first is that at the end of the nineteenth century, after two decades of falling prices and rapidly rising real wages, rather more than a quarter of the people in our towns were living at a standard insufficient or barely sufficient for subsistence. The second is that in the first quarter of the twentieth century there was a remarkable improvement in the position; and that by 1950 there is some evidence for saying that poverty, judged by subsistence-level standards, had virtually disappeared. The third is that the application of more generous standards, the raising of the poverty line to allow for something more than mere existence, continues to reveal a disquieting amount of 'near poverty'.

§ **6. The Causes of Poverty.** How has the improvement come about? In order to answer this question it is necessary to examine the findings of the social surveys in regard to the causes of poverty. To begin with, there is Rowntree's distinction between primary and secondary poverty. In the case of primary poverty, where the income of a family is insufficient for its basic needs, the problem is whether poverty arises because the income is exceptionally low, on account of low productivity or unemployment of the chief wage-earner; or because the needs are exceptionally high, as in families with an abnormally large number of children or dependants. In the case of secondary poverty, where income is sufficient but is mis-spent, the problem is to find out why it is mis-spent. Analysis along these lines will obviously throw light on the relative importance of wage-increases, full employment, social security benefits, education and welfare schemes, and

[1] D. Caradog Jones: *The Social Survey of Merseyside*, 3 vols., 1934.
[2] P. Ford: *Work and Wealth in a Modern Port*, 1934.

other factors, in the progress towards the conquest of poverty.

In all the surveys undertaken before the first world war it was quite clear that low wages were the principal cause of poverty. Booth found that, of the poverty in the East End of London in 1888, nearly two-thirds was caused by low wages and irregular employment, about one-fifth by 'circumstances' —illness, old age and large families; and the remainder (which was really secondary poverty) by 'habits'—drink, unwise spending and loafing. Booth did not separate low wages from unemployment and irregular work in his list of causes, but the relative importance of these three was probably much the same as in York, where Rowntree found that 52 per cent of the poverty in 1899 was caused by low wages and only 3 per cent by irregular work and 2 per cent by unemployment. It must be borne in mind, however, that 1899 was a year of high employment. 'Circumstances' accounted for rather less than half of the poverty in York, the chief causes under this heading being large families (22 per cent); death of the chief wage-earner (16 per cent) and illness or old age (5 per cent). Bowley's findings in the five towns confirmed the conclusion that, even when working full time, many wage-earners could not earn enough to keep a family of normal size out of poverty.

The surveys of the inter-war years showed the same causes at work, but in a different order. The rise in the wages of unskilled labour, the institution of Trade Boards and minimum wage schemes in certain occupations, and the fall in the cost of necessities, had all contributed to the reduction in the total amount of poverty and also reduced the proportion of the remaining poverty which was caused by low wages. The principal cause was now unemployment, alike (the dates are significant) in the five towns in 1923–4, in London in 1929 and in York in 1936. In the five towns Bowley at first assumed a full week's normal earnings for each household. When he took the actual earnings in the week of the enquiry the incidence of poverty was raised from 3·5 per cent to 6·5 per cent for the five towns together, and in Bolton it was almost trebled.

The same picture was apparent in the London Survey, where Bowley showed that full employment would have reduced the poverty in 1929 by one-half: instead of 10 per cent of the working population, only 5 per cent would have been below the poverty line.

Turning now to the post-war period, in 1950 only 2·77 per cent of the working-class population of York were in poverty, even by Rowntree's Human Needs Standard; and it is interesting to find that more than two-thirds of this remaining poverty was caused, not by low wages or unemployment, but by old age. Sickness accounted for about one-fifth; death, large families and low wages for about one-tenth and unemployment for none at all. Rowntree demonstrated the effectiveness of full employment and the social services in the cure of poverty by a set of calculations designed to introduce, as it were, the conditions of 1936 one by one into the environment of 1950. He showed that if, in 1950, unemployment had existed at the level of 1936, everything else remaining as it was in 1950, the amount of poverty would have been doubled. He also showed that if, in 1950, only those social services had operated which were in existence in 1936 (everything else, including unemployment, remaining as it was in 1950) the amount of poverty would have been about five times as great.

Unfortunately the causes of secondary poverty have not proved measurable with the same accuracy as those of primary poverty. For obvious reasons it is extremely difficult to obtain reliable information as to how income is being misspent. Rowntree's impressions fifty years ago were that the chief causes of secondary poverty were drink, betting and gambling, and ignorant or careless housekeeping, in that order. Recent surveys give the impression that drink is now a lesser cause and that gambling heads the list. There is no doubt about the seriousness of secondary poverty, and there is no shortage of case-studies or trenchant accounts of its consequences. But accurate measurement is not possible.

§ 7. Has Poverty in Great Britain been cured? It is now clear that each of the main causes of primary poverty has been matched by an appropriate remedy. Poverty caused by low wages, irregular employment and unemployment, has been largely resolved by the rise in real wages, by legislation relating to minimum wages and casual work, by the continuance of full employment, and by the payment of social insurance benefits to the unemployed. Poverty caused by illness has been mitigated by the provision of better health and welfare services, and by the payment of social insurance benefits in time of sickness. The aged and the widowed receive pensions, the large families benefit through family allowances. Any remaining cases of poverty can receive individual care from a special body called the National Assistance Board. Does this mean that poverty in Great Britain has been cured?

When we come to discuss the social services in detail (in Chapter VIII) the principles which underlie the legislation will be examined, to see how they have developed since the time when the only State social services were those provided by the Poor Law. In this chapter it remains only to discuss the results as revealed in the York Survey of 1950 and in other reports and enquiries, especially the annual reports of such bodies as the Ministry of National Insurance and the National Assistance Board. Broadly speaking, primary poverty has been cured in Great Britain; but there are four qualifications to this simple answer.

In the first place, there are still people who are in poverty because they are not able to qualify for insurance benefits and who, from ignorance, pride or prejudice, or from some higher motive, do not apply to the National Assistance Board. Two quite different groups of people come under this heading. One consists of persons who are on the borderline between employment and unemployment or between health and sickness. Through mental instability or chronic illness of some kind they are unable to earn enough to keep them out of poverty but not ill enough to claim sickness benefits, or sufficiently unemployed to claim unemployment benefits, or old

enough to claim a pension.   They should receive some help
from the National Assistance Board but for various reasons
they do not.   These people are probably not numerous, but
their cases are tragic, and any social worker can testify to their
existence.   The other group consists of people who are doing
work which is very poorly paid, not because they are unable
to do better, but from a sense of vocation.   Chief among
these are the clergy, some of whom willingly and without
complaint suffer poverty which impairs their physical health
and limits the effectiveness of their important work.

The second qualification concerns the effects of inflation.
The decade following the second world war saw a rapid rise
in the cost of living and therefore in the money cost of whatever standard is adopted for the measurement of poverty.
The poverty line was, as it were, rising automatically, but the
benefits paid under the various social security schemes rose
only intermittently and as a result of political discussion,
usually at the time of the Budget.   In York in 1950 the
principal cause of the poverty that remained was old age.
These were not people deprived of a pension, but people who
in nearly every case were receiving the statutory pension and
found it inadequate for subsistence.   Again the remedy was
to seek further relief from the National Assistance Board, but
many of them did not.   The scope of the problem over the
whole country was shown by the fact that at the end of 1955,
out of 4·8 million persons receiving pensions,[1] just over one
million *did* obtain further assistance from the National Assistance Board because their pensions were inadequate.   All this
raises considerable problems of economic and fiscal policy
which will be discussed later.   For the present we are merely
accounting for the substantial number of people who (in 1955)
are in poverty through old age.

The third qualification to the claim that poverty has been
cured raises again the question of definitions.   It was suggested earlier that as the *average* standard of living rose, so the

[1] Retirement Pensions, Contributory Old Age Pensions, and Non-
Contributory Old Age Pensions.

minimum standard which people regarded as tolerable tended to rise. The result is that by the time poverty, as defined by one standard, has been cured, public opinion has come to accept a new and higher standard, according to which a much larger percentage of the population falls below the poverty line. By 1952, for example, there was an influential group of opinion in Great Britain which regarded the standard suggested ten years earlier as the basis for the post-war social security payments as too severe. Poverty as it was conceived in 1942 might have been cured, but not as it was conceived in 1952. This social trend is obviously a good one, and one which must be recognised alike by politicians and economists. But its implications are far-reaching.

Finally, the problem of secondary poverty, although it cannot be measured, remains and comes into greater prominence as primary poverty recedes. Its root cause is deficiency of character and lack of education in the widest sense. Its cure lies to some extent in the sphere of economic and social influences but, for the most part, outside them. We can give instruction in good housekeeping, we can rescue children from parental neglect, we can limit the opportunities for gambling and drinking. But it is the moral quality of teachers and social workers, the moral influence of the Churches, and the personal example and service of those who are concerned about spiritual welfare, that will eventually cure the disease of secondary poverty. Charles Booth summed it up in these words:

'In regarding the conditions of life at their worst, and in seeking to improve them, there are two distinct tasks: to raise the general level of existence, but especially at the bottom level, is one: to increase the proportion of those who know how to use aright the means they have is another and even greater. Each of such efforts should aid the other.'[1]

[1] Booth: *op. cit.*, Final Volume, 1902, p. 201.

CHAPTER VII

VOLUNTARY SOCIAL SERVICES

§ **1. The Importance of the Voluntary Services.** In Chapter VI it was found that the relief and cure of poverty were being achieved in three ways: by the raising of all incomes through economic progress, so that even the lowest in the scale would eventually be above the poverty line; by economic policy, and especially employment policy, designed to enable most people to earn enough to supply their ordinary needs; and by the operation of the social services, many of which were aimed at those exceptional needs and circumstances which threatened the security of individuals and families.

A more detailed study of the social services must now be attempted in order to find out how they work, what economic principles and problems are involved in their operation, and how far they make up that modern Leviathan, the Welfare State. There is no convenient definition of a social service, and there are differences of political attitude to both the scope and the function of social services in a democratic society. But in order to limit the field of study, let us say that a social service provides for those personal economic and social needs which arise out of income insecurity and the handicaps of poverty. This definition excludes all those voluntary organisations whose primary aim is religious, political, commercial or cultural, even though they may provide incidentally for economic and social needs in the way here suggested. It also excludes those services of Government and local authorities which people enjoy collectively, such as defence services and street lighting, and those trading activities, such as public utilities, which are commercial rather than social services. Even so, the boundaries are vague: they exclude, for example, the Churches, whose primary concern is religious; yet most of the pioneers of voluntary social services were inspired, and many workers now engaged in all kinds of social service still are inspired, by religious ideals. Again, there is little apparent difference between provision of personal medical services by a hospital, which is included, and of collective services by a public health authority, which is not.

Having limited the field, we can now conveniently divide it into two parts: voluntary social services and public social services. The distinction does not rest on whether or not those who provide the services are paid for their work: many employees of the voluntary societies are salaried officials and many people give their services free to various branches of the public services. Nor does the distinction imply that voluntary social services are not subject to public supervision; their activities are often carefully controlled and information about them is published by public officials. Broadly speaking, the voluntary services, in this context, are those which have a substantial income from sources other than public funds. With certain exceptions, the scope of their activities is limited by the extent to which they can attract voluntary subscriptions and enjoy private endowments.

It is often imagined that the voluntary and public social services are mutually exclusive, like private enterprise and nationalised industry. It is better to regard them as complementary, and indeed the history of the voluntary social services suggests that there will always be a place for them in the most thoroughgoing Welfare State. What that place is likely to be in the future will be discussed at the end of this chapter. But it is important to know something of their history and traditions even where they have been partly superseded by the public social services.

In the first place, voluntary social services are characteristic democratic institutions. Experience in leadership, service to the community, tolerance in discussion, training in committee work, all that makes up that much-abused term 'good citizenship' is found at its best in the voluntary social services.

Nowhere is this better illustrated than in Professor T. S. Ashton's book on *The Industrial Revolution*:

'In the eighteenth century the characteristic instrument of social purpose was not the individual or the State, but the club. Men grew up in an environment of institutions which ranged from the cock and hen club of the tavern to the literary group of the coffee-house, from the "box" of the village inn to the Stock Exchange and Lloyd's, from the Hell Fire Club of the blasphemers to the Holy Club of the Wesleys, and from the local association for the prosecution of felons to the national Society for the Reformation of the Manners among the Lower Orders and the Society of Universal Good Will. Every interest, tradition, or aspiration found expression in corporate form. The idea that, somehow or other, men had become self-centred, avaricious and anti-social is the strangest of all the legends by which the story of the industrial revolution has been obscured.'[1]

Secondly, in every sphere of social service the voluntary services came first. In provision for times of illness, unemployment and old age, in education, in organised saving, in housing reform—the ground was first covered by voluntary action. One reason for this is that innovation is always controversial: all pioneers have been criticised, many have been ridiculed; and the public authorities cannot enter the field until it becomes less controversial and acceptable at least to a majority in Parliament if not to a majority of the electorate. Another reason is that the risks of social pioneering are too great. Many social experiments appear to have a greater chance of failure than of success, but the faith of the pioneers results in their being made none the less. Clearly the public authorities, with their responsibility to the taxpayer and the ratepayer, cannot afford to take risks of this kind. A third reason for the precedence of voluntary social services is that the scale of operation is, initially, quite small. The field of the

[1] *Op. cit.*, p. 127.

public social services is the whole country, or the whole area of a local authority. Most of the social services grew from small beginnings: a few individuals and a local leader, trying to provide for some local social need, and then extending their activities or inspiring others to form similar groups. Only when they become nation-wide in their scope does the possibility of public supervision, support or control, arise.

§ 2. The Friendly Societies. In contemplating the whole field of voluntary social services, just as in looking at the pattern of industry, the first impression is one of bewildering variety. This variety is a reflection of the varied needs and demands that gave rise to these institutions. The services planned by the State tend to be more uniform, more standardised and, in terms of volume of output, often more efficient. Voluntary services are not only more varied, but often more flexible (with the notable exception of certain charitable trusts) and therefore more efficient in terms of adaptability to individual and local needs.

In spite of their variety, however, it is possible to classify the voluntary social services for purposes of description and analysis. Two broad groups are distinguishable, inspired respectively by the motives of mutual aid and philanthropy. Lord Beveridge, in making this very useful division, defines the mutual aid motive as 'the desire to help one another in a common need for security against misfortune' and the philanthropic motive as 'the feeling which makes men who are materially comfortable, mentally uncomfortable so long as their neighbours are materially uncomfortable'.[1] The distinction between them is not only one of motive, but applies also to their method of organisation, their economic effects, and their relationships with the State. Mutual aid organisations were formed by a group of people getting together to help each other, and were essentially democratic; philanthropic societies were often set up by one person to alleviate want or distress among people who could not help themselves,

---

[1] Lord Beveridge: *Voluntary Action*, p. 9.

and were therefore more autocratic and dependent on the resources, of character, time and money, provided by the founder. The economic effect of mutual aid is the transfer of income from the fortunate to the unfortunate among people of the same social class and whose normal earning power and standard of living is similar; philanthropy tends to redistribute income from rich to poor. Finally, the Registrar of Friendly Societies is responsible for the registration of a wide range of mutual aid organisations, for the benevolent supervision of their activities, and for the publication of statistical and other information about them; the Charity Commissioners, on the other hand, have been more strictly concerned with ensuring the proper application of trust funds and have neither collected nor published information relating to the scope and finances of philanthropic institutions as a whole.

The typical mutual aid organisation is the friendly society. Originally, the friendly societies were small groups of people— small enough for them to be able to know and trust each other —who met regularly for 'good fellowship', and who contributed voluntarily to a common fund for the relief and maintenance of their sick, infirm and aged members, and of the widows and children of deceased members. Many such societies grew up in the seventeenth century and earlier, but in the main they were the product of the economic and social changes of the eighteenth century: the Industrial Revolution, urban and rural insecurity, and the insufficiency or misdirection of the Elizabethan Poor Law. By 1800 there were many hundreds of such societies, not only providing good fellowship and facilities for insurance against loss of income through sickness or death of the breadwinner, but catering also for other economic needs which could be satisfied in this way, in particular the desire to avoid a pauper funeral and the desire to save in an organised and regular manner, either for a special purpose or simply as a precaution. Most of them centred on either the churches or the public houses, and many of them displayed unusual imagination and humour in their choice of name and conditions of membership. There were, for example, the Improved Order of Total Abstinent Sons of the Phoenix Sick and Burial Friendly Society, the Amalgamated Order of Comical Fellows, the Loyal Order of Ancient Shepherds Friendly Society, and innumerable brands of Oddfellows, ·Foresters, Buffaloes, Anglo-Saxons and Rechabites, many of which survive to the present day under their original names.

These societies did not cater for the needs of the very poor: the normal earnings of their members would be high enough and regular enough for them to maintain their subscriptions and take part in the social activities of the club. On the other hand, they were not merely skilled artisan organisations, as is sometimes suggested: the stress laid by successive committees of enquiry on their importance as rate-relieving institutions implies that their members were living near enough to the poverty line to be potential claimants for poor-relief.

In course of time there have emerged five principal types of friendly society differing according to their economic organisation and purpose. First, there are the affiliated orders, of which the largest still existing is the Independent Order of Odd Fellows, Manchester Unity, Friendly Society. These are federal organisations with local lodges, grouped together into districts, which in turn are grouped together into 'unities'. The local lodges are small and independent, collecting subscriptions in order to provide benefits for their members in time of sickness. Life insurance is organised on a district basis, and the 'unities' are responsible for general policy but do not interfere in the day-to-day affairs or finances of the lodges and district branches. These orders are missionary in spirit: new lodges are sponsored not from above, but horizontally by the existing lodges, and the network grows like a strawberry patch. They combine, therefore, an emphasis on local independence with a realisation that there are economies of scale in regard to certain types of risk, against which insurance is better organised on a district than on a local basis.

The second type is the accumulating society, of which the best-known and largest is the Hearts of Oak Benefit Society.

These are strongly centralised in finance and organisation and, partly for this reason, offer a much wider range of insurances and benefits than do the Orders, which provide only sickness and death benefits.

In contrast to the accumulating societies are the dividing societies, small, local and independent, collecting small regular contributions from each member, giving him a benefit in time of sickness, assisting with medical and funeral expenses, and dividing, periodically, a large part of their funds among the members. The advantages of this system are obvious: the members have an interest in efficient administration, malingering is discouraged, and the periodic 'dividend' is a great attraction. But, having no reserves, many of the dividing societies were short-lived, and the longer-lived found it difficult to recruit young members, because of the disproportionate claims of the older members on the societies' funds. In more recent times, however, they achieved greater stability by carrying over substantial reserves from year to year.

While the dividing societies provide for both insurance and saving, the latter in a somewhat haphazard manner, the fourth type of friendly society, the deposit society, is primarily a savings bank and less of an insurance society. Members contribute both to an insurance fund and to a personal savings account, but there is considerable flexibility between the two, for the benefits in time of sickness are paid first from the insurance fund and later, if necessary, from the deposit account. At a normal rate of sickness, however, there is usually a surplus in the insurance account which goes to increase deposits; and these accumulate at interest until retirement. One society, the National Deposit Friendly Society, has grown to be the largest friendly society of any kind in the country, and the combination of insurance with 'organised saving' clearly explains the success of this type of society.

Lastly, there are the burial societies, whose purpose is both life insurance and the provision for a respectable funeral. It is often difficult for us to understand the deep-rooted concern which people had, and still have, about the character of their funerals. In part it was connected with the whole psychology of pauperism and the apparent disgrace of a pauper funeral; in part it was a feature of times when mortality rates, especially infant mortality rates, were much higher and occasional funerals were as serious a drain on family income as occasional sickness and unemployment. The innumerable local burial clubs of the eighteenth and nineteenth centuries were a direct response to this need, and although the whole business has changed in scope and organisation, there are still many friendly societies whose main function is to relieve working-class people of anxiety on this account.

There are several other types of friendly society, all retaining their original purpose of voluntary mutual insurance against various forms of economic insecurity. Where insurance could be provided satisfactorily and cheaply on a small scale, and where mutual fellowship and social activities were regarded as important, the societies remained small. In other cases, economies of scale in the spreading of risks and the opportunities of business organisation led to a rapid growth and sometimes to a complete change in character.

Many trade unions, for instance, began as friendly societies. Until the repeal of the Combination Acts in 1824, associations of workmen for any purpose were regarded with suspicion (this is why friendly societies formed before that date often attached the adjective 'loyal' to their titles); but later on, trade unions openly sought the legal recognition as a non-profit-making body which was provided by registration with the Registrar of Friendly Societies. The conflict between those who maintained that trade union funds should be used solely for the provision of friendly society benefits to their members, and those who sought to use them increasingly for the support of strikes and other forms of 'trade protection', is of course an important chapter in the history of trade unionism. But it is interesting to find that, even in 1955, 405 out of a total of 666 trade unions, and 8,517,000 members out of a total of 9,662,000, were registered with the Registrar of Friendly Societies; and that nearly a quarter of their total expenditure was on 'provident benefits'—chiefly sickness, accident, superannuation and funeral benefits.

While some friendly societies grew to take on a more political aspect, others changed into large-scale commercial undertakings. Particularly was this so in the case of the burial clubs, but it occurred also in other societies in which subscriptions were collected from people in their homes instead of being brought to a central meeting place. The former system inevitably placed considerable responsibility in the hands of the collectors and in course of time their job became an occupation by itself, rewarded on a commission basis. So began the business of 'industrial assurance', whose chequered history makes fascinating and not always wholesome reading. But here was a field in which the 'club' aspect of friendly societies was weak and mutual aid gave way to big business.

Another change in character is one that was already noticed in describing the deposit societies. Where the savings motive was important, friendly societies have tended to become more like savings banks than mutual aid clubs. Especially is this true of the building societies, which are now large-scale financial organisations for the borrowing and lending of money, but most of which began as small local groups of people helping each other to save in an organised manner with a view to owning their own homes.

At the end of the eighteenth century the combined influences of Government concern about combinations of workers for any purpose, local anxiety about the growing burden of the Poor Law, and the desire of the friendly societies to obtain official recognition and legal protection, led to the passage of the first Friendly Societies Act, known from its promoter, George Rose, as Rose's Act, of 1793. Societies had to register, and deposit their rules, with the Justices, and in return received certain privileges in regard to legal proceedings and exemption from tax. The Chief Registrar of Friendly Societies was first appointed in 1846. His periodic reports show that there are many other varieties of society than those we have described and that even in the middle of the twentieth century, they play a considerable part in our social and economic life. At one end are the trade unions, the building societies and the enormous network of the Co-operative Movement; at the other, there are still many local societies, some over 100 years old, others registered since the second world war.

The friendly societies were naturally affected by the development of national insurance. The Insurance Acts of 1911 and 1946 were important upward and downward turning points in their history; for the first used them as agents for the administration of the national scheme, and the second abandoned them. The Act of 1911 was the first measure of compulsory social insurance to be introduced in Great Britain and was viewed with some apprehension by the friendly societies, the trade unions and the industrial assurance companies. Their support was gained, however, by the wisdom of Mr. Lloyd George, who decided to administer Part I of the Act (relating to health insurance) through 'Approved Societies' which, after some argument about the dividing societies, came to include every type of friendly society. In consequence, the Civil Service was spared a formidable task, the knowledge and experience of the friendly societies was enlisted, and the societies were able to combine their own insurance business with the national scheme. The costs of administering national insurance were paid by the State, and the Approved Societies eventually found the arrangement to be much to their advantage. They grew in size and importance, their social insurance departments facilitated, rather than competed with, the business of their voluntary insurance departments, and the combined overhead costs of offices and staff were well subsidised.

In his plan for a new, unified scheme of social insurance against all the principal causes of poverty, Lord Beveridge proposed that the friendly societies should continue to be used as agents of the State. When the plan was put into operation, however, in the years following the second world war, this suggestion was not adopted. The National Insurance Act of 1946 came into force in July 1948, when the friendly societies had to curtail their activities severely, to reduce their staffs, and to overhaul radically their administrative and financial organisation. Many of their employees were absorbed into the new Ministry of National Insurance, but, from being an ally, social insurance has become more of a competitor with the insurance provided by the friendly societies. It was the intention of the new scheme to provide benefits at subsistence level; the contribution for State insurance was substantially increased; and, while many of the existing members of friendly societies continued to insure above the minimum provided by the State scheme, the recruitment of younger members became increasingly difficult.

The Chief Registrar of Friendly Societies did not publish any detailed reports between 1937 and 1952; but his reports for 1952 and subsequent years show clearly the effect of post-war social legislation. From the end of 1937 to the end of 1947, total membership of friendly societies[1] rose from 8,341,000 to 8,608,000, an increase of 3 per cent. Between 1947 and 1954 it fell to 6,503,000, a decrease of 25 per cent. The societies whose main business was the provision of sickness benefits suffered most severely, and in all types of society juvenile membership fell more heavily than adult membership. Among the societies with branches (the affiliated orders) the small branches with less than 100 members showed greater powers of survival than the large. The other types of society suffered most of their casualties among small societies, though to some extent this implied a solution of the problem by amalgamation. The difficulty of personnel seems to have been as serious as that of finance; the Registrar says: 'In the past these societies have been administered by men to whom the job was often a lifetime's hobby and whose enthusiasm helped to make up for any lack of technical equipment. It has become harder to find volunteers to carry on the work, and the death or retirement of a secretary is too often the signal for dissolution.'[2]

---

[1] i.e. friendly societies proper. The figures do not include collecting societies, assurance companies, industrial and provident societies, trade unions, building societies and other organisations coming within the Registrar's field.

[2] *Report of the Chief Registrar of Friendly Societies*, 1952, Part 2, p. 2.

For all this, the total funds of the friendly societies continued to increase, from £146 million at the end of 1937 to £203 million at the end of 1947 and £224 million at the end of 1954. If to these are added the enormous financial resources of the building societies, co-operative societies, trade unions and industrial assurance companies, whose progress has not been impaired by national insurance, it is clear that the Registrar's field supplies a substantial part of the investment capital of the country.

§ 3. **Philanthropic Organisations.** The variety of philanthropic organisations is so great as to defy classification. The National Council of Social Service, formed in 1919 'to bring together in council, nationally and locally, representatives of voluntary organisations and statutory authorities', publishes a list of some 300 organisations, under about 20 different headings, but these are only the main national societies. There are many others, national, regional and local, as well as some 110,000 charitable trusts, ranging from village funds disposing of a few shillings annually to the great national trusts whose endowments run into millions of pounds. Lord Beveridge, in his study *Voluntary Action*, gives an interesting and often exciting account of the vicissitudes of many of these organisations. In this section it is only possible to discuss their salient features and then to look at the special problems of the charitable trusts.

The first of these features is that hardly any philanthropic organisations are concerned with the direct relief of poverty: with money grants to those who suffer temporary or permanent loss of income. Many societies assist the unfortunate in this way, but that is not their main purpose. It was at one time the main purpose of almsgiving and poor relief, and is still the main purpose of mutual aid through friendly societies, of private and social insurance, and of 'national assistance'. But philanthropy has been more concerned with the circumstances of poverty than with poverty itself, with the provision of hospitals and schools and facilities for recreation, with the betterment of housing and family life, with the spreading of educational, social and cultural opportunities, with the solution of personal problems, with the provision of links between urban and rural communities, between working and professional classes, between the individual and the State.   In a sense, it has been concerned with secondary poverty, with the unwillingness or inability of people to provide all these things for themselves, less from lack of money than from lack of leadership and of expert help and advice.

The second feature is that most philanthropic organisations were founded by people of a particular class and with particular gifts.   With the outstanding exception of Lord Shaftesbury, the founders were middle-class people.   They had a certain amount of spare time and spare money, and were inspired with an enthusiasm for unselfish service and, usually, a religious idealism which enabled them to persevere when others would have despaired.   There were some who exhibited an old-fashioned patronage which is distasteful to the present generation, though it was accepted more sincerely in Victorian times than is often realised.   But we have only to read the lives of Elizabeth Fry and Octavia Hill, of the Rev. Henry Solly and Dr. Barnardo, of Shaftesbury and Baden-Powell, to appreciate philanthropy at its best.

A third characteristic is the adaptability of most philanthropic organisations.   Economic progress, the emergence of new needs and problems, the assumption by the State of responsibility for certain aspects of poverty, have led philanthropists to adapt their ideas and redirect their enthusiasm with surprising flexibility.

The best type of philanthropic organisation aims at 'helping people to help themselves' rather than providing services which make no demands on the time or effort or purse of the beneficiaries.   Nevertheless, the finance of this type of voluntary service represents a transfer from the richer to the poorer members of the community which is quite different from the mutual aid of the friendly societies.   Some organisations rely entirely on membership fees, but for the most part they derive their income from donations and endowments, from grants made by trusts and statutory bodies, from public subscriptions, and from the sale of goods and services to benevolent consumers who would not otherwise be disposed to buy them. An important privilege enjoyed by all non-profit-making organisations is exemption from the payment of income tax. The privilege extends to the refund, to the organisation, of tax in respect of 'covenanted' subscriptions, that is, regular gifts made by any donor for a period of at least seven years. With a high marginal rate of tax this amounts to a substantial concession. It means that if the donor is liable to pay income tax on part of his income at the rate of 8*s*. 6*d*. in the £, his choice lies between keeping 11*s*. 6*d*. for himself and paying 8*s*. 6*d*. in tax, and giving 20*s*. free of tax to any voluntary organisation he wishes to support; which provides a nice exercise in fiscal ethics.

One of the most interesting and significant of the philanthropic organisations of the nineteenth century was the Charity Organisation Society, formed by the Rev. Henry Solly in 1869. Its principles deserve careful examination, because they are of fundamental importance in the whole history of voluntary and public social services. Briefly they are that the conditions on which charitable aid is given should be related as closely as possible to the genuine needs of each individual; and that indiscriminate charity is wasteful, unfair and demoralising. The problem is as old as society itself. If beggars find that by certain behaviour and tactics they can obtain alms more generously and regularly, then that sort of behaviour is encouraged, and that sort of behaviour, rather than the genuine needs of the individual, becomes the condition on which alms are given. On the other side of the transaction, if charitable persons make it known that in certain circumstances they will dispense charity, potential claimants are encouraged to place themselves in such circumstances, whether or not these are evidence of genuine need.

The Charity Organisation Society felt that, in the mid-nineteenth century, there was a growing misdirection of the funds and energies of charitable people. It believed that individual treatment of each case of need on its own merits was essential in order to make the best use of the limited resources available, in order to distinguish between real need and mere importunity, and in order to discourage abuse. It therefore undertook an ambitious programme of individual case-work and compiled a register of applicants for relief, and of charitable organisations, distinguishing those who conformed to its principles from those who did not. The Society also undertook a great deal of valuable work on housing reform, on the 'voting system' for entry into certain public institutions, and on many other social problems.

The Society found, however, that rigid adherence to its principles brought it into sharp conflict both with voluntary societies who were not very discriminating in their provision of voluntary relief and with any State scheme for providing social services on a basis other than that of individual need. Thus, it opposed the Salvation Army for setting up soup kitchens on the Embankment at midnight and so encouraging hundreds of people who need not have been either homeless or hungry to attend the feast. It opposed Charles Booth and others for advocating a national scheme of old age pensions. It opposed, in the words of its biographer Mrs. Bosanquet, 'all plans for granting a stereotyped form of relief to large numbers of persons whose needs are very varying and only capable of being met by individual attention'.

In course of time the Society tempered its views, adapted itself to the new conditions resulting from the social legislation of this century, and continues to do work of incalculable value as the Family Welfare Association, which name it adopted in 1946. Its activities, however, are still based on the principle of family casework and the promotion of economy and efficiency in the administration of philanthropy.

§ **4. Charitable Trusts.** Among philanthropic institutions, the charitable trust is in a special position. It is a fund established for charitable purposes by a benefactor who lays down conditions regarding its use. Many of the philanthropic

14

organisations whose activities have already been mentioned derive part or all of their income from endowments of this kind, but the charitable trust by itself is a purely financial institution, and there are many trusts which are not concerned with social work and voluntary service in the practical sense but simply with the distribution of grants of money on certain conditions. Some trusts, like the Nuffield Foundation, are formed during the lifetime of the founder and given wide and flexible terms of reference so that, while remaining faithful to the founder's intentions, they can be adapted to changing circumstances. But most of them have been established by will, and in some cases the conditions laid down by the testator showed a lack of imagination, a carelessness of wording, and, be it said, a lack of charity which in course of time made them extremely difficult to carry out. Often the primary motive of the founder was the perpetuation of his own name (for example, by stipulating an annual oration in his memory) or the dispossession of his nearest relatives. Sometimes the income of the charity was to be shared among a limited number of poor people, and changing circumstances (for example, an increase in land values) so increased the income that the beneficiaries were translated into wealthy pensioners. Occasionally, the limitation of a charity to a particular parish attracted a large number of expectant residents of indifferent character and caused a substantial increase in the local Poor Rate, thus frustrating the purpose of the charity and exemplifying the dangers which the Charity Organisation Society saw so clearly.

The chief problem in regard to charitable trusts, however, has not been the unwisdom of some of the trust deeds, but rather the attitude of the law, which has always been to uphold the wishes of the deceased as precisely as possible. From earliest times charitable trusts (defined since 1601 by reference to the Statute of Charitable Uses of that year) enjoyed considerable privileges, and the law, being concerned to prevent misuse, could hardly encourage their adaptation to changing circumstances. The position was not unlike that relating to monopoly, where, as Professor Robinson has shown, 'When considering the public interest, the courts . . . measure it more by the interest that the sanctity of contracts should be upheld and property preserved, than by the interest that restraints which might conceivably lead to the raising of prices should be made difficult of enforcement'.[1] If for 'contracts' we read 'testaments' and for 'the raising of prices' 'the degradation of charity', there is a significant parallel in these two fields of social policy. Until the middle of the nineteenth century the only relaxation was the doctrine of *cy-pres*, by which the courts could divert charitable funds, the original purpose of which had become quite impossible of fulfilment, to the nearest similar workable purpose. Even so, both the redress of abuses and the alteration of the purpose of a trust under the *cy-pres* doctrine could be secured only through the Court of Chancery, and was a slow and expensive business. Public concern about the unsatisfactory state of many trusts led to the appointment of a Commission under Lord Brougham in 1818. Their enquiry was supplemented by that of the Poor Law Commissioners of 1834 and the Commission on Education of 1861.

Of the subsequent legislation the most important Acts were the Charitable Trusts Act of 1853 and the Endowed Schools Act of 1869. The former set up the Charity Commissioners as a permanent independent body to supervise charitable trusts and (since 1860) to approve modifications put forward by the trustees, within the strict limits of the *cy-pres* doctrine. The latter permitted a less strict modification of educational trusts subject to the approval of the Privy Council and, later, the Board of Education. There the matter stood until the appointment of a new Committee in 1950.

Discussion continued unabated during the remainder of the nineteenth century. It probably reached its height with the publication by Lord Hobhouse, one of the Charity Commissioners, of a gruesome book called *The Dead Hand*. He

[1] E. A. G. Robinson: *Monopoly* (Cambridge Economic Handbooks), 1941, p. 264.

argued, with many an illustration from his 'Charities Chamber of Horrors' (as Lord Beveridge aptly describes it), that there should always be a 'living and reasonable owner of property, to manage it according to the wants of mankind'. And yet, many charitable trusts were operating successfully and providing for social needs in a way that no public trustee could have improved upon. Why all this fuss about a few fossilised benefactions? Simply because the subject could not be separated from the general discussion about the relationship between voluntary and State social services and their place and purpose in the economy. There was the moral problem of the degrading effects of some charitable gifts and the social attitude to 'pauperism' (the condition of those receiving Poor Law assistance). There was the financial problem of making the best use of private and public money. And there was the economic problem of providing incentives to work and not interfering with the structure of wages. The philanthropists divided the field into separate plots and did what they thought best in the patch, large or small, which interested them. The Charity Organisation Society, with its principles of efficiency and individual casework, strove for discrimination, over the whole field, between those who needed help and those who did not. The Poor Law Commissioners, with their traditional doctrine of 'less eligibility', struggled to achieve a different kind of division: between those who could work and those who could not. Their aim was to administer poor relief in such a way that the able-bodied poor would be driven to seek employment rather than apply for relief.

The general discussion subsided with the social legislation of 1906–11, which seemed to provide the solution to the old Poor Law problem and inaugurate a new kind of partnership between State and voluntary action. The Charity Commissioners continued to give advice and assistance within the limits of their small staff and their restricted powers. Not until 1950 did a revival of interest in charitable trusts, resulting largely from Lord Beveridge's book *Voluntary Action*, lead to the appointment of a new committee, under the chairmanship of Lord Nathan. By this time a new wave of social legislation had shifted the balance between the voluntary and public social services. In areas of overlap the result was often the reduction of State benefits to allow for income received from charities, so that in effect many trusts relieved the taxpayer and the rate-payer rather than their immediate beneficiaries. Moreover, the need for a new definition of charitable trusts had become more pressing as a result of a court case in which it was decided that mixed trusts, partly for 'charitable' and partly for 'non-charitable' purposes, could not claim exemption from income tax. Finally, the fall in the value of money was steadily reducing the real value of many trust funds, which, under the Trustee Act of 1925, could be invested only in gilt-edged securities, with fixed rates of interest.

The Committee's Report (published in December 1952) dealt with all these matters. The main recommendation was that the doctrine of *cy-pres* should be relaxed and the Charity Commissioners and the Minister of Education given wider powers to reshape charitable trusts. They would pay due regard to the intentions of the founders and the views of the existing trustees and would maintain local and denominational interests. But they would be able to initiate schemes, instead of waiting for the trustees to submit them; they would have power to register all trusts and receive their accounts; and in some cases smaller charities would be merged into larger and more effective units. The Committee also favoured the setting up of a 'national common good trust', to finance new ventures and pioneer experiments in voluntary social service. Into it would go the property of people dying intestate and without next of kin (which amounts to about £100,000 a year and is now applied to the relief of the National Debt); and the donations and bequests of those who preferred this type of charity to the endowment of more local and specific causes. Amongst other recommendations, the Committee called for a rewording of the definition of charity and a limited extension of the range of trustee investments to include equity shares.

In 1955 a White Paper was published, expressing the view that the *cy-pres* doctrine was wide enough and that the power to initiate schemes should remain with the trustees; that 'common good trusts' should be local and voluntary; that a new definition of charity was undesirable, and new powers of registration unnecessary. Only in the matter of investments was a need for wider powers, involving a general revision of the Trustee Acts, recognised.

§ 5. Voluntary Service in the Welfare State.

The last hundred years have seen a gradual shift of opinion in regard to the respective roles of the voluntary and public social services. From the view that the family, the Church and voluntary action should provide for most ordinary cases of need, and the public social services step in where voluntary provision proved inadequate or unworkable, the trend has been to the opposite view that the public services should provide for all the 'basic' needs and the voluntary services deal with the exceptional cases. This trend has been largely associated with the development of social insurance. But social insurance is merely a device or technique. The Welfare State, as it is now called, is much more: it is a political concept, a society in which the public authorities assume the responsibility of ensuring certain minimum standards of income, of education, of health and of 'welfare' to every citizen.

It is possible to justify this trend on several grounds. In the first place, the voluntary services, having by their nature no powers of compulsion, cannot help those who do not want to be helped or redistribute income beyond the limits of voluntary giving. As a result, there tends to be a 'hard core' of people who, through destitution, lack of education or ill-health, eventually become a burden on society, and who might be saved from this plight by compulsory provision at an earlier stage. In the second place, there are economies of scale in organising social services on a nation-wide basis. Insurance risks can be spread over the whole community, the same departments (the post office, tax offices, labour exchanges and

so on) can be used for a variety of purposes, and routine benefits and services can be supplied by routine methods, requiring
less-skilled labour and taking advantage of all the economies
of large-scale administration. In the third place, it is only
fair to say that the pioneers of the voluntary social services
often looked forward to the day when their success would persuade the public authorities to take over the responsibility and
release them for service in some other part of the social field.

Nevertheless, there is nothing inevitable or irreversible about
the trend towards increasing public control, nor does it imply
a decreasing trend in the scope and importance of voluntary
activity. The Committee on Charitable Trusts stated cate-
gorically that 'so far from voluntary action being dried up by
the expansion of the (public) social services, greater and
greater demands are being made upon it'.[1] Above all, the
remarkable feature of the growth of social services in Great
Britain has been, not the antithesis between voluntary and
public services, but their complementarity and interdependence.
The empiricism which is characteristic of democracy has led
to almost as many different admixtures of voluntary and public
enterprise as there are different branches of social service.

We have shown that some voluntary organisations, the
friendly societies, required nothing more than legal protection
and recognition in order to carry on their work and regulate
their finances satisfactorily. The result was the appointment
of a public official, the Chief Registrar, who, without interference or control, became an adviser and friend, in quite
exceptional degree, to thousands of voluntary societies. This
is still the relationship, though from being the principal means
of provision against economic insecurity the friendly societies
became, from 1911 to 1948, the agents of a State scheme of
social insurance, and have become since 1948 an important
channel for voluntary *supplementary* provision above the
compulsory minimum provided by the State. We have
shown, too, that all charitable institutions have enjoyed the

[1] *Report of the Committee on Charitable Trusts*, 1952, Cmd. 8710,
para. 54.

special privilege of exemption from tax, and that this, combined with the special legal problems relating to trust funds, has led to the appointment of a public supervisory body, the Charity Commissioners. The function of this body has remained supervisory, although there is little difference between exemption from tax and a specific grant of public funds, which would normally carry with it some degree of public control. The benefits provided by charitable trusts sometimes supplement, sometimes overlap the benefits provided by public services. In many cases they have been adapted, with or without the assistance of the Commissioners, to the relief of special kinds of need and special cases of hardship not covered by the State services. In the case of hospital endowments, for example, the income which used to go towards the main costs of running the hospitals is now devoted largely to the provision of additional comforts and facilities which are not met out of the budgetary funds of the National Health Service.

Even where direct grants are made from public funds, however, the control of expenditure is often left in the hands of voluntary bodies. The Universities, for example, received nearly 70 per cent of their total income in 1954–5 in the form of Treasury Grants, but the allocation of this money was controlled by a University Grants Committee, composed largely of distinguished past or present members of the academic world, who report direct to the Treasury and not to the Ministry of Education. The Committee exercises no control in detail over the way in which the Universities expend the public funds allotted to them. The Citizens' Advice Bureaux, which perform the valuable function of providing skilled advice on personal problems and helping people to use the social services wisely, have the whole of their headquarters expenses paid by the Ministry of Health but are staffed entirely by voluntary workers and controlled by a voluntary organisation, the National Council of Social Service. Only a few of the many voluntary societies which receive grants from public funds have a Government representative on their governing body.

In some cases voluntary social services make arrangements with public services for sharing the work in a particular field. In the provision of homes for orphans and neglected children, for example, the local authorities and various voluntary societies work side by side. In other cases, notably the care of the aged, the public services provide certain standard benefits, such as pensions, and rely almost entirely on the voluntary services to look after the personal needs of each individual.

In future, therefore, the main activities of the voluntary social services are likely to be: (1) to provide supplementary benefits where the public services provide only a minimum; (2) to act as agents for the distribution of public funds where direct control by public authorities is not thought to be desirable; (3) to make arrangements with public services to share the work in particular fields; (4) to provide personal care and help where the public services cannot suitably do so; (5) to fill the gaps in the public services by dealing with exceptional cases of need; (6) to provide liaison between individuals in need and the services, public or voluntary, which can help them; (7) to pioneer new fields of social service; and, we might add, (8) to offer constructive criticism of the working of the public services and make representations in appropriate quarters.

We have been discussing *the voluntary services*, defined as those services which are not financed entirely out of public funds and controlled by public authorities. If we turn our attention to *voluntary service*, defined as service which is rendered to the community without monetary reward, we exclude the salaried employees of voluntary societies on the one hand, but we bring in, on the other hand, the large and growing army of voluntary workers who assist in the administration of the public social services. It is well known that in the educational system of England and Wales considerable use is made of the unpaid services of public-spirited men and women on local and national advisory committees. Less well known is the fact that the national insurance and national assistance schemes, although directly administered by public employees, both rely for their efficient working on voluntary service. Each scheme has an elaborate network of local advisory bodies (comprising, over the whole country, several thousand persons) which meet regularly to discuss local problems and decide difficult cases. Most remarkable of all, the detailed planning and daily management of the National Health Service is entirely in the hands of unpaid, part-time volunteers. About 10,000 people give their services to the regional hospital boards, hospital management committees, executive councils, and other bodies through which, each year, £400–£500 millions of public money is allocated.

If, in the absence of opportunities for voluntary service, these people would consume their time in leisure or in less 'useful' activities, the services which they now produce amount to an invisible increase in the national income and in economic welfare—invisible because, since they are unpaid, the value of their services (like those of the housewife) does not figure in the money measure of the national income. If they were paid for performing these same services, there would be a visible increase in the national income, but also an increase in their share of it.

The domain of voluntary service is not, however, as is sometimes suggested, a model of an ideal society, in which resources are devoted to the public good without any regulatory price mechanism or apparent profit motive. For the domain is narrow, in relation to the whole economy, and if it were extended into areas in which the services required were less obviously connected with the relief of poverty and suffering, some kind of price mechanism would become necessary, both to indicate the relative urgency of the demands for different services, and to provide incentives. Even within the accepted field of voluntary service it is often found that well-meaning persons waste their abilities by performing services which could be much better done by other voluntary workers, if the distributive mechanism were more efficient.

So much for the demand side, as it might be termed, in the

market for voluntary service: the change in the pattern of opportunities caused by the development of the public social services. There has also been a change on the other side, in the willingness and ability of people to give their time and energy to voluntary service and their money to voluntary societies. The *willingness* of people to serve the community voluntarily has probably been affected by a decline in religious influences. The *necessity* for such service certainly appears to many people to dwindle as the Welfare State expands. The extent of this attitude is difficult to assess, but recent social surveys suggest that it is widespread. The *ability* of people to give voluntarily has undoubtedly been affected by the redistribution of incomes, for which the growth of the public social services has partly been responsible. It may be that the whole structure of voluntary service, and especially the finance of the voluntary services, will in future be built on a broader base; that in place of a few people, mainly of the middle class, with substantial amounts of time and money to spare, there will be many people, of all classes, with smaller amounts of time and money to spare. In these circumstances the typical method of finance for voluntary organisations may be the Lord Mayor's Fund and the B.B.C. Appeal. The typical method of service may be that of the Women's Voluntary Services, through which a large number of women give occasional days and half-days to a great variety of activities, including all that goes under the headings of child welfare, old people's welfare, home-helps and hospital work.

CHAPTER VIII

PUBLIC SOCIAL SERVICES—THEIR STRUCTURE AND HISTORY

§ 1. The Structure of the Public Social Services. In the last chapter, while stressing the interdependence of the voluntary and public social services, we found it convenient to distinguish the voluntary services as those which derived all or part of their income from voluntary subscriptions and private endowments. Similarly, in this chapter the public social services may be designated as those which do not derive any income from voluntary sources but rely entirely on public funds: they are financed out of national and local taxation, compulsory insurance contributions and, to some extent, charges for the services provided. They are therefore the direct responsibility of a Minister and a central or local government department. But, as has been shown, they need not be organised by public officials, voluntary workers may play a part in their administration, and co-operation with voluntary organisations may be very close.

Many writers have attempted to classify the public social services for purposes of description and analysis. Some have emphasised their concern with the 'personal welfare' or 'individual well-being' of the citizen; have set out various sorts of personal need, and excluded all 'impersonal' services. Others have stressed the 'element of redistribution', have classified the systems by which income is 'redistributed', and excluded services which do not appear to result in any redistribution. A somewhat cumbersome vocabulary has grown up in recent years to describe the different groupings. There are security services and community services; nutrition services and rehabilitation services; environmental services and amenity services; geriatric services for old people and paediatric for young. But there is not general agreement about the meaning and use of all these terms, and it is better to avoid them as far as possible.

Stated in general terms, the mainspring of social policy may be said to be the desire to ensure to every member of the community certain minimum standards and certain opportunities. But, in more precise terms, it can be elaborated as follows.

First, extremes of poverty and inequality constitute a social problem to the solution of which the economist can contribute a great deal. He may be very strongly moved as a humanitarian, as a moralist, as a politician, but his special contribution as an economist is to analyse the economic causes of these social problems and to point out the economic consequences of the problems themselves and of the various remedies which may be suggested for them.

Secondly, the principle of diminishing marginal utility provides a general case, though subject to a number of qualifications, for assuming that, as a rule, a given addition to income will yield a greater increase in utility and total welfare, the lower down in the scale of money incomes it is applied.

Thirdly, if individuals or families lack the necessities of life, any increase in their real income to enable these necessities to be provided will yield a more than corresponding increase in the national income and in economic welfare, in so far as it improves their physical and mental efficiency. This is the problem of poverty; of meeting the 'common human needs' of people so that they can live a decent life and work with normal efficiency. The common needs may go unsatisfied either because income is exceptionally low, as in the case of irregular employment; or because needs are exceptionally high, as in the case of large families; or because the income, though adequate, is mis-spent. The first two result in primary poverty, the last in secondary poverty.

Fourthly, any increase in the real incomes of individuals and families beyond the point of providing the necessaries of life may also yield a more than corresponding increase in the national income and in economic welfare, if it improves their economic efficiency. This is the problem of inequality; of meeting those 'special needs' of different people which correspond to differences of ability, and providing exceptional opportunities to those of exceptional efficiency.

In all cases, the remedy may come about either through a general increase in total real income (by bringing into employment resources hitherto unemployed or increasing investment in productive capital), or through a redistribution of real income, without any increase in the total.

A general increase, by raising the incomes of all sections of the community, will clearly reduce the incidence of primary poverty, provided that the definition of the 'common needs' is not increased *pari passu*. It will also, by raising the margin of 'inessential' expenditure for all members of the community, reduce the incidence of secondary poverty, provided that the propensity to indulge in 'inessential' before 'essential' expenditure does not increase.

A redistribution, similarly, will probably reduce the incidence of primary and secondary poverty: for it is unlikely that an increase in the share of the 'poorer' classes will affect the physical efficiency of the rest of the community.

In the case of economic efficiency, however, the effect is not so clear. A general increase in the incomes of all sections of the community may reduce inequality in the sense of spreading opportunities in general without disturbing the pattern of 'special' opportunities, but it may still not provide special opportunities to some who could take advantage of them. A redistribution, on the other hand, may both spread opportunities in general and redistribute special opportunities, but it will also raise new social problems by disturbing the existing pattern of special opportunities; and beyond a certain point it will affect incentives and react unfavourably on the size of the national income.

Thus it may be that the most valuable social services are not commonly classed as social services at all: they are those aspects of economic policy which promote a high level of employment and a high rate of economic progress. Of course, some branches of the public social services, as commonly understood, assist in the promotion of a high level of employment. The whole system of labour exchanges, the schemes for the employment of the disabled, and the Re-establishment Centres of the National Assistance Board all help to reduce certain types of unemployment, and one of the aims of the health services is to get people back into work as quickly as possible. Further, the very increases in efficiency that we have been discussing are a constituent part (but only a part) of economic progress. As a rule, however, discussion of the operation of the public social services has been concerned less with the long-term general increase, than with the short-term redistribution of incomes and opportunities.

In this and the following chapters it will be convenient to divide the public social services into three groups, differing in their aims, their methods and their economic consequences, but all connected with the social problems of poverty and inequality. We shall first distinguish these groups and examine their financial implications; then discuss in detail the development of particular services; and finally turn to some general problems affecting the public social services as a whole.

Group I consists of the schemes of national assistance, social insurance, family allowances, and a few other services providing pensions and grants. The chief aim of these services is the removal of primary poverty. Their method is to ensure that every family has sufficient money income to satisfy the essential needs of all its members. Money benefits are accordingly paid to those who claim individual assistance or whose incomes are affected by any of the historical causes of primary poverty: unemployment, sickness, old age, widowhood, industrial injury, large families, and funeral and maternity expenses. In one respect only, the services are also concerned with secondary poverty: social insurance is compulsory because (among other reasons) many people 'discount the future' too heavily and neglect to make provision, even if they could well afford to do so, for times of exceptional misfortune or exceptional need.

The characteristics of these services are therefore that the benefits are given in the form of money (which means that the beneficiaries can choose how to spend or mis-spend them); that they are discriminate, being confined to those persons or groups who are threatened with poverty; and that they are limited, being designed to supplement incomes up to an objectively defined subsistence level only. The effect of the services is to increase the total of personal incomes (since they are transfer payments); but not to disturb the price structure; nor to compete directly for real resources except to the extent of the costs of administration.

Group II consists of the health, education and other services which provide benefits in the form of real goods and services. The aims of these are more diverse. They can only be said to be concerned with primary poverty if the definition of 'essentials' is extended to include a minimum amount of medical services and a minimum amount of education. This would seem reasonable enough, but in fact no such allowance was made in calculating either the poverty lines of the social surveys[1] or the subsistence levels of the services in Group I; because medical and educational needs are much more varied and irregular than physical needs: they cannot be converted into 'the cost of a minimum average amount' as can the needs for food, clothing and house-room.

The aims of the Group II services are, however, closely connected with secondary poverty. The benefits are provided in kind rather than in cash (and, in the case of education, compulsorily), partly because the beneficiaries, through ignorance or neglect, would not otherwise use their incomes to buy these services, beneficial though they are. If this statement reads a little strangely nowadays (who would not make sacrifices to obtain the best medical care and the best education?) this is itself evidence of the effectiveness of the services in mitigating secondary poverty. For the true value of these services is only

---

[1] In the social surveys, sickness was found to be a cause of poverty, not because medical services were expensive but because the wage earner could not go to work.

realised as people consume them, and the educational process is still going on.

The redistribution of opportunities must also be included in the aims of this group of services. There are three aspects to this process. First, the services are not, like those in Group I, limited to ensuring for everyone certain minimum standards; indeed, they are required to provide the 'best possible' health and education services. Secondly, individual needs for the services, although they are varied and irregular, and although they may be quite limited in some cases, will probably be catered for on a wider front, as it were, than if there were no public services. Thirdly, the needs are in many cases unlimited, not simply because the services are free, but because the borderline between incomplete and complete education, and between sickness and health (especially of the aged) is often indeterminate. Over the whole field, therefore, there is considerable scope for redistribution of opportunities, and the total need for this group of services may be so high that a choice has to be made between providing more opportunities for the many and bigger opportunities for the few.

The method of organizing these services is for the central or local authority to purchase goods and services and supply them to the beneficiaries free of charge[1] or at a nominal price. The characteristics of the services are, therefore, different from those of Group I. Since the benefits are provided in kind, the beneficiaries cannot choose how to spend or mis-spend them; these services are intended to discriminate among people according to their needs; but there is no objectively defined limit to their total volume. The effects of the services are also different. They do not directly affect the total of personal incomes but provide supplementary real income They do affect the price structure by removing some goods and services from the final consumers' market, and fixing the prices of

[1] The ambiguous phrase 'at zero cost' is sometimes used in this connection, but it is as well to avoid it. It does not mean, of course, that the services cost nothing to produce, but that they appear to cost nothing to the consumer.

others below their market value. And they compete directly with other users for the real resources of labour and capital.

Group III services consist of the subsidies on housing, food, and a few minor items such as school meals, milk in schools and welfare foods.

The immediate aim of these services is to reduce the cost of living, but—whose cost of living? They do not reduce the cost of living in general but merely the prices of certain commodities. It is widely held that, since most of the subsidised commodities are 'essential', and since the poor spend the whole of their money income on 'essentials', the ultimate aim of the subsidies is the prevention of primary poverty. But this is false logic. On the one hand, the consumers of a subsidised commodity are a collection of people of whom only a small proportion may be threatened with poverty. On the other hand many people living near the poverty line may not be able to take advantage of the subsidies. Thus the housing subsidies reduce the rents of houses built by local authorities; but many occupants of such houses have more than sufficient income to satisfy their essential needs and many families threatened with primary poverty do not live in subsidised houses.

Similarly, the Group III services are connected with secondary poverty only in a somewhat roundabout fashion. Certain 'welfare foods', such as milk for schoolchildren and orange juice for babies, are subsidised in order to encourage consumption; but there is no compulsion (as in the case of education services), nor is the subsidy 'one hundred per cent' (as in the case of free health services). The aim of reducing secondary poverty is therefore achieved only to the extent that the demand for the subsidised commodities is elastic.

Again, subsidies aim at the reduction of inequality, not by directly increasing the lowest incomes, but by making flat rate additions to the incomes of certain groups of consumers, so that, within these groups, those with lower incomes obtain a larger proportional increase than those with higher incomes. The method of the Group III services is to reduce the final supply price of certain commodities below their factor cost by paying the difference out of public funds. In this they differ from the so-called producer subsidies, which are paid to farmers and others in order to assist them to maintain their output and which are not directly aimed at assisting the consumer.

The characteristic of these services is therefore that the benefits are attached to certain commodities, so that only the consumers of these commodities can avail themselves of the services; that they are largely indiscriminate as between different income groups; and that they are limited either by the demand of consumers at the subsidised price or by some form of rationing. They do not affect the total of personal incomes, but they do affect its purchasing power. They alter the structure of prices. They do not compete directly for real resources except (as in the case of Group I) to the extent of the costs of administration.

§ 2. **The Finance of the Public Social Services.** Since the public social services spend public money, information about them is published in the accounts of the three responsible authorities: the central government, the local authorities and the National Insurance Funds. The extraction of the relevant figures is not an easy matter, however. Social service expenditure is scattered about under various headings in the official accounts, and even where a special return is published, the official definitions do not always correspond to those adopted by social economists and other unofficial investigators. Some services are financed by two different authorities. On the income side, central government taxes and local rates are levied not only for the social services but for other purposes as well; and the destination even of the contributions to the National Insurance Funds is not always clear, because these funds may have an annual surplus which is put into reserve and invested in Government securities. A further complication is that the three authorities make transfers among themselves. The central government makes grants to the local authorities and to the National Insurance Funds; these funds also earn national debt interest on the Government securities held by them; and they make a return grant to the central government towards the cost of the National Health Service. These transactions must be included when considering the income and expenditure of the separate authorities. But when social expenditure as a whole is being considered transfers from one public authority to another must be eliminated to avoid double counting.

From 1920 to 1939 the most valuable source of information was an annual White Paper published by the Treasury and known as the 'Drage' Return of *Expenditure on the Public Social Services*. During and since the war, figures for the calendar year have been available in the annual White Paper (now Blue Book) on *National Income and Expenditure*. Since 1949, however, the most useful source has been a specially prepared set of tables on social service expenditure, relating to the financial year and published in the May issue of the *Monthly Digest of Statistics*.

The collation of pre-war and post-war statistics and the reconciliation of the various accounts has been carried out by Mr. A. T. Peacock and Mr. P. Browning as one of a set of studies on *Income Redistribution and Social Policy*.[1] Messrs. Peacock and Browning have compared the situation in 1937/8 with that in 1947/8 (before the National Health Service and the post-war insurance scheme came into operation) and in 1950/1. Many of the figures in this section are derived from their work, but the figures for 1955/6 can now be substituted for those of 1950/1.

The general picture is given in Table IV, which shows the relative importance of the different services as spenders of public money. In this table the expenditure of the three public authorities is combined, so that, for example, expenditure on education by the central government and the local authorities appears as one figure. The services are arranged in the three groups distinguished in the last section. Consequently, the administrative costs of all the services are shown under Group II.

[1] Edited by A. T. Peacock, 1954. Chapter V: 'The Social Services in Great Britain and the Redistribution of Income'.

Table IV. Expenditure on the Public Social Services[1]
(in £ millions)

	1937/8	1947/8	1955/6
Group I			
National Assistance	37	13	100
Outdoor Relief	22	17	—
Non-contributory Old Age Pensions	46	50	19
Retirement Pensions	45	220	439
Sickness Benefits	21	27	104
Unemployment Benefits	37	19	19
Other Insurance Benefits	2	3	87
Family Allowances	—	57	111
Service Pensions	38	82	82
Miscellaneous Grants	2	25	41
Group II			
National Health Service	—	1	532
General Health and Hospital Services	47	126	—
Other Medical Services	13	26	19
Education	112	197	435
Child Care	1	8	16
Welfare of the Poor and Blind	17	28	—
Miscellaneous Services	—	—	15
Administration	17	46	127
Group III			
Food Subsidies	—	315	185
Housing Subsidies	22	55	82
School Meals, Milk and Welfare Foods	—	52	88
Other Subsidies	—	2	—
Total of Current Expenditure	**479**	**1,369**	**2,501**
Capital Expenditure			
Housing	⎫	224	311
Education	⎬ 88	23	87
Health	⎪	13	23
Miscellaneous	⎭	—	8
Total of Capital Expenditure	**88**	**260**	**429**

[1] Figures for 1937/8 and 1947/8 relate to Great Britain; those for 1955/6 to the United Kingdom.

The most striking features of this Table are the figures relating to insurance benefits, health and education services, and food subsidies. Expenditure in the form of insurance benefits was about the same proportion of total current expenditure (22–26 per cent) in 1937/8 and 1955/6. Within this category, however, significant changes have taken place since before the war. One consequence of the high level of employment since the war has been to reduce the cost of unemployment benefits from about 8 per cent in 1937/8 to less than 1 per cent of total social service expenditure in 1955/6. The changing age structure of the population, on the other hand, has increased the cost of retirement pensions from 9 per cent to 17 per cent.

Similarly, expenditure in the form of health and education services together was about the same proportion of total current expenditure (36–39 per cent) in 1937/8 and 1955/6; but, while the pre-war health services accounted for only 13 per cent and the education services for 23 per cent, the introduction of the National Health Service had almost reversed these proportions by 1955/6.

Food subsidies, on the other hand, did not exist before the war but accounted for 23 per cent of total current expenditure in 1947/8 and 7½ per cent in 1955/6.

Clearly the whole pattern of social service expenditure depends very much on what happens to these particular services, which in 1955/6 accounted for nearly three-quarters of the total. In the decade following the war the level of insurance benefits was raised, there was some attempt to stabilise the cost of the health and education services, and the food subsidies were cut, but there was no sign of any diminution in the preponderance of these services taken together.

Turning now from the particular services to the figures of total expenditure: it is a common practice to compare the grand total with some definition of the national income and to applaud or deplore, as the case may be, the changing proportions of the national income devoted to the social services. This is, however, a deceptive procedure. It is legitimate to compare the total of public expenditure on the social services with the total of public expenditure as a whole (including expenditure by the National Insurance Funds). This proportion, which was just over 40 per cent in 1955/6, shows the extent to which the social services compete with other public services (such as defence, national debt, roads, police, and the general expenses of government) in the *budgets* of the central and local authorities. Comparison with the national income does not, however, indicate the extent to which the social services compete with other users for the real resources of the community. The impact of social service expenditure on the national income is different for different types of social service: it varies in fact according to whether the services are in Groups I, II or III of our classification, and each group must be taken separately.

In the case of transfer payments (Group I) the direct effect of the social services is to increase personal incomes, and the significant relationship is therefore the proportion of such transfer payments to the total of personal incomes. Now, once received, personal incomes are then spent, saved or paid in taxes; and transfer incomes may be allocated among these uses differently from earned incomes, so that the eventual money claims on the real national income may be increased or merely redistributed. But these are secondary effects. The immediate impact of social services in Group I is on the proportion of personal incomes received without the recipients having made any contribution to national output. It is likely, therefore, that, the larger the proportion, the more the incentive to produce will be affected.

This is not to say, however, that the effect on incentives is related only to the size of this proportion. It depends also on how many people are affected and how far the effect is 'marginal' and touches their incomes at the margin, that is, at the point at which decisions are made about producing more or less. On the one hand, less would be produced if transfers were 50 per cent of personal incomes than if they were 5 per cent. On the other hand, 5 per cent which affected many incomes at the margin could be more significant than 10 per cent which affected only a few at the margin.[1]

These points must be borne in mind when looking at the figures in the first part of Table V, which shows that transfer payments through the social services amounted to between 5 and 6½ per cent of the total of personal incomes both before and after the war. In some cases, if the beneficiaries did not receive these transfers, they would work harder or continue to work instead of retiring. In other cases, they might regard the benefits as windfalls, and their incentive to work would be unaffected. In others, the benefits might raise their incomes to the point at which physical efficiency and both ability and willingness to work were increased.

The services in Group II operate differently. They make a direct claim on the real resources of the community by demanding beds and bricks and books, nurses and teachers and administrators. The significant relationship is therefore the proportion of expenditure on these services to the total real national income. This applies not only to current expenditure, but also to capital expenditure, which was shown separately at the foot of Table IV. We are not here concerned about whether capital is being maintained. We are simply measuring the extent to which the social services make direct purchases (at market prices) out of the current national product. Thus, current Group II expenditure can be added to capital expenditure and the total expressed as a proportion of gross national expenditure at market prices. The larger this proportion, the smaller the share available to other purchasers, private and public, of consumer goods and capital goods.

The second part of Table V shows that this proportion rose from 5·1 per cent to 8·1 per cent between 1937/8 and 1955/6. Again, the importance of the figures depends very much on the 'marginal' effect of these purchases: on how easily the

[1] If the revenue required for transfer payments is raised by direct taxation, the effect on the incentive to work is two-edged: some efforts go without reward; some rewards come without effort.

particular goods and services can be diverted from other uses or increased in total supply.

Table V. Public Social Service Expenditure and National Income (in £ millions)

	1937/8	1947/8	1955/6
1. Expenditure on Group I services: Transfer payments	250	513	1,002
2. Total of personal income before tax (including transfers)	4,952	9,489	16,117
1 as percentage of 2	5·1%	5·4%	6·2%
3. Expenditure on Group II services: Direct purchase of goods and services	207	432	1,144
4. Capital expenditure on social services	88	260	429
5. Total direct purchase of goods and services (3 plus 4)	295	692	1,573
6. Gross national expenditure at market prices	5,841	11,291	19,467
5 as percentage of 6	5·1%	6·1%	8·1%
7. Expenditure on Group III services: Subsidies	22	424	355
8. Consumers' expenditure at market prices	4,296	7,879	12,924
7 as percentage of 8	0·5%	5·4%	2·7%
9. Capital expenditure on social services	38	260	429
10. Gross fixed capital formation	845	1,218	2,926
9 as percentage of 10	10·5%	21·5%	14·7%

With regard to the services in Group III (subsidies) the direct effect of expenditure under this heading is to reduce the prices of consumer goods. They therefore supplement personal consumption, and the significant relationship is the proportion of this expenditure to total consumers' expenditure. The higher this proportion, the wider the gulf which these services create between the amount that consumers pay and the real value, in terms of factor cost, of the goods they consume. The subsidies are measured against total consumers' expenditure at market prices, rather than at factor cost, for the following reason. The amount of the subsidy is determined, not by some independent assessment of needs, as in the case of 'free' education and medical services, but by the effective demand of consumers in the market. Their pattern of demand, their decisions to buy more of this and less of that, is determined by the structure of market prices, including the market prices of taxed goods on the one hand and of subsidised goods on the other.

It should be borne in mind that the 'proportion' in the case of the Group III services is *supplementary*; and the third part of Table V shows that subsidies supplemented consumers' expenditure to a negligible extent before the war, by 5·4 per cent in 1947/8, and by 2·7 per cent in 1955/6.

Finally, there is a little more to be said about capital expenditure on social services. The amount of this is significant not only in relation to the gross national product (which was considered above), but also to that part of the gross national product which consists of capital goods and is usually called gross fixed capital formation. On the assumption of full employment, the higher the proportion of 'social service capital' to this item, the smaller the proportion available for other forms of capital investment, including private building and the maintenance and increase of productive capital in private and public industry. This does not imply that investment in social capital is unproductive: houses and schools and hospitals may contribute to the efficiency and mobility of labour. But the social services are clearly more prominent in the sphere of capital investment than in that of the real national income as a whole.

The last part of Table V indicates the practical importance of the problem. Expenditure on social service capital (mainly housing) absorbed 10½ per cent of total capital expenditure in 1937/8, 21½ per cent in 1947/8 and 14½ per cent in 1955/6.

We now turn to Table VI, which shows the distribution of current expenditure on the public social services among the three responsible authorities.

Table VI.   Expenditure on Public Social Services by Authorities (in £ millions)

	£ millions			Percentages		
	1937/8	1947/8	1955/6	1937/8	1947/8	1955/6
Central Government	128	660	1,141	26·7	48·2	45·6
Local Authorities	221	400	678	46·1	29·2	27·1
National Insurance Funds	130	309	682	27·2	22·6	27·3
Total Current Expenditure	479	1,369	2,501	100·0	100·0	100·0

It is plain that responsibility has passed increasingly into the hands of the central government.   While before the war the local authorities administered about one-half of expenditure on public social services, and the central government about one quarter, their respective roles were reversed after the war. In 1947/8 the picture was distorted by the enormous central government expenditure on food subsidies.   If these had been excluded, the local authorities would still have had the major share of responsibility in that year.   By 1955/6, however, the situation had altered more radically by the transfer to the central government of responsibility for poor relief and for nearly all the health services.   The only substantial expenditure controlled by the local authorities is now on education and housing.

Even so, Table VI does not indicate the full extent of central government predominance in either the pre-war or the post-war finance of the social services.   The National Insurance Funds, although a separate department of the public accounts, have always received supplements from the Exchequer and have become more closely linked with central government finance since the war; and the local authorities have become increasingly dependent on grants from the Exchequer.   Table VI shows who is responsible for spending the money required for the public social services.   Table VII shows who is responsible for raising it.

Table VII.   Sources of Income for Public Social Service Expenditure

	£ millions			Percentages		
	1937/8	1947/8	1955/6	1937/8	1947/8	1955/6
Central government taxation and income from property	280	1,049	1,717	54·9	71·7	67·3
Local government taxation	126	194	224	24·7	13·2	9·6
Insurance contributions by private employers and insured persons	104	221	591	20·4	15·1	23·1
Total Current Revenue	510	1,464	2,552	100·0	100·0	100·0

Thus, before the war, central government taxation was the source of more than half, and, after the war, nearly three-quarters of the income. Local rates provided about one quarter in 1937/8; 13 per cent in 1947/8, when they still supported poor relief and general hospital services, and only 9½ per cent in 1955/6.

All these figures relate to *current* income and expenditure (the difference between the totals being the annual surplus on current account of the National Insurance Funds). On the capital side, expenditure, both before and after the war, was almost entirely a local authority responsibility, but the borrowing powers of the local authorities were, already in 1939, largely channelled through the Public Works Loans Board. This meant that the loans were first raised by the central government and then passed on to the local authorities.

§ 3. The Development and Break-up of the Poor Law.   The Elizabethan Poor Law is rightly regarded as the first big landmark in the development of the public social services, for it was not until the sixteenth century that poverty became a social problem. The poor have always been with us, and some, especially widows, have from very early times been the subject of special compassion. In the Middle Ages, however, begging was a legitimate activity and almsgiving an accepted remedy. The guilds provided mutual aid among their members and a certain amount of relief to the poor of the towns. Hospitals, almshouses and other charitable foundations gave special help according to their different dispensations. Most of all, parish churches, and especially monasteries, gave generously and often indiscriminately to those who knocked at their doors. There were vagrants who got into mischief, but their problem was one of vagrancy rather than of poverty; and after a short, sharp punishment they could be sent back to their parish of origin, there to work or beg.

By the sixteenth century the balance of this system had been seriously disturbed. On the one hand labour was becoming more mobile. Enclosure was detaching the peasants from particular bits of land, and the ranks of free labour were swelled by disbanded soldiers and unemployed cloth workers. On the other hand, the dissolution of the monasteries and religious guilds removed the principal source of poor relief. Vagrancy and poverty were no longer distinguishable, and the history of the Poor Law contains a catalogue of attempts to maintain this distinction in the face of changing economic conditions. Most of the crises in this history arose through inability to deal with unemployment and low wages as two of the causes of poverty, or to recognise mobility of labour as one of the cures.

The framework of the Poor Law was built up empirically between 1531 and 1601. The preamble to an Act of 1531 set out the problem:

'Whereas in all places throughout this Realm of England, Vagabonds and Beggers have of long time increased, and daily do increase in great and excessive numbers, by the occasion of idleness, Mother and Root of all Vices, whereby hath insurged and sprung, and daily insurgeth and springeth, continual Thefts, Murthers, and other sundry heinous offences and great Enormities, to the high Displeasure of God, and the Inquietation and Damage of the King's People, and to the marvellous Disturbance of the common weal of this Realm. And whereas many and sundry good Laws, strict Statutes, and Ordinances have been before this time devised and made, as well by the King our Sovereign Lord, as also by divers his most noble Progenitors Kings of England, for the most necessary and due Reformation of the Premisses; yet that notwithstanding the said numbers of Vagabonds and Beggers be not seen in any part to be minished, but rather daily augmented and increased into great Routs and Companies, as evidently and manifestly it doeth and may appear; Be it therefore enacted etc. . . .'

At first, the Justices of the Peace were given power to grant begging licences to 'poor, impotent and aged persons', and to punish the able-bodied unemployed and send them back to find work. Next, licensing was replaced by parish relief, out of funds voluntarily subscribed; poor children were to be apprenticed, and the able-bodied punished more severely. Then, a compulsory tax on property replaced the voluntary subscriptions and the parish authorities were instructed also to provide materials on which the able-bodied unemployed could be set to work. Finally, the building of hospitals, almshouses and workhouses by the parish authorities was authorised. The Act of 1601 merely consolidated all these regulations and established a system which lasted, subject to periodic strains, for three centuries.

In principle it was not very different from the modern system of social security: compulsory taxation providing relief for the sick and aged, 'education' for the children, and 'public works' for the unemployed. It attempted, as recent legislation has done, to separate out the causes of poverty and match them by appropriate remedies. It went further in trying to separate those who ought from those who ought not to be assisted—there was power to compel families to provide for their own poorer members where they were able to do so; and power to deter and punish those who would not work.

It is not easy to discover how rapidly or how thoroughly the Poor Law was put into operation during the seventeenth century. London, Norwich and some other towns had already developed similar systems of relief[1] before the national legislation was introduced. In some parishes the law did not become effective for many years. One consequence of this uneven development was that some parishes became more attractive than others to those seeking assistance. The resulting migration caused such alarm that the 'Act of Settlement' was passed in 1662, giving power to the Justices to send immigrant claimants for relief, or new residents who might become claimants, back to their parish of origin in certain circumstances. This and subsequent legislation regarding settlement created far more problems than it solved. It perpetuated local differences in the scale of poor relief. It caused some parishes to devote more time and resources to the task of getting rid of claimants than to that of assisting them. And it restricted the mobility of labour throughout the eighteenth century. Adam Smith complained that 'The scarcity of hands in one parish . . . cannot always be relieved by their superabundance in another, as it is constantly in . . . countries where there is no difficulty of settlement.'[2]

Meanwhile, by the beginning of the eighteenth century, the Poor Law was going astray in other respects. The cost of out-relief was increasing rapidly because many people became 'registered' for regular assistance who were not entirely destitute but simply earning irregular incomes, or keeping alive

---

[1] Some of them based on earlier schemes introduced in certain European towns. A very interesting account of these is to be found in F. R. Salter: *Early Tracts on Poor Relief*, 1926.

[2] Adam Smith: *Wealth of Nations*, Cannan Edition, Vol. I, p. 142. But Sir Frederic Morton Eden: *The State of the Poor*, 1797, Vol. I, p. 296, thought that Adam Smith overestimated the restrictive effects of the settlement laws.

large families, and so claiming grants in supplementation of their wages. Indoor relief, however, was not flourishing, and the workhouses were half empty. Accordingly, in 1722, an Act was passed authorising parishes to apply the 'workhouse test' and refuse relief to any who would not enter the workhouse and there do such work as was assigned to them. Further, parishes were allowed to contract out the running of workhouses to private persons who could then 'take the benefit of the work labour and service' done in them.

At first the measure appeared to achieve its purposes. Many workhouses were bought or built (parishes could combine for this purpose); the net costs, per head, of indoor relief appeared to be much lower than those of out-relief; and many people chose not to apply for relief at all rather than submit to workhouse discipline. But during the eighteenth century the whole system came into disrepute. Public opinion was roused about the appalling conditions in the workhouses, where the various types of poor could hardly receive the distinctive treatment implicit in the original Poor Law. The costs of running them increased in the third quarter of the century and high prices and bad harvests made the need for relief more widespread.

In 1782 a new Act, known from its promoter as 'Gilbert's Act', abolished the contracting system, improved the parochial organisation of the Poor Law, and closed the workhouses to able-bodied paupers. The way seemed open once again for the separate treatment of different types of poverty: 'The aged, infirm and impotent are to be brought into poorhouses; the idle and dissolute are to be kept at houses of correction; and the poor infants in their tender years are to be placed out with proper persons. Those who are completely able and willing to labour are to be hired out where work can be procured for them.'[1] In 1795 the legislation was further improved. Authority was given for 'industrious poor persons . . . under circumstances of temporary illness or distress' to receive relief

[1] Thomas Gilbert: *Plan for the Better Relief and Employment of the Poor.*

in their homes.   And a long-overdue relaxation of the settlement laws, while still insisting that applicants for relief could be sent to their parish of origin, allowed the independent labourer seeking work much more freedom of movement.

But legislation was not enough, for these were years of exceptional distress, especially in the countryside.   The new wave of enclosures, which had gathered strength in the second half of the eighteenth century, affected particularly the common wastes, woods and pastures on which the poorer inhabitants relied for fuel and grazing.   Being thus deprived of part of their income in kind, they were all the more affected by the rise in the cost of food consequent upon bad harvests and the war with France.

For those who remained in employment on the land, a rise in wages was the obvious remedy, and the possibility of a minimum wage, which the Justices could have established locally, was much discussed.   A Bill to encourage it was introduced in the House of Commons but rejected on the opposition of William Pitt, who argued that a minimum wage was too inflexible because it did not take account of the size of families. The same conclusion had been reached earlier at a meeting of Berkshire magistrates in the hamlet of Speenhamland.   But, in place of a minimum wage they recommended a device which found such popularity (though less in the North than in the South of England) that it soon dominated the whole system of poor relief.

The argument was disarmingly simple: wages were too low for subsistence; the cost of subsistence depended on the price of bread and the size of the family; therefore wages should be supplemented (out of the poor rate) by allowances which varied on a sliding scale according to the price of bread and the size of family.   The scale itself was equally straightforward: when the price of a gallon loaf (8 lb. 11 oz.) was 1s., the cost of subsistence for a labourer was reckoned to be 3s. a week, for his wife 1s. 6d. and his children 1s. 6d. each; and wages were to be supplemented up to the appropriate amount for each family. For every increase of 1d. in the price of the gallon loaf, the

16

subsistence level was to be increased by 3*d*. for the labourer and 1*d*. for his wife and each child.

What was wrong with the system? There was nothing wrong with the assumption that large families or irregular employment were causes of poverty and that the payment of allowances out of public funds would be an appropriate remedy. Nor was anything wrong with the principle that the amount of relief should vary with the cost of living. These ideas may have been exactly 150 years in advance of their time (they were officially recognised in 1945–6), but they were sound enough. The fallacy implicit in the Speenhamland scheme was that poverty caused by low *wage rates* should be remedied by supplements to wages out of public funds, instead of by an increase in wage rates. The promoters urged farmers to raise wages. But the system gave them no incentive to do so. The large farmer benefited from a plentiful supply of cheap labour and paid a *relatively* low poor rate. The small farmer who worked his own farm with his family obtained no benefit and paid a relatively high poor rate. The labourer himself had no incentive to earn a higher wage, less incentive to save, and some incentive to have a large family. How far the increase in population between 1800 and 1830 was encouraged by this system it is difficult to say. But there is no doubt that the increase in the cost of poor relief would have been much less if it had not been tied to wages.

Thus the centre of gravity shifted, as Gilbert had hoped it would, away from the workhouse. But beyond that, Gilbert's plans, and the intentions of the original Statute of Elizabeth, seemed as far from fulfilment as ever. Very few parishes took advantage of the Act of 1782 and the whole policy of making separate provision for different types of poverty was overwhelmed by the allowance system, which appeared to be 'pauperising' everybody, including the able-bodied employed earning a full week's wage.

This was therefore the chief concern of the Royal Commission appointed to enquire into the operation of the Poor Law in 1832. Its most influential members were the economist

Nassau Senior and the brilliant administrator and disciple of
Bentham, Edwin Chadwick. These two were mainly responsible for the voluminous Report[1] published in 1834. The
Report presented a mass of information on the evil effects of
the system of poor relief as it had developed during the previous half-century, stressing particularly the differences in
moral and economic status between the independent labourer
and the person receiving relief. The gross inequality of the
burden of rates in different parishes; the impossibility of preventing fraudulent applications for relief; the demoralising
effect on the recipients of out-relief and their families; the
hindrances to an increase in wages resulting from the allowance system—all these were illustrated and proven with
well-marshalled evidence.

The main recommendations of the Commission related to
three matters: the treatment of the able-bodied poor, the
administration of the whole system, and the organisation of
workhouses. On the first matter they proposed that out-relief
for the able-bodied should cease except for medical relief
and the apprenticeship of children. An able-bodied person
who could not earn his living as an independent labourer
would be offered maintenance in a workhouse, a special and
separately administered workhouse where he would do useful
work: *but*—'the first and most essential of all conditions, a
principle which we find universally admitted, even by those
whose practice is at variance with it, is that his situation on the
whole shall not be made really or apparently so eligible as the
situation of the independent labourer of the lowest class.'[2]

Here was the famous principle of *less eligibility* which
became the keynote of Poor Law administration for the next
seventy-five years. By making the condition of the recipient
of relief less attractive than that of the lowest wage-earner, it
aimed at ensuring that the poor laws would not interfere with
the wage system; that independent wage earners would not be

[1] *The Report from His Majesty's Commissioners for Inquiring into the
Administration and Practical Operation of the Poor Laws*, 1834.
[2] *Report*, p. 228.

tempted to accept relief as a desirable alternative; and that recipients of relief would be encouraged to aspire to the status of independent labourers, an aspiration to be supported by the example of work in the workhouse which, though hard and unprofitable, must be well-regulated and useful.

The administrative reforms sought to remove the parochial basis of the system by grouping parishes together into larger units called 'Unions' under the supervision of Boards of Guardians, who would replace the Justices and parish over-seers. This would permit economies of scale, both financially and in the organisation of workhouses, and, incidentally, contribute to the solution of the settlement problem. Uniformity in the scale and standards of relief was to be achieved among the various Unions by placing the whole organisation under the control of three Poor Law Commissioners appointed by the Crown.

Finally, there were to be separate workhouses, with distinctive and appropriate aims and methods, for the aged, the children, the able-bodied women and the able-bodied men. (Out-relief of the aged, and apprenticeship of children outside the workhouse would be continued, but not, of course, out-relief for the able-bodied.)

All these recommendations were incorporated in the Poor Law Amendment Act of 1834.

How did it work out? The story is told in great detail in Sidney and Beatrice Webb's *English Poor Law History*. We can only deal briefly with the main feature: the doctrine of less eligibility. It solved, as it was meant to do, the problem of the allowance system; but it did not solve the problem of poverty. First, it assumed that not only the status but also the standard of living of the lowest-paid independent wage-earner was more desirable than that of the pauper. This was not necessarily so, for the paupers had to be maintained at 'subsistence' level and many wage-earners were living at or below that level. Secondly, it assumed that the independent wage-earner did not require any assistance. This depended, however, not merely on his wage, but on his needs, and even if his wage were sufficient for 'normal' subsistence, the needs of his family might well be abnormal. Thirdly, the doctrine assumed that the able-bodied worker *could* achieve independence as a wage-earner, if persuaded or forced to do so. It assumed opportunities for employment; but these would be fewer at some times and places than at others, so that in fact there might be no choice for him.

In regard to status, the doctrine succeeded only too well. The sharp distinction between the social class of the independent wage-earner and that of the able-bodied pauper became a feature of the entire system and left a mark which later attempts to distinguish between the deserving and the undeserving poor failed to erase. This did not mean that the distinction was wrong or that it was unimportant. There was no lack of evidence even at the end of the nineteenth century, that if relief were not strictly administered a large number of people would find dependent poverty less uncomfortable than independent poverty. The tragedy was not that many people, faced with this choice, would choose the former, but that many who had no choice were forced to accept it.

The situation might have been much less acute if the plans relating to workhouse administration had been carried out. If, as was intended in 1834, the institutions for the aged poor had become, not workhouses, but old people's homes; those for children, schools; those for the sick, hospitals; and those for the able-bodied, training establishments, even under severe discipline; paupers might have come to be regarded as a class requiring special care (as were the recipients of private charity) rather than as social outcasts. It is unfortunate that Chadwick is more often remembered for his association with the doctrine of less eligibility (a doctrine which he inherited from Bentham) than for his rigorous advocacy of separate treatment for different types of poor. He became one of the new Commissioners but was soon diverted into the field of public health administration and, as one writer[1] says: 'The extent to which the general mixed workhouse became the solution most

[1] Mr. Brian Rodgers, of Manchester University, in an unpublished paper on 'Less Eligibility—The Influence of an Idea'.

favoured by the Guardians was an indication of Chadwick's loss of control of the machine.'

The general mixed workhouse was the undoing of the Poor Law. A deterrent regime for the able-bodied poor could not be combined with more generous treatment for other classes of poor under the same roof and the same governor. There were enquiries into conditions in the workhouses; there were administrative reforms (the Commissioners were replaced in 1847 by a Poor Law Board under a minister responsible to Parliament); there were changes of policy from 1870 in regard to out-relief for the aged; there was a Royal Commission on the Aged Poor in 1895. But the central problem of pauperism remained until the end of the century.

The appointment of a new Royal Commission in 1905[1] came at the end of a period of lively public discussion on poor law policy. One group of opinion stood firmly by the principles of 1834, rigorously applied. It was represented in its extreme form by James Davy, Chief Inspector of the Poor Law Division,[2] who wanted to apply the doctrine of less eligibility to *all* classes of poor and even reached the point of saying that the unemployed 'must suffer for the general good of the body politic'. Another group of opinion was concerned to define the respective spheres of the Poor Law and the voluntary services. It originated in 1869, when George Goschen, President of the Poor Law Board, had issued a memorandum suggesting that only the wholly destitute should be dealt with by the Poor Law, and those with some, but inadequate means, by the philanthropic organisations. The Webbs called this the 'parallel bars' theory because its advocates insisted that the public and voluntary services should work side by side, with no overlapping. Yet another group, led by the Charity Organisation Society, strove to establish a variant of the parallel bars theory, by which the voluntary services would

---

[1] Royal Commission on the Poor Laws and the Relief of Distress.

[2] The Poor Law Board became the Poor Law Division of the Local Government Board in 1871, but without any change in its functions or character.

deal with the 'deserving' and the public services with the 'undeserving' poor. This the Webbs called the 'cowcatcher theory', because it would sweep up some of the destitute who would otherwise become a burden and expense to the public authorities. A fourth group, represented by Joseph Chamberlain, favoured social insurance on the German model. A fifth, which included Charles Booth and Lloyd George, devised schemes for giving unconditional State pensions to the aged. A sixth—Sidney Webb, Bernard Shaw and the Fabians —opposed the whole Poor Law system and sought to replace the 'parallel bars' by the 'extension ladder'. They maintained that the ordinary local government committees concerned with education, health, etc., aided by a sort of almoner, called a 'Registrar of Public Assistance', could ensure a minimum level of welfare to every citizen. The task of the voluntary services would then be to 'raise the standard of civilised conduct and physical health above the comparatively low level which could be enforced by public authority'.[1]

The Poor Law Division and the Charity Organisation Society were strongly represented on the Royal Commission, and the Majority Report, published in 1909, expressed their view. The Fabians were represented by Beatrice Webb, not Sidney; but the Minority Report was obviously a joint product. The manuscript was in Sidney's handwriting, and together they republished it (without Treasury permission) in a much more readable form than the official edition.[2]

The Majority Report was a more attractive document than is generally acknowledged. It showed a more humane and constructive approach than the Report of 1834; it abandoned the idea of the workhouse test; and it recognised the importance of the voluntary societies. Its emphasis was not on tests or

[1] M. P. Hall: *The Social Services of Modern England*, p. 296.

[2] An exercise in demand theory is provided by the Webbs' claim that '... altogether five separate editions of the Minority Report were ... simultaneously on the market, at widely differing prices, and they did not apparently, interfere with each other's sales'. The statistics are in a footnote to p. 718 of S. & B. Webb: *English Poor Law History*, 1929, Vol. II.

deterrence, but on curative treatment. It proposed that in every district there should be, under the Public Assistance Authority (which would replace the Boards of Guardians), a Voluntary Aid Committee and a Public Assistance Committee. Those in need would go first to the Voluntary Aid Committee which would try to ensure their 'treatment' by some voluntary agency. In particular 'temporary need, due to non-recurrent causes', whether of the sick, the aged, the children or the able-bodied unemployed, would be dealt with by private charity. Cases of 'chronic distress or destitution' would be passed on to the Public Assistance Committee, which would provide either allowances or treatment in specialised public institutions, according to people's needs.

So far, so good. There would be discrimination, for which the Charity Organisation Society had been fighting. There would be specialised treatment, which the mixed workhouse had failed to provide, and the need for which had been newly endorsed by the surveys of Booth and Rowntree. Private charity would be encouraged and used to its limits (the maximum of cowcatching) and public assistance would be so administered that the 'stigma of pauperism' would fade away. The difficulty arose in the attempt to draw the line between the voluntary and public areas. A clear division was essential 'because the charitable public will not contribute . . . towards a purpose for which they are also taxed or rated', and the line could only be drawn by 'making the public assistance in some way less agreeable'. This was fatal. The ghost of less eligibility stalked on to the stage once more.

The Minority pointed out that since 1834 the whole structure of local government had expanded. Various local authority committees had grown up for education, health, mental deficiency, pensions and employment. Surely these bodies could deal with the poor as well as the rest, and so avoid duplication, segregation and any suggestion that the destitute were in a different social class? Moreover, these committees were concerned with prevention, as well as relief, of poverty, and in due course the problem of destitution would be resolved by attacking its causes rather than by treating its consequences.

We need not go further into the details of these great Reports. The clarity and common sense of the Minority Report, aided by the propaganda of the Webbs' 'National Committee to promote the Break-up of the Poor Law', won for it a well-deserved reputation. Its principles were not officially accepted. But the Poor Law was nevertheless broken up by a succession of Acts which dealt more effectively with the causes of poverty.

Already by 1909 various Education Acts had enforced the attendance of children and their proper feeding and medical treatment, at school. The Workmen's Compensation Act of 1897 had introduced compulsory insurance against industrial accident for employees in certain industries. The Old Age Pensions Act of 1908 had provided non-contributory pensions at the age of 70. It is true that the receipt of pensions was subject to a means test, and that some parents were required to pay, and others were not, for the services provided through the schools. But the vital difference between the new legislation and the old Poor Law was that the condition of receiving relief was not *destitution*, with all its social and political implications. In other words, under the new regime there were State beneficiaries, and there were poor persons, but there were no *paupers*.

There followed the Trade Boards Act of 1909, by which statutory minimum wages were established in certain trades; the Labour Exchanges Act of 1909, creating a system for the organised mobility of labour; the National Insurance Acts of 1911 and 1920, which set up compulsory insurance schemes for the payment of benefits and the provision of medical services in times of sickness and unemployment; and the Widows', Orphans' and Old Age Contributory Pensions Act of 1925. The relation of all these to the causes of poverty was discussed in Chapter VI. Their effect was to remove from the scope of public assistance successive groups of people who in the nineteenth century had no alternative sources of

relief to the Poor Law and private charity. Had it not been
for the heavy unemployment of the inter-war years, public
assistance would have become, what the National Assistance
Board of 1948 (discussed in Chapter IX) was intended to be,
a residual authority dealing only with a few odd cases.

CHAPTER IX

NATIONAL INSURANCE AND ASSISTANCE

§ **1. National Assistance.** There was furious campaigning on behalf of both the Majority and the Minority of the Royal Commission from 1909 to 1911, but officially the Poor Law system remained exactly the same in organisation and, apart from some relaxation in the standards of out-relief, in policy. The National Insurance Act of 1911 was widely thought to solve the problem without placing too much power in the hands of the voluntary societies on the one hand or Government officials on the other. Criticism and counter-criticism died down. Insurance, prosperity and the demands of war reduced the number of claimants for relief. The Ministry of Health replaced the Local Government Board as the central authority in 1918; and with the widening of the franchise in the same year, came also the abolition of the rule under which those in receipt of poor relief were disqualified from voting.

Towards the end of 1920, the post-war unemployment problem began to show itself. The number of persons receiving relief had been less than half a million since 1917. By December 1920 it had risen to 568,000; by the end of 1921 it was $1\frac{1}{2}$ million, and in subsequent years it never fell below 1 million. Most of these were able-bodied unemployed.

The strain was too great for the system to bear. Conditions varied enormously from one district to another in regard to the incidence of unemployment, the burden of the Poor Rate, and the methods of relief. Some Guardians paid much higher rates of relief than others; some took account of family resources in an effort to reduce the cost of relief, others deliberately adopted more generous standards. Some tried to continue a form of workhouse test, others abandoned it. The

Councillors of Poplar, a poor district with heavy unemployment, went to prison in support of their refusal to levy rates for the London County Council until the Poplar Guardians received some outside help. As a result all the Metropolitan Unions were given increased grants from the Common Poor Fund which London had maintained for certain special cases of relief since 1867. Some Unions began to borrow, went bankrupt, and were 'taken over' by the Ministry of Health. Year by year the need became more urgent for a wider unit of administration and finance than the Poor Law 'Union', and for some kind of national provision for the unemployed. The Local Government Act of 1929 and the Transitional Payments Scheme of 1931 were designed to meet these needs.

The first of these transferred the administration of poor relief to the borough councils and county councils, still under the general supervision of the Ministry of Health. The councils each appointed Public Assistance Committees and the actual cases were dealt with by District Relieving Officers. The raising of money, however, was the responsibility of the councils, and so was the duty of 'providing assistance otherwise than by way of poor relief' wherever possible. Thus the Public Assistance Committee became merely one of several council committees interested in the welfare of the poor; and the break-up of the Poor Law, as envisaged in the Minority Report of 1909, was made possible.

In the particular field of unemployment relief, however, a new kind of 'parallel bars' theory was developing. In 1931 the unemployed were receiving financial assistance in three ways. Those who still satisfied the ordinary conditions of unemployment insurance were drawing 'standard' benefits, as of right, from the Insurance Fund. Those who had exhausted their rights to benefit were drawing 'extended' benefits, subject to a test of means, also from the Insurance Fund; but for this purpose the Treasury was lending money to the Fund at a rapidly increasing rate, in order to keep it solvent. Those who had no insurance record at all were obtaining benefit from the Public Assistance Committees, subject to all the conditions attendant upon receipt of poor relief.

The Transitional Payments Scheme transferred the second group from the Insurance Fund to the Public Assistance Committees. The claimants could still apply through the Labour Exchanges, but they were dealt with by the Public Assistance Committees, who thus dispensed one set of benefits out of money provided by the Exchequer and another out of local Poor Law funds. They were noticeably more generous with the former than with the latter. There was a great deal of ill-feeling about the whole business, and in 1935 a new national body was created, with a separate network of local offices, to assume responsibility for the unemployed who had exhausted their right to insurance benefit. This was the Unemployment Assistance Board, which, partly on account of its more liberal policy, partly because it operated uniformly throughout the country, partly because, although it applied a means test, it was entirely free from Poor Law associations, was rapidly acknowledged to be a more satisfactory method of relief than the Public Assistance Committees. Accordingly, on the outbreak of war, the duty of assisting persons in distress on account of the war was given, not to the Public Assistance Committees, but to the Assistance Board, as it was called from 1940 onwards. To this body also was given the task of supplementing pensions for those whose statutory pensions proved inadequate.

Under the stress of war conditions a great many administrative problems which in normal times would have been debated and discussed at great length were solved by sheer pressure of events.[1] One of these was the difficulty of deciding what resources should be taken into account in determining the needs of an applicant for relief. Under the old Poor Law, the family of an applicant could be pursued all over Great Britain, if necessary, and made to contribute to his support. Under Public Assistance, the members of his household were

[1] Professor R. M. Titmuss's *Problems of Social Policy* in the Official History of the Second World War, demonstrates this point admirably.

expected to contribute, but the practice varied from one Union to another. During the war it was laid down[1] that only the resources of a husband, wife or dependant of the applicant, residing with him or her, would be taken into account, either by Public Assistance Committees or by Assistance Boards. This was an important departure. The measurement of poverty, as we showed in Chapter VI, depends on the relationship between needs and means. We noted a tendency to a more generous definition of needs in successive social surveys. Here was a more generous definition of means.

One of the principles governing post-war social legislation was that most cases of need would be adequately met either by social insurance and family allowances, or by the medical and welfare services, so that 'assistance' in the sense of money grants to individuals on the basis of a personal assessment of needs, would be of minor importance. Another principle was that nearly all services would be financed on a national scale. The local authorities would still play their part, not only in the administration of education and housing services, but in the provision of accommodation and services for the aged, and for the blind and other handicapped persons. But the cost would be met largely by the Exchequer, and all money grants (or 'domiciliary assistance') to those in need would be provided on a national scale.

Let us first see how the latter principle worked out. With the passing of the National Assistance Act of 1948, the Assistance Board became the National Assistance Board and took over all the functions of its predecessor and those of the Public Assistance Committees. As the first annual report of the new Board put it: 'The division (of assistance) between the Board and the Local Authorities could be explained as a matter of history, but could not be defended by rational considerations: it was wasteful in administration and confusing to the public.'[2]

[1] In the Determination of Needs Acts, 1941 and 1943.
[2] Report of the National Assistance Board for the year ended 31 December 1948, p. 9.

With the disappearance of the Public Assistance Committees the last vestiges of the Poor Law, and of locally financed relief, were abolished.[1] The main function of the new National Assistance Board was thus the provision of a uniform type of assistance grant to those who had previously received extended unemployment benefit, supplementary pensions, or domiciliary relief. It also became responsible for the payment of non-contributory old age pensions; for allowances to blind persons and people receiving treatment for tuberculosis; for the provision of 'reception centres' for 'persons without a settled way of living' (this, in new terminology, meant casual wards for vagrants); and for the 'resettlement' of Polish immigrants who were being maintained in camps and hostels at the end of the war.

Returning to the first principle: it seemed likely that most of this work would be of steadily declining importance. In course of time more and more of the unemployed and the aged would receive adequate benefits from social insurance. The non-contributory pensioners would eventually pass away. The Poles and some of the vagrants would be 'rehabilitated' in such a way that they could earn their own living. Only a few special cases who had fallen through the net of social security, and a hard core of super-tramps, would remain.

This view of the relegation of the National Assistance Board to a position of minor importance was felt to be desirable because, although it would no longer have Poor Law associations, it would be the only branch of the social security system to apply a means test. Means tests, according to another

[1] 'It is of some interest to note that this development, though not envisaged in either the Majority or Minority Reports of the Poor Law Commission of 1906–1909, was discussed by the Poor Law Commissioners of 1832–4, who reported that many persons for whose judgment they had a great respect had proposed that the relief of the poor should be made a national instead of a parochial charge, and be both provided and administered under the direction of the government. Though the Commissioners recognised that the proposal would have a value in putting an end to the law of settlement, they felt bound to reject it partly because they considered it impossible that the Exchequer should be called upon to bear a burden which seems to have amounted at that time to about £7 million a year.' (*Ibid.*, p. 9.)

principle, were to be avoided as far as possible, most benefits being provided 'as of right'.

The basis of National Assistance Board payments is a standard weekly amount for single persons, married couples and children of various ages, to which is added the actual rent in each case. Further additions can be made in special cases, at the discretion of the Board's officers, and deductions are made for earnings, insurance benefits or family allowances received by the claimant or his dependants living with him. Capital resources up to £75, and war savings, are ignored. Non-dependent members of the household are expected to contribute to rent only. The system is clearly a fair and flexible one, but it does involve elaborate enquiry into individual financial circumstances.

The experience of the first six years of the National Assistance Board considerably altered the picture. In the first place, the scope and expenditure of the Board, so far from declining, increased year by year. In December 1948 the Board had 1,400,000 cases on its books. In December 1954 there were over 2 million. In 1949, the first full year of its operations, its expenditure was £80 million. In 1954 it was £130 million. More than two-thirds of the increase was assistance in supplementation of national insurance benefits. One in every four of the persons receiving retirement[1] pensions, one in five of those receiving unemployment benefit, and one in six of those receiving sickness benefit, finding their insurance benefits inadequate on account of the rise in prices, were obtaining further assistance from the Board.

The consequences of this unforeseen development were important. Administratively it placed on the National Assistance Board a burden of work which it was never intended to bear. From the point of view of principle, it weakened the

[1] Retirement pensions are those to which contributors become entitled under the National Insurance Acts, on retirement from work. Old age pensions are those to which uninsured persons become entitled, under the Old Age Pensions Act, on reaching the age of 70.

basis of the insurance scheme, which was that insurance benefits, drawn without means test, would be adequate in nearly
all cases.   Financially, it diverted to the Exchequer, i.e. the
general taxpayer, payments which should have been a charge
on the Insurance Fund.

In the second place, the reputation and prestige of the
National Assistance Board also increased year by year.   It
discharged its main functions with an efficiency and understanding which not only overcame the deep-rooted prejudice
against public assistance, but also removed, in many cases,
much of the resentment against means tests as a technique of
discriminatory relief and individual case work.   This showed
up most clearly in the numerically less important duties of the
Board, the guidance into regular employment of cases with a
bad history of casual work and maladjustment.   It was
apparent also in the success with which the Board carried out
a number of additional tasks that were thrust upon it between
1948 and 1953.   Thus, it became responsible for assessing the
means of persons who applied for legal aid, free welfare foods,
pensioners' tobacco coupons, and the refund of charges imposed by the National Health Service.   It provided advances
of wages in the first week of a new job; it assisted the families
of persons on strike; it refunded the bus-fares of patients
going to and from hospital; it paid the cost of domestic help
in times of illness.

All this is described, with illustrations from individual cases,
in the Annual Reports of the National Assistance Board, which
breathe an air of human understanding and personal interest
that makes them about the most readable documents that have
ever come out of any government office.   On the one hand,
therefore, the principle of 'benefits as of right' implicit in the
post-war social insurance scheme was being undermined and
benefits subject to a means test were becoming more common.
On the other hand, the means tests themselves were acquiring
quite new and much more hopeful characteristics.   How far
the second development offset the first is not within the scope
of the present discussion.

17

§ **2. The Growth of Social Insurance.**   The idea of compulsory national insurance as a method of provision against economic insecurity arising from sickness and old age was much canvassed at the end of the nineteenth century.   The experience of the friendly societies showed that sickness was an insurable risk and that contributory pensions, which combined insurance with organised saving, were also feasible, at least among the classes of people who belonged to such societies.   The German experiment, begun in the 1880's,[1] suggested that, if the employer and the State, as well as the employee, contributed, the system could be extended to classes of the working population who were unable or unwilling to join friendly societies.   The surveys of Booth and Rowntree gave, for the first time, some idea of the scope of the problem by revealing the relative importance of sickness and old age among the causes of poverty.

Unemployment insurance on a national scale was not generally regarded as practicable.   At the time of the Royal Commission the trade unions provided unemployment insurance for about $1\frac{1}{2}$ million of their members, but they were nearly all among the highly skilled and highly paid.   On the Continent, the only example of official unemployment insurance before 1900 was in the Swiss canton of St. Gallen where, in 1894, a scheme based on contributions from workmen earning less than 5 francs a day, supplemented by local and cantonal subsidies, failed ignominiously through bad adminis-

[1] Bismarck introduced this legislation with the avowed object of defeating the socialists by making the State itself socialist.   Insurance against sickness was introduced for industrial workers in 1883.   Employees contributed two-thirds, employers one-third, and the scheme was organised through all kinds of approved societies, including trade unions and voluntary clubs.   Accident insurance followed in 1884 'to rouse the labouring population to a consciousness of the blessings attending the peaceful development of the unified Fatherland, and withdraw the ground from those revolutionary elements that would work for the overthrow of Divine and human institutions'.   The employers bore the whole cost and were required to form associations for mutual protection in meeting their liability.   Old age and invalidity insurance came in 1889.   Employers and employees contributed equally and the State provided a subsidy as the expenditure of the fund required it.   This was organised through the post office by a system of stamped cards.

tration.   The real stumbling block, however, in all the schemes discussed at this time was not so much the administrative problem of defining genuine unemployment as the actuarial problem of predicting its incidence.   Apart from epidemics, death rates and sickness rates could be forecast within a reasonable margin of error.   Unemployment rates did not seem to obey any known rules of probability.

By the time of the Royal Commission Report, industrial accident and old age had already been partly provided for. The Workmen's Compensation Act of 1897 established the principle that an employer was liable for the payment of compensation in the event of death or incapacity suffered as a result of accident in certain industries.   Until that time it had been necessary for the employee to prove negligence in order to obtain compensation.   In 1906 the scope was extended to cover nearly all manual workers and also to include industrial diseases.   The significance of the Workmen's Compensation Acts in the development of social insurance was that they made insurance compulsory but left it entirely in private hands. It is often assumed that compulsory insurance inevitably implies a State-organised scheme and a contribution from public funds. Accident insurance, from 1897 to 1946, included neither. The whole burden was placed on the employers, who could, of course, make contracts with commercial insurance companies.

The Old Age Pensions Act of 1908 was not an insurance scheme.   All persons, on reaching the age of 70, became entitled to claim a pension, paid out of public funds, subject to a means test.   The importance of this legislation was that within a year it was providing pensions outside the Poor Law system for about half a million old persons.   It therefore contributed to the break-up of the Poor Law, and also narrowed the possible field for social insurance, while the Reports of the Royal Commission were still unpublished.   The administration of these non-contributory pensions was transferred to the Assistance Board in 1940 (when supplementary pensions based on individual need were added) and to the National Assistance Board in 1948.

The Majority Report of 1909 suggested the appointment of a special committee to formulate a national scheme of unemployment insurance, which would include unskilled workers and be partly financed by public funds. But, characteristically, they favoured the Ghent type of scheme (also adopted in a number of other Continental towns) whereby the first provision would be made by the trade unions, friendly societies and 'organisations of a similar character which may be brought into existence' and the State would add a fixed amount to the benefits paid by these organisations.

The Minority, somewhat unexpectedly, were against any form of national insurance, for administrative and political reasons.

'To keep the separate accounts for half a century of all these millions, to register them in their changes from industry to industry and from place to place, and to receive and manage all the contributions, would in itself be a colossal task, and to enforce against the defaulters the obligation of payment would be an impossible one.'

'Any attempt to *enforce* on the people of this country— whether for supplementary pensions, provision for sickness or invalidity, or anything else—a system of direct, personal, weekly contributions must, in our judgment, in face of so powerful a phalanx as the combined Friendly Societies, Trade Unions and Industrial Assurance Companies, fighting in defence of their own business, prove politically disastrous.'[1]

It was for very similar administrative and political reasons that Lloyd George *did* introduce compulsory national health insurance administered through approved societies, and unemployment insurance administered through the labour exchanges, in 1911. He did not, as the Majority had suggested, and the Minority had feared, use the trade unions in the organisation of unemployment benefits, or make State insurance a sort of supplementary activity to that of the volun-

[1] S. and B. Webb: *The Break-up of the Poor Law*, 1909, pp. 349–50 (their italics).

tary bodies. The compulsory scheme was to be the basis, with voluntary societies providing additional benefits as their members required.

The National Insurance Act of 1911 was in two parts. Part I set up the health insurance scheme for all manual workers and non-manual workers earning less than £160 a year.[1] Contributions were paid by insured persons, their employers and the Exchequer in the actuarial ratio 4:3:2—this was the basis of Lloyd George's slogan 'ninepence for fourpence'— but in practice the shares varied for different classes of contributor, and the actuarial ratio did not, of course, represent the ultimate distribution of either the incidence of the contributions or the source of the benefits. There were four kinds of benefit: sickness benefit, consisting of a cash payment for a limited period; disablement benefit, paid at a lower rate after 26 weeks of absence from work; medical benefit, consisting of free practitioner services and drugs; and a maternity grant. The main principle of the scheme, as of all schemes of social insurance, was that benefits were paid without means test, on the strength of the contribution record of the insured person. Friendly societies, trade unions, and other non-profit-making societies could register as approved societies and collect contributions and distribute benefits for the national scheme in conjunction with their own schemes. Persons who were not members of societies were dealt with by local Insurance Committees, which also administered the whole system of medical benefits and 'panel' doctors.

Part II of the 1911 Act was more tentative. The unemployment insurance scheme applied in the first place only to a limited range of industries. The whole scheme was administered through the labour exchanges, but there was a cautious provision for special arrangements to be made with trade unions to refund them part of the unemployment benefit which they paid to their members as an alternative to direct payment. The tripartite contributions to the unemployment fund were based on the ratio 3:3:2 and it was assumed, for actuarial

[1] Raised to £250 in 1919 and £420 in 1942.

purposes, that the average rate of unemployment in the insured industries would be about three weeks in the year, or 6 per cent. The period of benefit was limited to fifteen weeks in any one year and the rules for adjudication of the right to unemployment benefit included powers to refuse benefit to persons on strike and to those who declined a reasonable offer of employment.

In all cases, both contributions and benefits were on a flat rate basis, and this principle has been observed throughout the history of social insurance in Britain. The justification of it is as follows: benefits must be the same for all insured persons, since they are intended only to provide the bare necessities of life; the rules of insurance require that persons receiving the same benefits must pay the same premium; therefore contributions must be the same for all. In other countries, both contributions and benefits are proportional to income. The main disadvantage of the flat rate system is that it limits the level of the insured person's contribution to the amount that the poorest can pay.

In 1914, out of an occupied population of between 16 and 17 millions, the number insured under the health scheme was 13·7 millions and under the unemployment scheme 2·5 millions. It seemed already that the schemes were working out, administratively and financially, better than had been expected, and the low unemployment of the war years assisted the process of consolidation. During and after the war unemployment insurance was extended, and in 1921 covered about 11 million persons, compared with 15 million who were in the health scheme by that time.

It soon became apparent, however, that social insurance was wholly inadequate in a period of heavy and prolonged unemployment. As we saw in the last section, the Insurance Fund had to resort to borrowing; the people who most needed help exhausted their right to benefit; and attempts to deal with the problem by adjusting the rates of contribution and benefit had little effect.

On this last point, the conflicts of principle during the 1920's are clearly revealed in the historical section of the Report of the Royal Commission on Unemployment Insurance published in 1932.[1]   In 1911 the standard rate of unemployment benefit had been fixed 'as an assistance to tide over short temporary spells of unemployment'.   The rate was increased in 1919 and again in 1920, but by less than the increase in the cost of living. A Committee of 1923 maintained that the purpose of unemployment benefit was 'to supplement private effort in mitigating distress due to involuntary unemployment'. In 1924 the Minister of Labour justified an increase in the rate of benefit by appeal to the principle that 'an honest man . . . though he be unemployed . . . shall be paid a sum of money which at any rate will keep him from starvation'.   A Committee of 1927 advocated that benefits should be 'definitely less in amount than the general labourer's rate of wages'.   In 1931 the benefit rates were cut, not because the cost of living had fallen, but in order to economise public expenditure.   The idea that social benefits should be at subsistence level, suggested in the 1924 pronouncement, was still in conflict with the ideas of 1834, that they should not interfere with wages, and of 1909, that they should not discourage voluntary effort.   And the whole situation was of course confused by the existence of other authorities providing unemployment relief at other rates and by different methods.

Meanwhile the case for extending social insurance to the field of pensions became more pressing.   The Act of 1908 had granted State pensions to persons over 70, but it was clear that a great deal of the poverty caused by old age was among people in the age group 65–70 who had retired involuntarily and become dependent on public assistance; and that widows under the age of 70 were similarly placed.   The Widows', Orphans' and Old Age Contributory Pensions Act of 1925 introduced the first national scheme of contributory pensions.   The new scheme was grafted on to national health insurance.   Briefly, widows and orphans of persons who had been insured under the health scheme became entitled to a pension without any

[1] Cmd. 4185, Final Report, paras. 27–57.

means test; persons then insured under the health scheme, on attaining the age of 70, acquired similar rights; and two years later pensions were paid to all insured persons from the age of 65. In addition, anyone not compulsorily insured under the health scheme could insure separately and voluntarily under the contributory pensions scheme. In 1926, therefore, about 17 million people became insured for contributory pensions (compared with 16·4 millions for health and 11·8 millions for unemployment), and the non-contributory pensions, subject to a means test, applied only to the uninsured population.

We are not here concerned with the details of this legislation or of many smaller Acts amending the rates of contribution and benefit and the conditions of payment[1]; but with the way in which social insurance superseded poor relief as the principal method of alleviating poverty. At this point it is useful to take stock of the situation as it was in 1939. How far had social insurance justified itself? And what more was required? To begin with the credit side of the account: in the first place, it was clear that in providing benefits as of right and without means test, insurance had psychological and administrative advantages as compared with assistance. However tactful and understanding an assistance officer might be, however thoroughly the vestiges of the Poor Law were swept away, there remained a vast difference between divulging one's resources in order to seek assistance, and claiming a contractual insurance payment on the evidence of a stamped card. And, however efficient and skilled an assistance officer might be, he could deal with far fewer cases by individual personal enquiry than could an insurance clerk of inferior skill by routine methods of administration.

Secondly, experience suggested that in *normal* circumstances four of the causes of poverty—sickness, unemployment, old age and widowhood—were insurable risks. Normal circum-

[1] They may be found in W. A. Robson (ed.): *Social Security*, 3rd Edition, 1948; in the Beveridge Report, *Social Insurance and Allied Services*, 1942, Appendix B; P.E.P.: *British Social Services*, 1937; and many other books.

stances would imply the avoidance of large-scale unemployment, a reasonable stability in the level of prices, and, in the case of old age, a contribution period appropriate to the actuarial requirements of a pension fund. In the inter-war years it could be said that social insurance had to contend with abnormality in all these respects, but especially in regard to unemployment. During the 1930's, however, the work of Keynes was becoming generally known and offered the prospect of avoiding cyclical unemployment, and research into the problems of industrial location seemed to point the way to a reduction of structural unemployment.

Thirdly, the nation-wide scope of social insurance had been fully justified. The spreading of risks over the whole community yielded economies of scale which were not available even to the largest friendly societies and insurance companies; and the disadvantages and inequalities of parochial and regional finance, which had so bedevilled the Poor Law system, were completely avoided.

Fourthly, the compulsory nature of national insurance was also vindicated. Even for those who could afford to insure voluntarily against periods of sickness, unemployment and old age, the tendency was often to discount the future too heavily, so that they did not make adequate provision and became a burden to the community in one way or another. More significant, however, was the fact that the risk of poverty was usually greatest among those with the lowest incomes, so that any voluntary insurance scheme, which imposed a premium appropriate to the risk in individual cases or groups, would require the highest contributions from those least able to pay them, and *vice versa*. By spreading the risk over the whole community and imposing the same *average* premium on all contributors, the national insurance scheme did not violate any actuarial principles, but it did remove the relationship between premium and risk in individual cases, and compulsion was necessary to make it work.[1]

[1] A simplified example may help to explain this point. Suppose that half the population consists of sedentary workers, who die a natural

Fifthly, the tripartite system of contributions had also proved acceptable. Again, the reasons were partly psychological and partly financial. The insured person's contribution gave him a stake in the scheme and, rightly or wrongly, created the impression that it did not involve much in the way of redistribution. It was often argued, for example, that the beneficiaries 'had a right to the benefits because they had paid for them', or that 'the workers were paying for their own insurance'. The employer's contribution was supposed to give him an interest in the welfare of his employees, and the State contribution to represent the community's share of responsibility for the banishment of poverty. The economic fact was, however, that the beneficiaries could not afford to pay for their own insurance, so that some subsidy from other sources was necessary. Whether the employer's contribution, being a tax on wages, came ultimately from the wage-earner, or the profit-earner, or the consumer (in the form of higher prices) depended on conditions in the industry and in the market. Whether the State contribution came ultimately from the owner of capital, the earner of income or the consumer depended on the distribution of Exchequer revenue between direct and indirect taxation. In any event, social insurance was more than a glorified system of mutual aid, redistributing income between the fortunate and the unfortunate, between the present and the future, between the young and the old. It also redistributed from rich to poor. In other words, without the employer's and Exchequer contributions, the contributions of the insured persons (at a flat rate) would have become so high as to create

death at an advanced age, and the other half of deep-sea divers, whose accident rate is very high. The former could insure their lives at a low annual premium, the latter only at a very high one. If the two groups are combined in one insurance scheme, an average premium can be charged which is appropriate to the total risk. But if both groups are offered the same premium, the sedentary workers will under-insure, the deep-sea divers will over-insure, and the scheme will fail. It is necessary to compel the 'good risks' to take out a certain (minimum) amount of insurance at the average premium and limit the 'bad risks' to the same (maximum) amount in order to make the scheme work. This is what social insurance does.

new cases of poverty as fast as the benefits relieved the existing ones.

Lastly, the administration of social insurance worked, not always smoothly, but satisfactorily. By making use of the experience and machinery of the approved societies, and by issuing insurance stamps and paying benefits through the post office,[1] the Government departments were able to carry out a task which, as the Webbs had feared, would otherwise have been impossible. The elaborate machinery for adjudication of claims also worked, and, in particular, the attempts to abuse unemployment insurance were far fewer than had been expected.

Now for the debit side of the account: first and foremost was the problem of mass unemployment, the disastrous effects of which, not only on social insurance, but on many other aspects of the social economy, have been repeatedly mentioned.

Next, there were the problems created by the piecemeal growth of social insurance. The whole organisation, like that of the original Poor Law, was built up gradually and empirically. Consequently it was complex and unco-ordinated, and contained curious anomalies and gaps. For a State-organised system (in contrast to private enterprise) such complexity and lack of co-ordination was undesirable. Public administration, using powers of compulsion and distributing public money, is expected to observe traditions of fairness and equality of treatment among its customers. Perhaps it did not matter that non-contributory pensions were administered by the Treasury, contributory pensions by the Ministry of Health, and supplementary pensions (from 1940) by the Assistance Board, under different sets of rules. More serious was the fact that, for several years, the Public Assistance Committees and the Assistance Board were running in parallel with the social insurance departments, providing different benefits, and imposing different standards, for the same set of people. Again, it was difficult for employers to understand why there

---

[1] Except unemployment benefit, which was paid by the labour exchanges.

had to be separate cards and stamps for unemployment, and for health and pensions insurance. The division of the entire field of relief into means test payments and insurance payments could be explained historically but not rationally. The fact that insured persons received medical benefit, but their wives and families did not; that children's allowances were paid to the widows and orphans of insured persons after their death, but not while they were alive; all these and many more oddities called for a general overhaul of the system.

A third problem arose out of the failure to relate insurance benefits to subsistence needs. In the case of *assistance* payments, it was not essential that the benefit itself should cover the whole cost of subsistence. There were standard rates of assistance benefit, and they sometimes amounted to a subsistence income, but the essence of such payments is that individual needs and means can be taken into account and the benefit adjusted upwards or downwards to fill the gap in each case. Social insurance, in doing away with individual casework, assumes that, since certain circumstances—sickness, unemployment, old age—are major causes of poverty, the payment of benefits to categories of people who are in these circumstances will effectively relieve poverty. The payments are made to people, not because they are destitute, but because they are sick, unemployed or aged. This is a more efficient way of relieving destitution, from the administrative point of view, on two conditions: that these categories of people continue to account for most of the potentially destitute, and that the payments provide a subsistence income to the beneficiaries. But there was no generally accepted rule that social insurance payments should be at subsistence level. It was frequently argued that most of the beneficiaries would have some other resources, or at least that they ought not to be discouraged from finding other resources; and that in the last resort those who were still in need could supplement their insurance benefits by assistance benefits—a practice which destroyed the whole basis of social insurance.

The approved society system also had its problems. Each

society was a separate financial unit, able to realise a surplus or deficit for its members out of the administration of the contributions collected compulsorily from them. The intention was to give the societies an interest in efficient administration by allowing them to distribute surpluses in the form of additional benefits. Societies varied considerably in size and efficiency, with the result that, including the additional benefits, insured persons paying equal compulsory contributions received unequal benefits. In voluntary insurance, such bonuses were quite acceptable, but not in a State-subsidised scheme, especially one in which the standard benefits tended to be below subsistence level. This and several other disadvantages of the approved society system were examined by the Royal Commission on National Health Insurance of 1926. The majority of this Commission reported, a little hesitantly, that the system should nevertheless be continued; a minority were in favour of replacing the approved societies by the local authorities as administrative agents.

All of these principles and problems, and many more, were considered by an Inter-Departmental Committee, appointed in 1941, 'To undertake, with special reference to the inter-relation of the schemes, a survey of the existing national schemes of social insurance and allied services, including workmen's compensation, and to make recommendations'. The Chairman was Sir William Beveridge, who signed the Report and took sole responsibility for the recommendations. The Report was presented in 1942 to the Minister concerned with problems of post-war reconstruction.

§ 3. **The Beveridge Report and After.**   The Report on *Social Insurance and Allied Services*, which soon became known as the Beveridge Plan, was far more than a reorganised insurance scheme. Conceived in the darkest days of war, it was a programme of prophetic faith and vision, which looked forward to a post-war world in which there should be social security in its widest sense. It sought to capture the unity of purpose which people had found under the stress of war and project it into the realm of peacetime reconstruction. It discerned, in the manner of John Bunyan, five Giants on the Road to Reconstruction: Want, Disease, Ignorance, Squalor and Idleness; and it set about forging the weapons for slaying the first on the assumption that the others would also be destroyed and the broad highway of social progress lie open.

It is important to stress the breadth of vision which inspired the Report because, although most of the recommendations were concerned with a comprehensive scheme of social insurance, Beveridge realised that the abolition of want was only partly attainable by insurance. If we compare the study of the causes of primary poverty (in Chapter VI) and that of the development of social insurance (in the last section), we find that at least three of those causes were not insurable risks: low wages, 'abnormal' unemployment and large families. By 1942 poverty caused by low wages had been largely cured by a general increase in real wages and by an improvement in the relative earning power of unskilled labour. 'Abnormal' unemployment, Beveridge stipulated, must be abolished by a full employment policy, so that 'normal' unemployment could be treated as an insurable risk. With regard to families, the difficulty was not simply that large families were not an insurable risk or that in the 1940's large families were likely to be a significant cause of poverty, but that family size was a principal cause of differences of need, as distinct from differences of means. In other words, social insurance was chiefly appropriate to interruptions in earning power, and the case for family allowances was independent of this. Beveridge therefore stipulated a system of family allowances, paid to all families and financed entirely by the Exchequer, as another essential element in the post-war social security system. To full employment and family allowances he added a national health service, 'providing full preventive and curative treatment of every kind to every citizen without exceptions, without remuneration limit, and without an economic barrier to delay recourse to it'.[1]

[1] *Report*, para. 437.

With these three prerequisites, the Plan proposed a unified system of social insurance which would be 'comprehensive, in respect both of the persons covered and of their needs. It should not leave either to national assistance or to voluntary insurance any risk so general or so uniform that social insurance can be justified'.[1]   There would be one Ministry responsible for the whole scheme; one weekly contribution, with a single card and stamp, in respect of all benefits; and one national insurance fund into which all contributions would flow and out of which all benefits would be paid.   The tripartite system of contributions (by the insured person, the employer and the Exchequer) was to be preserved, the actuarial ratio for most of the benefits being 5:5:2; but for unemployment benefit the contribution was to be on the basis of each paying one-third; and the 'security budget' attached to the Plan included estimates for the cost of national assistance, family allowances and the national health service, all of which were to be met entirely by the Exchequer.   Over the whole range of benefits the Exchequer contribution would amount to about one-quarter.

The proposed insurance benefits consisted of retirement pensions; sickness, accident, unemployment and widows' and guardians' benefits; maternity, marriage and funeral grants. It was summed up as 'social security from the cradle to the grave' or, as a modern poet expresses it, 'from womb to tomb'.

The Plan provided for the whole population between the ages of 16 and 65 to become contributors, except that housewives would acquire the right to all the appropriate benefits on the strength of their husbands' contributions.   Beveridge wanted to retain the services of the approved societies under a new arrangement which would ensure that the benefits paid on behalf of the State scheme would be uniform and adequate. He also suggested that, in addition to the national health service, there should be services, associated with the payment of money benefits, for the retraining of the long-term unemployed, the rehabilitation of the disabled, and the promotion

[1] *Report*, para. 308.

of schemes for reducing industrial accidents and diseases. Social insurance could also be a means of implementing general economic policy. The problem of the ageing population could be mitigated by providing increased retirement pensions to those who remained at work after the normal retiring age. And employment policy would be supported, not only by the ordinary increase in expenditure and reduction in revenue of the insurance fund in times of depression, and *vice versa* in times of prosperity; but also by the deliberate adjustment of contribution *rates* in order to stimulate or curb effective demand.

No outline, such as has been attempted here, can give any indication of the full scope and far-reaching possibilities of the Plan. There was general admiration for its boldness and thoroughness, and some justifiable doubts about its economic and financial implications. To understand the subsequent history, it is most useful at this point to examine more closely two of its principles, which Beveridge called the contributory principle and the subsistence principle.

Beveridge laid great stress on the psychological importance of the contributory principle. He maintained that if benefits were to be paid as of right, the insured person must be convinced that he had a fixed claim on the insurance fund, dependent only on his fulfilment of the contribution conditions. The evidence given to the Committee showed that this conviction was most successfully upheld by the contributory system, even though the insured person's contribution was purely nominal. 'The insured persons . . . like to pay', he wrote; '. . . they should not be taught to regard the State as a dispenser of gifts for which no one needs to pay' and 'the insurance document . . . provides automatically the record by which the insured person's claim . . . can be tested'.[1]

He admitted that the case for the employer's contribution was weak, except in regard to accident insurance. It did not vary with the employer's profits or capacity to pay, but simply according to whether he happened to be a large or a small user of labour. Nevertheless, it was justified by a number of argu-

[1] *Report*, para. 274.

ments which amounted to saying that the employers ought to have a stake in the scheme. As for the Exchequer contribution, it was necessary, as it had been in the pre-war schemes, in order to make social insurance pay its way.

The contributory principle was also justified on the ground that it made the scheme a genuine insurance scheme, which was actuarially sound. What exactly did this mean? In private insurance, it would require adherence to four rules: first, that the risks must be calculable; secondly, that the premium is adjusted to the risk in each case; thirdly, that for a fixed premium the insured person receives a fixed benefit; fourthly, that over the period of the insurance contract the premiums cover the benefits. In social insurance, the rules could be slightly modified, but without destroying the actuarial soundness of the scheme. The first rule could stand: statistics were available to the Government Actuary enabling him to calculate mortality rates and sickness rates and accident rates with as much accuracy as any private insurance company; and for unemployment it was assumed, on the advice of Beveridge, that $8\frac{1}{2}$ per cent of the working population should be taken as the average rate for the post-war period.[1]

The second rule could be maintained by arguing that, if insurance were made compulsory, and the risk of poverty, from any cause, spread over the whole insured population, then a uniform average premium could be charged to everyone alike; and further, that, if the amount of insurance in each case were fixed (so that people could not opt for larger or smaller benefits by paying larger or smaller contributions), the contributions actually paid by the insured person could be purely nominal. The third rule could stand, and was in fact stoutly defended by Beveridge when he emphasised that 'insured persons should realise that they cannot get more than certain benefits for certain contributions'.[2]

The fourth rule takes us into deeper water. In social insurance the annual contributions of the three parties are so

[1] *Report*, Appendix A, para. 14.
[2] *Report*, para 274.

calculated that they could provide a fund out of which the benefits can be met when they become due.   The same is true of the premiums in a private insurance scheme.   But this does not mean that the income and expenditure of the fund will balance in any one year.   In any type of insurance the risks may be averaged over a period of years, and in the case of pensions the contract may cover the whole working life and period of retirement of the insured person.   A private insurance company balances income and expenditure each year by payments into and out of a reserve fund.   Social insurance contributions are not funded in this way. A current balance is kept in hand to meet day-to-day fluctuations.   Beyond this amount, annual surpluses are transferred to a reserve fund under the control of the National Debt Commissioners and invested in Government securities.   The interest on the investments forms part of the current income of the insurance fund, but the capital cannot be drawn on 'save in very exceptional circumstances'[1] and with the specific authority of a resolution of the House of Commons.   This implies that normal annual deficits, when they arise, are to be made good, not by drawing on the reserve fund, but by increasing the Exchequer contribution.   Moreover, it was proposed in the Beveridge Plan, as it was in the Contributory Pensions Act of 1925, that pensions should be granted immediately to older members of the insured population at a higher rate than would be justified by their past contributions.   The Exchequer payment into the national insurance fund can therefore consist of three slices: the first is the actuarial contribution of the Exchequer, in a fixed ratio to the contributions of insured persons and employers; the second is an Exchequer subsidy to provide pensions for those who have not yet earned them; the third is an annual payment to balance the current account.   In private insurance the first would be classed as a premium, the second as an *ex gratia* payment, and

[1] *Second Interim Report by the Government Actuary* (on the National Insurance Act, 1946), for the year ended 31 March 1951, para. 10.   The possible nature of the exceptional circumstances has never been officially disclosed.   The balance of the reserve fund in March 1955 was £1,069 millions.

the third as a drawing on reserves.   In social insurance they may in practice be indistinguishable.

'The proportion (of total expenditure) met by the Exchequer . . . is much greater than the part of the actuarial contribution allocated to the Exchequer . . . in addition the Exchequer takes the strain of admitting the existing population of all ages for the ordinary benefits of the Plan at the same rate of contribution as is charged to new entrants at age 16.   Further, owing to the fact that it does not extinguish its liability by a series of deficiency payments to an accumulative fund, but makes good the annually emerging excess of current expenditure over current income, there is a deficit in perpetuity, the charge on the Exchequer not being reduced when, in due course, the present insured population has passed away.'[1]

All this means that the scheme, while still a contributory scheme observing some of the technical rules of insurance, is entirely dependent on variable Exchequer grants for its solvency, and therefore differs radically from any commercial insurance scheme.

The other principle to which Beveridge attached great importance was the subsistence principle.

'The rates of benefit or pension provided by social insurance should be such as to secure for all normal cases an income adequate for subsistence, on the assumptions (a) that assistance will be available to meet abnormal subsistence needs; (b) that voluntary insurance and saving to provide for standards of life above subsistence minimum will be encouraged and made easy.'[2]

Thus Beveridge proposed to settle the argument which had been going on since 1834 about the relationship between benefits and wages, and between benefits and saving.   His

[1] *Report*, Appendix A, para. 89.   [2] *Report*, para. 193.

subsistence level was determined objectively, by the methods of Rowntree and Bowley (who personally advised him). There were, however, two important differences from the practice of the pre-war social surveys. For the purpose of insurance benefits, family needs would be those of single persons and married couples only, since children would be provided for by family allowances, whether the family was in receipt of benefit or not. And, instead of including the actual rent of each household, as Rowntree and Bowley had done, Beveridge took an average rent in order to preserve uniformity of benefits. This was a difficult choice, defended on the ground that, though expenditure on rent could less easily be reduced during a temporary interruption of earning than expenditure on clothing, fuel, light and even food, yet higher rents would normally indicate higher standards of living, and it was not the object of social insurance to support higher than subsistence standards. Beveridge made his calculations at 1938 prices and assumed that prices after the war would be 25 per cent above 1938. He also added the following paragraph connecting the contributory principle with the subsistence principle:

'Whether or not the scale of benefits suggested here as a basis of discussion be adopted, the relation between benefits and contributions remains. To give benefits at rates 25 per cent or 50 per cent above those suggested here means increasing the contributions of each of the three parties of the scheme in the same proportions, or increasing the share of one party to the contribution by less and of another party or parties by more. In so far as an increase of the rates of benefit and contribution suggested here was made necessary by change in the value of money, that is by a level of prices after the war materially more than 25 per cent above the level of 1938, that would be a difference only in money terms. Wages and other incomes will presumably rise roughly in proportion to prices, and contributions in terms of money can be raised without representing a larger proportion of wages. In so far as increase of the rates of benefit and contribution above the scales proposed was dictated by social policy and not by change in the value of money, that would represent a decision to put the national minimum higher than bare subsistence.'[1]

Nevertheless, one exception to the subsistence principle was proposed. To grant full subsistence pensions to all persons of pensionable age from the outset of the new scheme would impose too heavy a burden on the Exchequer. 'Too heavy' in this context meant more than Beveridge's advisers in the Treasury felt would be reasonable, especially in view of the proposal which we noted above, that many pensioners would come into the scheme too late to be able to make adequate annual contributions. It was therefore suggested that for a transition period of twenty years, pensions should be paid on a scale gradually rising to subsistence level, with assistance pensions granted meanwhile, to ensure that nobody was in want.

So much for the Beveridge Plan. The Government accepted most of its proposals in a series of White Papers published in 1944[2] and in due course they were embodied in five Acts of Parliament: the Family Allowances Act, 1945; the National Health Service Act, 1946; the National Insurance Act, 1946; the National Insurance (Industrial Injuries) Act, 1946; and the National Assistance Act, 1948. The main departures from Beveridge were four. The approved society system was abandoned. Family allowances were not provided for the first child of school age, but for the second and subsequent children only; and insurance beneficiaries received increases of benefit in respect of all their children. The graduated pension scheme was not accepted, and full pensions were granted immediately at a level between Beveridge's initial and ultimate

[1] *Report*, para. 295.
[2] Cmd. 6502, February 1944: *A National Health Service*. Cmd. 6550, September 1944: *Social Insurance, Part I*. Cmd. 6551, September 1944: *Social Insurance, Part II (Workmen's Compensation)*. The White Paper on *Employment Policy*, Cmd. 6527, May 1944, was also relevant.

rates.   As for the subsistence principle, it was not accepted in the Coalition Government's White Paper in 1944, the arguments being that it would entail frequent variations of the benefit rates, that it would require adjustments for different localities, and that 'the right objective is a rate of benefit which provides a reasonable insurance against want and at the same time takes account of the maximum contribution which the great body of contributors can properly be asked to bear'.[1] It was, however, officially accepted on the introduction of the National Insurance Bill in 1946, though the pronouncement was in very general terms,[2] and there was no reference to any objective standards.

The Ministry of National Insurance was set up in 1944 and the Insurance Acts came into force, together with the National Assistance Act, in July 1948.   Every five years the Government Actuary is required to 'report to the Treasury on the financial condition of the National Insurance Fund and the adequacy or otherwise of the contributions . . . to support the benefits'. The Minister then has to 'review the rates of benefit'.[3]   The first quinquennial review was due in 1954, by which time the adventure which Beveridge had likened to the Pilgrim's Progress had become more akin to Gulliver's Travels: one of the expected giants, unemployment, proved to be a mere dwarf; and a new giant, inflation, found the warrior ill-equipped and threatened to destroy him altogether.

An unemployment rate in the post-war period of $8\frac{1}{2}$ per cent had been suggested as a working basis, allowing a good margin of safety, for the calculation of insurance risks, rather than as the level which Beveridge, or the Government, expected in reality.   Even so, compared with pre-war experience, or the

[1] Cmd. 6550, para. 13.

[2] 'The leading rates must be fixed initially at figures which can be justified broadly in relation to the present cost of living. . . . I believe that we have in this way endeavoured to give a broad subsistence basis to the leading rates . . . definite arrangements should be made for a review of the rates from this point of view at periodic intervals.' (The Minister of National Insurance, Mr. James Griffiths, in the House of Commons, 6 February 1946.)

[3] *National Insurance Act*, 1946, sections 39 and 40.

history of the period which followed the first world war, it was not unreasonable. But many economists and politicians hoped that, by good fortune or deliberate policy, it could be kept as low as 3 to 5 per cent.

From 1944 to 1948, it varied between 1 and 3 per cent, and from 1948 to 1954, apart from the short recession in textiles in the middle of 1952, it remained between $1\frac{1}{2}$ and 2 per cent. The effect on the National Insurance Fund was so to increase its income and reduce its expenditure that from 1948 to 1951 it had an annual surplus, in spite of the pension burden, of between £100 millions and £150 millions (roughly a quarter of the total income of the Fund). Not all of this surplus was attributable to high employment, but most of it was, and from October 1951 the Government Actuary was instructed to assume 'an average long-term rate of unemployment of 4 per cent, instead of $8\frac{1}{2}$ per cent' and 'in assessing the short-term prospects, a rate of unemployment of $1\frac{1}{2}$ per cent up to March 1954, and $2\frac{1}{2}$ per cent in 1954–55.'' [1] The Exchequer contribution was reduced, but not those of the other parties, and at the same time the pension rates were increased, without any increase in contributions. The combined effect was to reduce the surplus in the Fund to £97 millions in the financial year 1951/2 and £23 millions in 1952/3. From October 1952, the Actuary, 'on Government instructions, adhered to the rate of 4 per cent for the long-term average (of unemployment) but, in assessing the annual income and expenditure for the next few years, adopted transitional rates of 2 per cent up to 1953/4 and 3 per cent for 1954/5, rising to 4 per cent thereafter'. [2] Thus official policy was busy adjusting itself to the facts of the post-war employment situation and also attempting to combine a short- and long-term assessment of risk, while keeping a weather eye on the state of the Fund from year to year.

---

[1] *Third Report of the Ministry of National Insurance, for the year 1951*, Cmd. 8635, para. 102.

[2] *Report of the Government Actuary on the Financial Provisions of the Family Allowances and National Insurance Bill*, 1952, Cmd. 8518, para. 11,

From the beneficiaries' point of view, however, the major problem of the post-war period was inflation, and in this respect official policy adjusted itself too little and too late. The standard rates of benefit were fixed in 1946 when the National Insurance Act was passed, at the Beveridge subsistence level, allowing for an increase in prices over 1938 of 31 per cent. This was the increase indicated by the Ministry of Labour's cost-of-living index. The Act was not to come into force until July 1948, but the new rates were introduced for all existing pensioners (though not for unemployment and sickness benefits) from October 1946. When, in 1948, the full scheme came into operation, the rates were not changed, although the monthly average of the Ministry of Labour index for that year was 41 per cent above 1938. They remained unchanged until 1951. In March 1951 the index was 57 per cent above 1938, and an Act was passed increasing the benefit rates for pensions only to this level; but the increase did not come into effect until October 1951, by which time the index had jumped to 69 per cent above 1938. In 1952 a further Act raised all the standard rates to 69 per cent above 1938 and was said to have 're-established the principle of uniform rates for the main National Insurance benefits and broadly restored their purchasing power to the July 1948 level'.[1] It had indeed, but the gap that had arisen between 1946 and 1948 was still uncovered, and the index in 1952 was 77 per cent above 1938.

At the end of 1954, for the first time, an attempt was made to jump ahead of the rising cost of living. A new Act increased, from April 1955, all the weekly rates of benefit 'to an extent which provided a margin over the amounts strictly necessary to restore the purchasing power of the benefits to that provided in 1946'.[2] The new rates were about 103 per cent above the Beveridge 1938 level, and the monthly average of the Ministry of Labour index in 1955 was about 95 per cent above

[1] *Fourth Report of the Ministry of National Insurance, for the year 1952*, Cmd. 8882, para. 7.
[2] *Report of the Ministry of Pensions and National Insurance, for the year 1954*, Cmd. 9495, para. 7.

1938. The index did not catch up until the spring of 1956.[1]

Even if the rates had been adjusted more frequently and more carefully, however, it is doubtful if in real terms they would have provided the Beveridge subsistence income, because the official index number was far from representative for the period 1938 to 1947. The Working Class Cost-of-Living Index in use until 1947 was based on a pattern of working-class expenditure which was sadly out of date, and several items in the index had been deliberately subsidised during the war in order to keep the index down. To that extent they also kept the cost of living down, of course, but the joint result of subsidy and rationing was to raise the prices of a number of essential commodities which were wrongly weighted or did not figure at all in the index. The deficiency was partly remedied by the use of a new Interim Index of Retail Prices from 1947 onwards, but it was generally considered that in making comparisons with pre-war consumption standards, the *London and Cambridge Economic Service* Index of Retail Prices was more suitable. In 1946 this index showed an increase of 54 per cent above 1938, compared with the official 31 per cent used for the original standard benefit rates. In 1955 the *L.C.E.S.* Index was 142 per cent and the official index 95 per cent above 1938, while the standard rate of benefit was 103 per cent above Beveridge's 1938 subsistence income.

We can now summarise the experience of the post-war period. First, the contributory principle was considerably modified. In 1951, when the unemployment risk was re-assessed, the Exchequer contribution was reduced, but the

[1] The following are the actual weekly rates of benefit for a single person and a married couple under the various Acts:

	Coverage	Payable from	Single Person	Married Couple
1938 Beveridge	All benefits	—	19s.	32s.
1946 Act	Pensions only All benefits	October 1946 ⎫ July 1948 ⎭	26s.	42s.
1951 Act	Pensions only	October 1951	30s.	50s.
1952 Act	All benefits	October 1952	32s. 6d.	54s.
1954 Act	All benefits	April 1955	40s.	65s.
1957 Act	All benefits	February 1958	50s.	80s.

others were not; and when pensions were increased it was 'not thought necessary on actuarial grounds to raise the contributions payable by insured persons and employers; nor is other fresh income required for this purpose in the next few years'.[1] In the following year, however, the general increase in benefits (including pensions) was matched by an increase in contributions of all three parties, the actuarial contribution for pensions being based on the assumption that contributions were made from the age of 16 onwards. In his Quinquennial Review at the end of 1954, the Government Actuary suggested that for future increases in pensions, the rate of contribution should be somewhat higher than the actuarial rate calculated on the above basis, in order to ease the burden on the Exchequer of providing higher pensions for existing pensioners and those who did not begin at 16. This new basis was adopted when contributions and benefits were raised in April 1955. And so the Beveridge rule that people must not get higher benefits without paying higher contributions was at first ignored, then observed and finally exceeded.

Secondly, the subsistence principle was virtually abandoned, for, in spite of attempts to catch up with rising prices, official policy appeared to view with equanimity the growing supplementation of benefits by the National Assistance Board. By December 1951 over a million insurance beneficiaries, including $\frac{3}{4}$ million pensioners, were receiving supplementary benefit from the N.A.B. The number increased steadily up to December 1954, when $1\frac{1}{4}$ million beneficiaries, including a million pensioners, were being supplemented. In 1955 the substantial increase in insurance benefits reduced, for the first time, the number of N.A.B. claimants, but in December 1955, there were still over a million, nine out of every ten being retirement pensioners.

Thirdly, the pursuit of the principles of social insurance was beset by serious political and administrative difficulties. Public opinion clamoured for an increase in retirement pensions,

[1] *Report of the Government Actuary on the Financial Provisions of the National Insurance Bill*, 1951, Cmd. 8212, para. 9.

because of the plight of the aged; but hardened against increases in employees' contributions, because they amounted to a regressive tax; and it became increasingly difficult to explain why both these aspects of public opinion should not be placated by plundering the substantial reserves of the insurance funds.

Administratively, on the other hand, it was clear that frequent adjustments of contributions or benefits would place an intolerable burden on the Ministry of National Insurance. The description, in the Annual Report of the Ministry, of how the changes were carried out in 1952, reads like an account of the invasion of Normandy. And well it might, in a department with 29 million customers (including 600,000 Smiths, 9,000 of them plain John Smith), out of which 9 million were affected by the 1952 Act.

Thus from several points of view, it looked as though 'genuine' social insurance could only operate successfully in a period of stable prices.

Finally it became increasingly clear that the main justification of a universal social insurance scheme was on psychological grounds. People felt that they had an unashamed right to the benefits because they had paid a contribution. That in itself was of paramount importance, but there was little more to it than that. The direct correlation of *changes* in benefit and *changes* in the contribution of insured persons, to which Beveridge attached great importance, had become considerably fogged by the system of variable Exchequer contributions necessitated by the granting of equal pensions to everyone. The justification of social insurance as a device for relieving poverty without means tests sounded hollow in the ears of the million beneficiaries who were drawing both insurance and assistance benefits. And it was doubtful whether the checking and filing and stamping, first by employers and then by officials, of millions of stamped cards (which the insured persons rarely saw) was worthwhile when the scheme was comprehensive and compulsory; for the number of people who on examination of their cards did *not* fulfil the contribution requirements which entitled them to benefit was negligible.

CHAPTER X

OTHER PUBLIC SOCIAL SERVICES

§ 1. Family Allowances. Family allowances are payments made in supplementation of wages or other regular income to take account of differences in the size of families. This implies that normal earnings do not take account of differences in the size of families, since they are based on productivity and not on needs. But it does not imply that normal earnings are necessarily insufficient for an earner with dependants. The needs of income earners differ for a number of reasons; physical, occupational, social, and according to their opportunities and the size of their families. To some extent differences of earning power will correspond to differences of need; especially is this true of occupational needs. To some extent the maintenance of incomes at a certain minimum level (by the establishment of minimum wages and the provision of insurance benefits) will be sufficient to cover differences of physical need and to spread opportunities. To some extent normal earnings will be sufficient to provide adequately for a normal size of family. But the differences of need which are least likely to be provided for by the wage system are differences of family size. This is the basis of the general case for family allowances, whether they are paid by employers, or out of a voluntary fund, or out of taxation.

The particular case for a compulsory scheme of family allowances, with or without support from public funds, rests on the argument that large families are a principal cause of poverty, or on general grounds of population policy. The poverty argument has two aspects. A significant proportion of the poverty found in the social surveys was directly attributable to largeness of family. And the prevalence of poverty from all causes was higher in the larger families than in the smaller because many families otherwise above the poverty line tended to sink below it during those periods when their children were growing up and not yet earning. The population argument may be in general sociological terms: that 'part of the total national income . . . should be directed down a new channel . . . to those individual citizens who were undertaking the rearing of the citizens of the future, in order to make sure that they had the means for this task.'[1] Or it may be specifically aimed at raising the birth rate. In Great Britain the level of family allowances (about 5 per cent of the weekly earnings of an unskilled labourer for the second and each subsequent child under school-leaving age) is hardly sufficient to influence the decisions of parents regarding the size of their families, but it does, together with other services and income tax relief, lighten the burden of parenthood considerably. In France, on the other hand, allowances for the first child amount to about 20 per cent of the average Departmental wage, for two children about 60 per cent, and for three about 100 per cent, with a further 30 per cent for each additional child: a bounty which parents can hardly fail to take into account.

In Great Britain the only legislation exclusively devoted to family allowances was the Act of 1945,[2] which provided weekly payments, financed entirely by the Exchequer and without means test (but subject to income tax), for the second and subsequent children from the time of their birth to the completion of their education. It was not merely the result of a recommendation in the Beveridge Report or of the Memorandum issued by the Coalition Government in 1942,[3] but the culmination of a campaign which had been waged for a quarter

---

[1] Lord Beveridge, in the Epilogue (Chapter IX) to *Family Allowances* by Eleanor Rathbone, 1949, p. 270.

[2] We should not forget, however, that between 1795 and 1834 the Speenhamland system probably provided family allowances on a bigger scale than any other scheme before or since, until 1945.

[3] Cmd. 6354: *Family Allowances*, Memorandum by the Chancellor of the Exchequer, May 1942. (The Beveridge Report was published in November 1942.)

of a century under the leadership of Miss Eleanor Rathbone, M.P. Her book *The Disinherited Family*, published in 1924,[1] combined accurate analysis with persuasive writing in a way that made it at once an important contribution to social economics and a political handbook for the Family Endowment Society, founded in 1927.

Before 1945 family allowances had been largely confined to three classes of people. Certain professional bodies had central funds out of which the salaries of their members were supplemented according to the age and number of their children; the Methodist Connexion, for example, have had such a scheme for over a century. A few industrial firms provided allowances for their employees. And most of the assistance and insurance services (but not health and contributory pensions) varied their scales of benefit according to the size of family. One of the results of this was that the receipts of a large family in time of unemployment or disability in some cases exceeded their earnings during work.

In the inter-war years, however, there was little progress apart from the inclusion of allowances in nearly all the new schemes for supplementing insurance and assistance benefits. Beveridge introduced family allowances for the teaching staff of the London School of Economics in 1926, and other University institutions followed suit. The (Samuel) Commission on the Coal Industry recommended the formation of a pool out of which allowances would be paid to miners, but the proposal foundered in the welter of the General Strike. At the beginning of the second world war, Keynes advocated the immediate introduction of family allowances, paid by the State, as part of a scheme to finance the cost of the war. His argument was that the severe taxation and high level of saving which the war would require should be coupled with the guarantee of certain minimum standards of consumption. To this end he put forward a plan for deferred pay, a cheap ration and family allowances.[2] The first and second were intro-

[1] Enlarged and republished in 1949 under the title *Family Allowances*.
[2] J. M. Keynes: *How to Pay for the War*, 1940, pp. 27 *et seq.*

duced, in the form of post-war credits and food subsidies, and were still on the scene fifteen years later. The third was not adopted, but it was at least the earliest piece of social legislation to be put into effect after the war.

The historical approach, however, which was essential for the analysis of the economic problems of social assistance and insurance, is not of much use in the discussion of family allowances. It is more interesting to examine some of the theoretical problems to which they give rise. Let us take two of them and ask: What are the relative merits of different methods of financing family allowances? and, How much should they be?

For the first question we assume that the payment of flat-rate allowances has been made compulsory in respect of all children of employed persons (other children being provided for by supplementary insurance and assistance benefits). One method of carrying it out would be simply to place the burden on employers and instruct them to pay the allowances. We saw that the Workmen's Compensation Act adopted this method for industrial injury benefit. It would not require any additional taxation or any official machinery apart from an inspectorate. It would, however, be open to two serious objections. First, it would work out unjustly as between one employer and another, and as between industries with a high proportion of labour costs and those with a low proportion. Secondly, it would inevitably lead to discrimination against workers with large families, for, however sympathetic he may be, an employer cannot afford to engage family men at high wages (including the allowances) if his competitors are free to engage bachelors (of the same efficiency) at lower wages.

A second method would be to instruct employers to work in groups and contribute, in agreed proportions, to a pool out of which allowances would be paid to the children of employees in all firms in the group. This is the method adopted in France. It avoids inequity between one employer and another; it avoids the danger of discrimination; and from the employers' point of view it is equivalent to a uniform increase in wage costs. In time of stable prices, or where demand is elastic, it

would probably work out partly in lower profits and partly in
unemployment. In a situation of rising prices and inelastic
demand the main burden would probably be passed on to the
consumer, but if allowances were a high proportion of wages,
and wages were a high proportion of total costs, the level of
wages would tend to be kept down below what it would otherwise be. This result is generally recognised to have occurred
in France. 'The extension of the system of children's allowances has in effect been accepted [in France] as an alternative
to larger wage increases in a period of rising prices.'[1]

A third method would be to incorporate all family allowances in the social insurance scheme and finance them by tripartite contributions. This would avoid placing the whole
burden on employers, on the one hand, or the Exchequer, on
the other; and the employee's contribution would not affect
incentive, since it is not a marginal tax. The case against this
method is merely that children are not an insurable risk. It is
possible for the actuary to make estimates or assumptions
about the birth rate, which would probably be much more
accurate than his assumptions about the unemployment rate.
But, for all its deficiencies, social insurance is insurance: it is
either provision against risks to which every insured person is
subject but which he hopes to avoid, such as sickness or unemployment or early death; or provision for benefits which
every insured person hopes to enjoy, such as pensions and a
respectable funeral. Families, large or small, do not fit into
either of these categories. It is true that maternity grants are
paid out of the National Insurance Fund, but their cost is a
negligible part of the Fund's expenditure. Family allowances,
if incorporated in the Insurance Fund at their present level,
would require an increase in contributions of between 10 and
20 per cent.

A fourth method is the payment of allowances entirely out
of Exchequer revenue. The chief objection to this method on
its introduction is usually that the cost is too high for the

[1] *Report of the Royal Commission on Population*, Cmd. 7695, 1949
para. 447.

Exchequer to take at one bite, but allowances may be introduced gradually; and the gross cost to the Exchequer can be partly offset by the amount which is recovered in income tax.

For the other question we assume that the principle of family allowances and the source of the funds have been agreed, and we ask: How much should be paid? This is really a series of questions: What is the cost of a family? How far should family allowances aim at removing the financial burden from the parents? If not altogether, on what basis should allowances be paid?

The cost of a family could be defined in terms of subsistence standards. But these are less reliable for children than for adults, because they vary according to age, and they vary according to the number of children. Every mother knows that the 14-year-old costs much more to feed and clothe than the 4-year-old, and that three children do not cost three times as much to feed and clothe and house as one child. Moreover, we are interested, not in the cost of children in isolation, so to speak, but in the *additional* financial burden placed on parents as a result of having one, two, three or more children: the marginal cost of children. Some evidence on this matter was provided by an enquiry, made in connection with the Report of the Royal Commission on Population, into the actual expenditure of families at different levels of income in which there were 0, 1, 2 or 3 children.[1] It was found, as might be expected, that expenditure on the children varied with income, with the willingness of parents to reduce their own standard of living for the sake of the children, and with the actual number of children.

In considering the possible scale of family allowances, therefore, it is necessary to decide, first, whether they should vary according to income, age and the number of children, and secondly, how much account should be taken of the parents' willingness to make sacrifices. For any child in any family, there are three possible levels at which allowances could be paid. They could cover the whole additional cost of the

[1] A. M. Henderson: 'The Cost of a Family', *Transactions of the Manchester Statistical Society*, 1947-8.

child, and so remove the financial burden from the parents and allow them to enjoy the same standard of living as they enjoyed before the children arrived. Or, the allowances could exceed this amount and give them the opportunity to spend more on the children, or on themselves, or both, as a result of having a family. Or, they could fall short of the 'marginal cost' and so allow for the willingness of parents to make some financial sacrifice. The first would at least guarantee that poverty arising out of the cost of maintaining children would be avoided, and might even encourage parents to have more children. The second would actually make it profitable for them to have more children. The third would reduce the financial burden of parenthood, and would have some influence on the incidence of poverty.

The Beveridge Report and the Royal Commission on Population both arrived at the same conclusion: 'The cost of maintaining children should be shared between their parents and the community.'[1] 'Even as an ultimate aim we do not think it desirable to relieve parents of the whole financial cost of maintaining any of their children.'[2] The actual allowances paid under the 1945 Act were 5s. per week for the second and subsequent children under school-leaving age. It was assumed that normal wages would be sufficient to maintain a family of one child, and this method was preferable to the alternative of paying a lower rate for all children

'as making a large reduction in the cost of the allowances to the community with no hardship to parents, and as increasing the proportion of the total cost borne by the community as the size of the family increases, this makes the allowances more effective in preventing want and increases whatever influence they may have in encouraging large families.'[1]

In 1952 the weekly rate was raised from 5s. to 8s.

[1] *Report on Social Insurance and Allied Services*, para. 417.
[2] *Report of the Royal Commission on Population*, para. 452. A number of interesting subsidiary questions are also discussed in this part (Chapter 17) of the Report.

In short, the allowances do not vary with income or age, and they do not cover the whole marginal cost of children; but they do, together with income tax allowances and welfare services, relieve the burden of parenthood considerably; and, being at a flat rate, they provide a greater degree of relief per child as the size of the family increases, because the cost does not rise proportionately with the number of children.

§ **2. The National Health Service.** In Great Britain, at the beginning of this century, general medical services were obtainable through five separate channels. Those who could afford them had private doctors, and paid fees which often varied according to the doctor's estimate of the patient's capacity to pay. Those who belonged to friendly societies were sometimes insured for medical services as well as for sickness benefit; in which case the society paid part or all of the doctor's bill and the cost of drugs. Some societies made contracts with doctors and paid them capitation fees on condition that they provided medical services, when required, to the societies' members. The voluntary hospitals (financed largely by endowments and public subscriptions) supplied treatment for in-patients and out-patients, often free of charge, but otherwise at a charge which the patient, or those who sponsored his treatment, could afford to pay. These three channels, therefore, were maintained by fees, mutual aid and philanthropy. The other two were maintained out of local rates. The Poor Law authorities provided institutional and domiciliary medical services for the destitute; and the Public Health authorities, though mainly concerned with preventive medicine, sanitation and the like, were looking after a steadily increasing number of the sick poor in hospitals and at home, in their attempts to prevent epidemics and isolate infectious cases.

It was these Public Health Committees of the local authorities that the Webbs wished to see expanded into a national health service. They would do away with the separate treatment of the destitute; their practitioners would be better qualified than many of the friendly society doctors; and they would start with a tradition that the Webbs regarded as essential for the proper development of all the social services: an emphasis on prevention as well as cure.

The system set up under the National Insurance Act of 1911 was not in charge of the Public Health authorities, but of local Insurance Committees composed of representatives of the several interested parties. The working of the system of 'panel' doctors and free drugs for those insured under the health scheme need not be described here.[1] It was cumbersome, but it did work, and, for most of the insured members of the population, it provided better medical services than they had previously known. It also found favour, after strong initial opposition, with part at least of the medical profession; for the panel system provided a fixed income to its doctors and was attractive to a young practitioner newly setting up in practice. Its greatest drawback was its limited scope. It did not cover those in uninsured occupations or those whose incomes exceeded the limit for national insurance. It did not go beyond free doctors and free medicines; specialist services, nursing services, medical appliances and many other branches of medical service were excluded. And it applied only to the insured persons themselves, and not to their wives and families.

Many of these gaps were covered by new schemes of voluntary insurance. The most interesting were the various hospital savings funds, through which a large number of people paid small weekly contributions to the hospitals and in return were given free treatment when they required it. The system had two advantages when compared with ordinary insurance and mutual aid schemes. The contributors were still glad to contribute, even if they never 'got anything back', because they were helping a good cause. The hospitals, like all voluntary institutions, preferred even a small guaranteed regular income, supplemented by irregular donations and subscriptions, to a system consisting entirely of irregular gifts. In their limited field, the hospital savings schemes probably pro-

[1] The most detailed study is that of Hermann Levy: *National Health Insurance*, 1944.

vided a pattern for the structure of the voluntary services in the Welfare State.[1]

In spite of all this, however, the limited scope of the pre-war insurance scheme and the inadequate finances of the voluntary hospitals were the two strongest arguments in the case for a national health service. The case was reinforced by developments in medicine using more expensive drugs and more elaborate equipment, the cost of which forbade their unlimited use by every doctor and hospital and required some system of allocation on a regional, if not a national basis. In addition it was said that the local Insurance Committees were so busy administering the panel system that they completely lost sight of the preventive aspect which had been stressed in 1911. Further, there were more general arguments. Although health insurance had shaken off the distinctive garb of the Poor Law, there were distinctions of class between those who were 'on the panel' and those who were not; and it was argued that the health of the nation, and the economic efficiency and social well-being which depended on it, were a communal responsibility calling for a 'comprehensive national service'. More precisely, the argument implied that the *additional* resources required for the national health service represented a 'social input' or investment which would yield a more than corresponding increase in the output of the beneficiaries, and in social welfare.

Could not the gaps have been filled by an extension of health insurance, by a more adequate use of the local authority powers to build public hospitals, and by the merging of Insurance Committees and Public Health Committees so that the mechanism would be simpler and preventive medicine would be encouraged? Would there not still have been a useful field for private practice and voluntary hospitals, to offset the dangers of top-heavy organisation, political influence, and

[1] *Vide* discussion at the end of Chapter VII. Those familiar with Church finance will recognise that the 'Envelope Schemes', which are becoming increasingly popular for the collection of freewill offerings, follow the same pattern.

restricted freedom which sometimes arise in comprehensive national institutions? The answer is probably: yes, had it not been for the experience of the war. It was that experience which prepared the ground for the acceptance of the national health service proposed in the White Paper of February 1944. The danger of air attack necessitated, during the war, a nationally organised system through which medical services and equipment could be immediately applied where they were most needed. The Ministry of Health took control of hospital accommodation and added new buildings, beds and facilities to meet the needs of the emergency. Distinctions, real or imaginary, between different classes of people, became meaningless in face of air-raids and the clearing-up that followed them. All this was of tremendous importance at a time when post-war reconstruction was widely regarded as a job which would command the same national solidarity as had the task of winning the war.

The discussion of the case for and against a national health service was influenced not only by a certain fusion of wartime and peacetime objectives, but also by two subsidiary arguments. It was argued that the national health service should be separate from the insurance scheme and paid for by the Exchequer and, to some extent, out of local rates. There were financial reasons for this: it was felt that the insurance contributions required for the money benefits of the insurance scheme were already as much as employers and insured persons could be asked to bear. But there was also a significant difference of principle. The basis of the insurance schemes (and of assistance and family allowances) was the guarantee of a *minimum* income; they were designed to prevent primary poverty. The aim of the health services (as of the education services) was to provide the 'best possible' services—if not a maximum, at least an optimum, which would distribute the available services as nearly as possible according to need. It assumed that these needs could be determined objectively, on medical grounds, and that in total their satisfaction would not place an unreasonable burden on either the budget or the real national income. But, as we noted earlier,[1] there was, especially in view of new discoveries in medical science, no 'technical' limit to the amount and cost of services, drugs and equipment which many people, in particular the aged, could use if they were available.

Coupled with this was the question of charges. It was argued that if the health service were divorced from national insurance and freed from the limitations of a 'national minimum' policy, it would have to be provided entirely free of charge. This, however, did not necessarily follow. The principle enunciated by the Webbs in the Minority Report, by Beveridge, and by the Government in 1944,[2] was that access to the best medical and other facilities should not *depend* on whether people can pay for them; which is quite different from saying that nobody must pay for anything. Certainly, any scheme of 'part-payment' would have to distinguish between those who could, and those who could not afford to pay; it would imply a means test, even if people were so grouped as to avoid individual investigation of means. But this was a separate issue.

In other words, the argument that a national health service would make available all the medical and other facilities that people needed did not carry with it the obligation either to provide these services without limit or to provide them without charge.

The National Health Service Act of 1946 came into force in July 1948 and imposed on the Minister of Health the duty 'to promote the establishment in England and Wales of a comprehensive Health Service designed to secure improvement in the physical and mental health of the people of England and Wales, and the prevention, diagnosis and treatment of illness'. There was a separate and similar Act for Scotland.

The Minister has the advice of a Central Health Services Council of 41 members, with a majority of doctors; and of a number of technical committees. Neither the Ministry of Health nor the Council, however, actually administer the

[1] See p. 209.   [2] Cmd. 6502, p. 5.

health service. For this there are three types of authority, all composed of voluntary, unpaid members: Regional Hospital Boards, Executive Councils, and the County and County Borough Councils.

The hospital and specialist services are organised in fourteen regions, in each of which there is a Regional Hospital Board. The boards take decisions affecting the region as a whole and appoint management committees to do the daily work of running the hospitals. The teaching hospitals have their own governing bodies, and the medical schools are separately financed through the University Grants Committee. The Executive Councils, one in each major local authority area, administer the 'general medical services' provided by doctors, dentists, opticians and chemists. The local authorities— county and county borough councils—are responsible for ambulances, maternity and child welfare services, health-visiting, and a number of similar services. The Act also provided for an entirely new type of institution, the Health Centre, in which the local authorities and Executive Councils would have a joint interest. Here accommodation would be provided in each locality for those activities which could not be carried out conveniently in the separate hospitals and surgeries, or in the homes of patients. The Health Centres would contain, for example, the welfare clinic run by the local authority; they would house special equipment and provide facilities which all the doctors in the area could use, they would bring together specialists and general practitioners, they would be centres for health education.

It was unfortunate that during the first few years of the operation of the National Health Service, public attention was almost entirely concentrated on the rising costs of the service, to the neglect of its achievements. There was no doubt, from the reports both of the Ministry of Health and of other observers, that it removed a great deal of anxiety and led to a much earlier diagnosis of illness among people who had previously failed to seek medical advice and treatment for financial reasons. There was no doubt that a large part of the enormous, unexpected and much-publicised demand for dentures and spectacles in the early years of the service came from patients who had postponed adequate dental and optical treatment longer than they should have done. There was ample evidence that the resources, whether of hospital accommodation, skilled personnel, or equipment, were being more fully utilised than they had been previously.

The main problems, apart from the inevitable administrative difficulties of a new nation-wide organisation, were those connected with the unexpectedly·large demand for all branches of the service, and the apparently uncontrollable increase in its total cost.

The Beveridge Report estimated that the gross cost of the health service would be £170 millions a year. In the first year, 1948–9, it was £218 millions; in the second and third, over £400 millions. In part, the increase could be explained by an increase in prices greater than the 25 per cent above 1938 assumed by Beveridge; in part by the fact that the Beveridge estimate was admittedly based on the slenderest statistical information. Chiefly, however, it was the result of the enormous latent demand for medical services which became effective on the introduction of a free service. For the hospitals this meant an acute shortage of accommodation, longer waiting lists, and a marked rise in the cost of wages and salaries, which account for about 60 per cent of hospital costs. The general practitioners were remunerated on the basis of a fixed fee per patient, irrespective of the amount of medical attention required; the intention being to encourage efficiency by giving the better doctors an opportunity to increase their salary by taking on more patients. The cost of their services increased only in proportion to the number of patients, and the higher demand for service per head worked itself out in crowded surgeries and less thorough medical attention. The dentists fared much better: their charges varied according to the work done, and, while they also had long queues, efficiency was fully rewarded. Thus, when the doctor did more prescribing per patient, the higher cost went into the pharmacist's account; when the dentist and optician prescribed more, they shared the benefit with the manufacturers of false teeth and spectacles.

The structure of professional incomes in the Health Service had been examined by an Inter-Departmental Committee,[1] and a scale of salaries worked out which, it was thought, would take account of the age and skill of general practitioners, dentists and specialists and also be appropriate to their relative status and their different 'occupational needs'. Briefly, the policy was to narrow the gap in the pre-war distribution of incomes between dentists (30 per cent of whom earned more than £1,000 in 1939) and general practitioners (57½ per cent of whom earned more than £1,000 in 1939); and between general practitioners and specialists (87 per cent of whom earned more than £1,000 in 1939). It was felt that dentists had been underpaid, and it was feared that general practice might fail to recruit the more able doctors unless the 'area of overlap' in the salaries of the three groups were increased. In the result, however, the dentists were able to race ahead of the general practitioners, and the specialists were given a minimum scale and a system of 'distinction awards' which placed them so high that at the age of 40, for example, only about 5 per cent of general practitioners could earn as much as the lowest-paid specialists unless they deliberately sacrificed quality of service to quantity of patients. In 1952 and 1953 changes were introduced which improved the relative position of the general practitioner. The whole story provided an interesting example of the difficulties of a controlled price system which could not adjust itself adequately to changes in demand and supply conditions in inter-related markets.

In 1951 it was decided that a ceiling of £400 millions should be fixed for the cost to the Exchequer[2] of the National Health

[1] The Spens Committee, which published three Reports: Cmd. 6810: *Remuneration of General Practitioners*, May 1946; Cmd. 7402: *Remuneration of General Dental Practitioners*, May, 1948; Cmd. 7420: *Remuneration of Consultants and Specialists*, May, 1948.

[2] In addition, about half of the local authority services are financed out of rates, and an annual sum of about £40 millions is paid by the National

Service. This was not an estimate of what an efficiently organised health service ought to cost; it was simply the limit of an over-taxed Chancellor's tolerance. In consequence, any increase in cost in one branch of the service could be met only by economies elsewhere. Either efficiency would have to be increased (more services provided with the same resources or the same services provided with fewer resources) or direct charges would have to be imposed on consumers for the services provided. Such charges were imposed, amounting to part of the cost of dentures and spectacles, a nominal charge of one shilling for each prescription form, and a contribution of £1 towards the cost of a course of dental treatment. The purpose of the charges was partly to increase revenue and partly to reduce demand. The actual effect was to provide an additional £5 millions of revenue in 1951–2 and £15 millions in 1952–3; and to reduce significantly the demand, not only for dentures and spectacles, but also for what is called 'conservative' dental treatment,[1] though it was obviously very difficult to say how far the decline in demand resulted from the imposition of charges, and how far it represented the completion of non-recurring treatment applied for in the early years of the service.

By 1953 the 'ceiling' was still £400 millions a year, but the main problem was still unsolved: how to establish a consistent set of principles by which limited resources, real and financial, could be directed towards the satisfaction of needs which, if not unlimited, were always likely to be far greater than the resources available. There were complaints that the hospitals had no proper costing system, that doctors prescribed expensive

Insurance Fund towards the cost of the Health Service. This last amount was based on the cost of medical benefit under the pre-war Health Insurance scheme and there is very little logical justification for its continuance. It has been partly responsible for a widespread belief that the whole of the National Health Service was financed by insurance contributions.

[1] 'We are all in favour of conservatism,' the Labour Minister of Health is reputed to have told a conference of dental practitioners in 1951. He meant that where a dentist was in doubt whether to patch up teeth, or extract them and supply dentures, he should choose the former and less costly alternative.

drugs too freely, that accounting on an annual basis encouraged waste and prevented any part of the service from developing an interest in more efficient operation.   In the same year the Minister of Health appointed an independent committee 'to review the present and prospective cost of the National Health Service; to suggest means, whether by modifications in organisation or otherwise, of ensuring the most effective control and efficient use of such Exchequer funds as may be made available; to advise how, in view of the burdens on the Exchequer, a rising charge upon it can be avoided while providing for the maintenance of an adequate service'.

All this was mainly concerned with current expenditure. The situation with regard to capital expenditure was that, although fuller use was made of existing accommodation in all branches of the Health Service, there was very little new building.   Hospital accommodation, amounting to about half a million beds in 1949, had increased by only 1 per cent three years later, and the building of Health Centres had hardly begun.

The Report of the Guillebaud Committee[1] was published early in 1956.   For the first of its tasks, 'to review the present and prospective cost of the National Health Service', it was assisted by a parallel enquiry,[2] carried out for the committee, into the whole question of defining and analysing the costs of a public service with extremely intricate financial arrangements. 'For the first time the modern technique of social accounting has been applied in an expert manner to one of the major sectors of the social services.'[3]   This analysis showed up the defects of the Appropriation Accounts (on which the Government's policy decisions were made) as indicators of the true cost to public funds.   It also revealed that, although the gross cost to public funds had increased by 20 per cent between 1949/50 and 1953/4, and the net cost, allowing for the charges imposed in 1951, by 16 per cent, much of the increase was the

[1] *Report of the Committee of Enquiry into the Cost of the National Health Service*, Cmd. 9663, 1956.

[2] Brian Abel-Smith and R. M. Titmuss: *The Cost of the National Health Service in England and Wales*, 1956.

[3] Foreword by C. W. Guillebaud to Abel-Smith, *op. cit.*

consequence of rising prices. At constant prices the rise in net cost over the period was only 3 per cent. Moreover, from the point of view of the use of real resources, the Health Service had absorbed a steadily declining proportion of the gross national product: 3·80 per cent in 1949/50 and 3·42 per cent in 1953/4.

These findings certainly disposed of the fear that the Health Service was claiming an alarming and growing share of the nation's resources. Nevertheless it was still true that the actual money charge on the Exchequer was increasing year by year, and that this continued to worry the Chancellor. Further, it is arguable that health services may be adequate and expanding without necessarily absorbing a growing proportion, or even the same proportion of a rising national income. If the real national product increases by 12 per cent, as it did between 1949/50 and 1953/4, we may, as a nation, enjoy more health services, but not necessarily 12 per cent more. In short, the discovery that the Health Service absorbed a declining proportion of the gross national product was interesting but not surprising.

The Committee's findings in regard to the future trends in the cost of the National Health Service did much to dispel the fear that the changing age structure of the population, combined with developments in medical science, would result in people living longer and longer in order to enjoy more and more expensive diseases. They estimated that population changes by themselves would, over twenty years, raise the cost of health services by as little as 8 per cent; of which $4\frac{1}{2}$ per cent was attributable to the increase in the total population and $3\frac{1}{2}$ per cent to the increase in the proportion of old people. In particular, they found that the costly facilities of hospital care, especially for mental and chronic illness, were mainly needed by the single, the widowed and the divorced. 'The married state and its continuance thus appear to be a powerful safeguard against admission to hospitals in general and to mental and "chronic" hospitals in particular.'[1]

[1] *Report*, p. 49.

As for efficiency of the Service, the committee did not recommend any major changes in the administrative or financial structure. Nor did they discover any 'built-in' system that would provide an incentive to greater efficiency in the hospital services, which accounted for more than half the total cost of the National Health Service. They did, however, recommend an overhaul of the costing systems employed in hospitals.

On the question of charges, the Committee favoured a continued charge for dentures as long as the shortage of dentists remained. They thought that when the Chancellor could afford it, he should arrange to remit the charge for a course of dental treatment to those who kept themselves 'dentally fit' by regular visits.[1] They also thought the charge for spectacles prevented some people from having them who ought to have had them; so that, when resources were available, this charge should be abolished. But they did not urge the removal of the shilling charge on prescriptions. Here, then, was an interesting combination of expediency, morality and economics in the use of the price system.

Turning to capital expenditure, the Committee deplored the virtual cessation of hospital building since 1938 and recommended the expenditure of £30 million a year on new building in the seven years from 1958 to 1965. They also urged that special accommodation should be provided by local authorities for old people who were not well enough to be properly cared for in their own homes but not ill enough to require hospital treatment.

Finally, with commendable frankness, the Committee stated that there was no economic or objective touchstone for establishing how much a national health service ought to cost. It must be a political decision.

'It is clear that the amount of the national resources, expressed in terms of finance, manpower and materials,

[1] Cf. the Ordinance which the Swiss reformer Zwingli promulgated for the poor-relief fund established in Zurich in the sixteenth century: '. . . relief shall not be given to . . . those who without good reason do not attend sermons. . . .' (F. R. Salter: *Early Tracts on Poor Relief*, p. 101.)

which are to be allocated to the National Health Service, must be determined by the Government as a matter of policy, regard being had to the competing claims of other social services and national commitments, and to the total amount of resources available.'[1]

Nor did they see any prospect that, as the health of the nation improved, the need for health services would be lessened:

'It is still sometimes assumed that the Health Service can and should be self-limiting, in the sense that its own contribution to national health will limit the demands upon it to a volume which can be fully met. This, at least for the present, is an illusion. It is equally illusory to imagine that everything which is desirable for the improvement of the Health Service can be achieved at once.'[1]

§ 3. **Welfare Services.** The Table of Expenditure on the Public Social Services on p. 213 included a number of minor items which may broadly be called 'Welfare Services'. In this section we shall describe five of these: school meals and milk, other welfare foods, child care, local authority assistance services, and rehabilitation services. From the accounting aspect, they come under various headings. The first two are classified as subsidies in Group III, the third and fourth as 'real services' in Group II, the last as a transfer payment in Group I. But this classification is not rigid or important, for these services have a functional affinity which is much more significant: they all provide special forms of assistance to special classes of people.

(*i*) *School meals and milk.* An Act of 1906, 'probably the earliest example of relief from public funds being given to a specific section of the population by an agency other than the Poor Law',[2] empowered local education authorities to provide

[1] *Report*, p. 243.
[2] M. Penelope Hall: *The Social Services of Modern England*, 1952, p. 168.

milk and meals to elementary schoolchildren who were 'unable by reason of lack of food to take full advantage of the education provided for them'. By 1939 about half the authorities were providing meals and about 85 per cent were providing milk. The meals were only intended for children who were undernourished, and they were not supplied free of charge unless the parents were necessitous. Milk, on the other hand, was supplied, under the Milk Act of 1934, to all schoolchildren who wanted it at the rate of a third of a pint per day for a halfpenny, or free of charge in necessitous cases.

The war helped to change the character of this, as of many other services. Children had to be fed at school, not because they were poor or undernourished, but because their mothers were working in factories; and by 1944 the service had come to be accepted as an essential ancillary to the education services. So far from being justified on the ground that undernourished children could not do their lessons properly, it almost became part of the curriculum, as a means of teaching them good table manners. The Education Act of 1944 made it a duty of local education authorities to provide meals and milk for all children in maintained schools who wanted them. The White Paper on Social Insurance[1] said that free meals and milk, together with the school medical and dental services and the payment of family allowances, would represent a general contribution by the State to the needs of families with children.

Since 1944 meals have been duly provided, but at a charge of 9d. per day,[2] which covers about half the cost; and an annual count has revealed that between 45 and 50 per cent of the day pupils in primary and secondary schools in England and Wales have dinner at school. In Scotland, school dinners seem to be less popular; roughly 35 to 40 per cent partake. And in Northern Ireland the percentage is only 20. In England and Wales and in Scotland there was a noticeable drop in 1953 which may have been attributable to the end of meat rationing.

[1] Cmd. 6550, 1944, paras. 50–51.
[2] Raised to 1s. in February 1957.

A special enquiry conducted in 1955/6[1] found that, according to the teachers, the reasons most commonly given for taking dinner at school were: 'The journey from home to school is long or difficult', 'Mother is at work', and 'It suits the mother's convenience'. The main reasons for not taking dinner at school were: 'There is a midday dinner at home and the parents like the children home for it', and 'Children are faddy and do not like the meals provided'. There was some evidence that parents of large families could not afford to pay the charge, but equally there was evidence that many parents could afford to pay the full cost.

Milk continued to be provided at a halfpenny per third of a pint until 1946, when the charge was abolished. The proportion of children taking milk in schools in England and Wales increased from about 75 per cent before 1946 to about 85 per cent in subsequent years, and there was a similar increase in Scotland and Northern Ireland. The reason is presumably not that parents could not afford halfpennies but that their payment and collection was a nuisance. On the other hand the wastage of milk is probably much greater when it is free, but this may be a small price to pay for the great benefits that children derive from the cultivation of the milk-drinking habit.

The gross cost of school meals and milk in 1955/6 was £73 millions; the net cost after deducting payments for meals was £51 millions. Both services are administered by the local authorities but the cost is covered by a grant from the Exchequer.

(ii) *Other welfare foods.* School age is by no means the earliest stage at which the social services become interested in the welfare of children. Indeed, services are provided for them before they are born. Under the National Health Service Act every local health authority has to provide maternity and child welfare clinics where expectant and nursing mothers, and children under 5, can receive the special care and attention they need. The clinics are staffed by qualified

---

[1] Ministry of Education: *Report on an Inquiry into the Working of the School Meals Service* (1955–56).

doctors, nurses and dentists, and are often in a better position to give advice about the special problems of mothers and young children than is the general practitioner. Health visitors are also appointed to visit mothers and young children in their homes.

In conjunction with these services, there is a Welfare Foods Service, through which all expectant mothers, and children under 5 years old, are entitled to one pint of milk a day at the special subsidised price of $1\frac{1}{2}d$. a pint.[1] Supplies of orange juice are also guaranteed to them at a subsidised price, and cod-liver oil and vitamin preparations free of charge. The milk and orange juice are also supplied free to those unable to pay for them. Milk foods at special prices, or free of charge, are provided for babies who do not take liquid milk.

It is widely recognised that these services have made an outstanding contribution to the health of children in Great Britain. Attendance at clinics is not compulsory, but the efforts of the health visitors, and the fact that the welfare foods are available at little or no charge, have overcome reluctance and prejudice to a remarkable degree. Here is a case in which free or subsidised services, even when supplied to people who could afford to pay the whole cost, have been fully justified.

The gross cost of the welfare foods in 1955/6 was £38 millions; the net cost was £36 millions; all of which was financed by the Exchequer.

(*iii*) *Child care*. The responsibility of caring for children deprived of a normal home life is shared in about equal proportions between voluntary agencies and public authorities. In 1945, the total number of such children was 125,000, of whom about 40,000 were in voluntary homes, about 40,000 in local authority institutions, and the rest in Approved Schools, remand homes and foster homes. The names of the largest voluntary societies are well known: Dr. Barnardo's Homes, The Church of England Children's Society, The National Children's Home, The Catholic Child Welfare Council; and

[1] Raised to 4*d*. a pint in February 1957.

there are many smaller ones. The local authority institutions were, until 1948, under the Ministry of Health as part of the Poor Law system, except for Approved Schools and Special Schools, under the Home Office and the Ministry of Education. Approved Schools take children removed by order of a court either as delinquents or as 'in need of care and protection'. Special Schools look after physically and mentally handicapped children.

The wide differences in the standards of care among these institutions, and especially the unsatisfactory treatment received by children in some foster homes, roused public opinion in 1944 and led to the appointment of a Committee of Inquiry. *The Report of the Care of Children Committee*, known as the Curtis Report,[1] showed that in some cases the conditions in institutions and foster homes were highly unsatisfactory. It blamed the division of responsibility, and the inadequate supervision of the boarding out and institutional maintenance, both by voluntary and by public bodies, of deprived children. It recommended that one Department should be responsible for the care of all deprived children, that rules should be established and enforced in regard to the placing of children in homes or with foster parents, and that all voluntary homes should be inspected, though not otherwise interfered with.

Within a very short time the Children Act of 1948 was passed. The Home Office was designated as the central authority for child care. Local authorities were required to establish Children's Committees and to appoint Children's Officers to look after all aspects of child care. Children in the care of local authorities may be boarded out with suitable foster parents, or where this is not practicable or desirable, placed in a children's home run by the local authority or a voluntary organisation. The homes in which children are boarded out must be inspected and approved, and the local authority itself must maintain adequate homes and hostels.

[1] Cmd. 6922, September 1946.

This is a form of social service in which personal relationships mean everything, and no amount of legislation or finance can guarantee that the care and affection which children have not received in their own homes will be provided elsewhere. But legislation and public money can at least ensure that efforts to promote child care in its most beneficial form will not be hampered by lack of supervision or lack of resources. Current expenditure on child care in 1955/6 amounted to £16 millions, of which about half came from the Exchequer and half from local rates. In addition capital expenditure of £1 million was incurred by local authorities.

(*iv*) *Local authority assistance services.* It was observed in Chapter IX that the National Assistance Board provided not only money grants, but also accommodation, for those in need. Such accommodation is of three kinds.

First, there are Reception Centres for persons without a settled way of living, which really means shelters for tramps. The Centres are managed by local authorities on behalf of the Board, which pays for them out of Exchequer funds. While they are enjoying temporary shelter, attempts are made to persuade vagrants to adopt a more settled way of life and take up regular employment.

Secondly, there are Re-establishment Centres for those whose general health and willingness to work have suffered through prolonged unemployment. People may be transferred from Reception Centres or recommended by Assistance Board officials from among those who have been receiving regular grants. They remain at the Re-establishment Centre for a period of weeks or months and are toned up and assisted into habits of regular employment. There is at present only one Re-establishment Centre, at Henley-in-Arden, but the Board also makes use of similar centres run by voluntary organisations.

The third type of accommodation is not only set up and organised, but largely financed, out of rates, by the local authorities. It is commonly called 'Part III accommodation' because Part III of the National Assistance Act of 1948 specifically deals with local authority services. 'It shall be the duty of every local authority,' says the Act, 'to provide residential accommodation for persons who by reason of age, infirmity or any other circumstances are in need of care and attention which is not otherwise available to them." Old people's homes run by local authorities come under this heading, and collaboration with voluntary organisations concerned with the welfare of old people is very close.

Finally, the local authorities have power to assist handicapped persons, that is the blind, the deaf and dumb, the crippled and the disabled. They can arrange for them to be cared for by an appropriate voluntary organisation. They can set up special workshops for them, provide instruction, special training and recreational facilities.

All this involved, in 1955/6, current expenditure of £15 millions, nearly all of which was financed locally, and capital expenditure of £2½ millions.

(v) *Rehabilitation services.* In fact, very few disabled persons are cared for under the National Assistance Act, because the Disabled Persons (Employment) Act of 1944, administered by the Ministry of Labour, provides much better things for them. A register of disabled persons is kept, and once registered they become entitled to special courses of rehabilitation and training wherein they can learn to do normal work as far as possible. They may then be employed in one of the Ministry of Labour's own factories for disabled men, called Remploy Ltd. In this form of sheltered employment they are paid full weekly wages based on outside trade union rates irrespective of their individual output. Alternatively, they may enter a designated occupation, such as that of lift attendant or car park attendant, in which vacancies must be offered first to disabled persons. Or, they may find employment in an ordinary industrial firm which participates in the National Scheme for Disabled Men and thereby undertakes to employ a certain proportion, usually 3 per cent, of disabled persons among its labour force.

Current expenditure on rehabilitation and training of disabled persons in 1955/6 was £3 millions, all of which was paid by the Exchequer and disbursed by the Ministry of Labour.

§ **4. Subsidies.** Subsidies enable producers to supply goods and services at a cost higher than the market price; they enable consumers to buy goods and services at a price lower than the factor cost. These are merely two ways of saying the same thing. But although it is the same thing, the way of saying it determines whether or not subsidies are to be classed among the public social services. If their main purpose is to assist the producer, they are not social services; if it is to assist the consumer, they are.

It is not easy to classify all subsidies in this way, especially since their purpose may change from time to time. In 1936, for example, food subsidies were not regarded as a social service, but as a means of assisting agriculture; in 1946 they were regarded as a social service and were distinguished, in the official statistics, from such purely agricultural subsidies as grants for attested herds, acreage payments and fertiliser subsidies; in 1956 food and agricultural subsidies were officially lumped together and treated as assistance to agriculture. It is to some extent a matter of opinion, but we have chosen, in Chapter VIII, to include among the public social services food subsidies; housing subsidies; subsidised school meals and milk, and welfare foods. Housing subsidies were discussed in Chapter III, section 5, and school meals, etc., in section 3 of this chapter.

Before the war only housing subsidies were regarded as a social service. Of the other pre-war subsidies, those paid to the cattle, milk, herring and tramp shipping industries were primarily intended to benefit existing producers; and those paid to the sugar beet and civil aviation industries were to encourage expansion, partly for military and strategic purposes. During the war the Board of Trade and Ministry of Supply subsidised a number of raw materials, and fuel and 'utility' cloth were also subsidised. The purpose of these was to offset increases in cost, especially of imported materials, which would otherwise have raised the prices of finished products and, thereby, the cost-of-living index.

The same principle applied to the wartime food subsidies, first introduced as part of a policy for providing a cheap basic ration for the whole community. The emphasis was on the avoidance of inflation rather than of poverty. It was understood that if the cost-of-living index were kept stable the trade unions would restrain their demands for higher wages. The rising cost of supplying food, both home-produced and imported, was therefore accompanied by a corresponding increase in subsidies, and by 1946 the 'trading losses of the Ministry of Food', as they were officially called, amounted to £237 millions. In 1947 they reached £296 millions and in 1948, £390 millions.

The Chancellor then decided that they must not be allowed to exceed £400 millions. Their limitation, however, was no easy task, for their original purpose had almost been forgotten and they were now defended as an essential ingredient of the social services. Certainly, inflationary pressure was as great as ever; and higher food prices would cause a rise in the cost-of-living index and stimulate wage demands. But most emphasis was laid on the importance of food subsidies in preserving the real standard of living of the poorest members of the community, particularly pensioners and wage-earners with large families. To relieve the budget by cutting food subsidies would therefore only increase the pressure for higher pensions and family allowances, both of which would have to be met by the Exchequer.

In the elections of 1950 and 1951 the food subsidies became a political issue of the first importance. On one side were those who argued that they were wasteful of public money, because they provided equal benefits to all consumers, rich and poor, while only the very poor, who spend a high proportion of their income on subsidised foods, really needed the benefit. On the other side were those who believed that all social service benefits *should* be spread equally over the community; and that any form of discrimination was out of keeping with the basic

principles of modern social services.   Again, some argued that
the two classes who benefited most, pensioners and wage-
earners with large families, could be adequately compensated,
if subsidies were abolished, at much lower cost to the Exchequer.   Their opponents replied that many other individuals,
not classifiable in this way, would suffer and be driven to seek
relief from the National Assistance Board; thereby greatly
extending the scope of means tests in the framework of the
social services.   Another argument was that the subsidies were
responsible for prolonging the period of food rationing: if
demand had not been inflated by low prices, supplies would
have been adequate for the abolition of food rationing much
earlier.   The reply was that if, as this argument implied, the
demand for food was price-elastic, the abolition of food
subsidies would represent an undesirable policy of 'dear food'
and 'rationing by the purse'.   If the demand for food was not
price-elastic, subsidies did not prolong rationing.

One writer suggested that the amount of benefit received
through food subsidies by the average working-class family
was at least equalled by the amount of indirect taxes paid by
the average working-class family.   Why not reduce subsidies
and taxes *pro rata* and avoid the cost of administration, the dis-
tortion of the price mechanism, and the interference of the State
in the free decisions of consumers as to how to allocate their
expenditure between bread and beer?   The ensuing discussion
ranged over all the points we have mentioned above, and ended
with a Hogarthian caricature of a Welfare State in which food
was dear and drink cheap, starving wives fought drunken
husbands over the size of housekeeping allowances, and wage-
earners flourished on cost-of-living bonuses while the professional and middle classes were ground under by the rise in
prices.[1]

When the dust settled and the Chancellor resumed his study
of the Budget, he was probably most influenced by two considerations: the competition of·other claimants to a share in
£400 millions of Government revenue, and the argument that,

[1] Correspondence in *The Times*, 18 October to 15 November 1951.

whatever the food subsidies were supposed to do, there were probably cheaper ways of doing it.   In the 1952 budget the ceiling for food subsidies was boldly reduced to £250 millions and pension increases were granted as a compensation to those likely to be hardest hit by the rise in prices.   Since that time they have hovered between £150 and £250 millions, but the situation has been blurred by administrative changes.   Under the old system, farmers sold their produce to the Government at fixed prices and the Government re-sold it to the public, the resulting trading losses of the Ministry of Food being the measure of the food subsidies.   Under the new system, first introduced in 1954, farmers sell their produce in the open market but each farmer is compensated, in the form of subsequent 'deficiency payments', to the extent that his realised price falls short of the standard price determined by the Government. The amount of food subsidies therefore fluctuates with changes in market conditions, and they have lost some of their consumer element and become rather a means of paying home producers higher prices than those prevailing on the world market.

EPILOGUE

THE CHANGING AIMS OF THE
SOCIAL SERVICES[1]

IT is not the task of the social economist to say what the aims
and objectives of the social services, or of any other branch
of the social system, ought to be. He can assume certain aims,
such as the achievement of the maximum economic welfare,
and examine the working of the economic system, or the social
services, in relation to those aims. Alternatively, he can take
the objectives set by the politicians, such as the maintenance
of a certain level of national self-sufficiency, and show the
relative contributions of different policies to that end. Sometimes, however, he can also point out that where there appears
to be only one aim, there are in fact several; that they may not
be consistent; and that they need to be distinguished or recon-
ciled in order to avoid confusion in the discussion of policy.

Such a situation has developed in regard to the social services
since the end of the war. Until a few years ago it was widely
assumed that the aims of the social services were, first, the prevention and relief of poverty and, secondly, a limited redistribution of opportunities. Recently, however, more diverse aims
than these have been assumed and it has become clear, not
only that there is a wide choice of aims but also that there is a
different set of aims according to how far ahead one cares to
look. There are short-term aims of policy: considerations
which dominate political discussion about social service
expenditure at the time of the budget. In the middle dis-
tance there are broader aims: social objectives to which
appeal is often made in order to justify short-term policy.
Finally, there are long-term aims: different conceptions of the

[1] A more topical version of this section appeared in an article by the
writer in *Lloyds Bank Review* for July 1953.

eventual place and purpose of social services in a democratic society.

A study of official pronouncements and Parliamentary Debates in the post-war period shows that adjustments in the finance of the social services were governed by three principal considerations. First, there was the need for more elbow-room in the budget. By 1949 social services expenditure, including subsidies, accounted for nearly 40 per cent of total central government expenditure, and the fact that this was a growing proportion made the Chancellor's task exceptionally difficult. Budget decisions are essentially marginal decisions—matters of spending a bit more here and saving a bit more there—and the health services and the food subsidies were clearly crowding out non-social-service expenditure. Secondly, there was the need to choke off demand for scarce resources. The imposition of charges in the National Health Service, which was described in Chapter X, was an obvious example. Thirdly, there was the need to maintain a reasonable relationship between insurance and assistance payments and the cost of living.

It is essential that these budgetary needs should be examined and debated, but no sensible decisions can be made, unless the needs are seen against a broader backcloth. The larger view, however, reveals at least five aims of social policy, not all of which can be pursued simultaneously.

The first of these aims is the relief of primary poverty, or, to use Beveridge's words, the removal of want. The task of the social services then falls into three parts: to decide where the poverty line shall be drawn, to discover who is below it, and to bring them up to it or just above it. It has been shown that ideas about the poverty line and the subsistence level vary from time to time and from place to place; that the assessment of poverty may be made individually or by grouping people into categories based on the causes of poverty; and that assistance and insurance payments are, with certain reservations, an efficient method of relief. The main point is that once the relief of poverty is accepted as an over-riding aim, any cut in the social services must take the form of either lowering the poverty line or discriminating more effectively between those who can and those who cannot afford to pay for the means of subsistence. A means test, in the widest sense, becomes a logical and an essential instrument of policy.

Much the same is true of the second aim: the relief of secondary poverty, which lies at the root of the health and education and welfare services. Here the social services are provided in kind, not only because the beneficiaries could not afford them (if that were the sole cause there would be no reason for not providing them in cash) but because the State thinks it knows better than the individual what is good for him. Here, too, the efficiency of the services must be judged by the precision with which they assess and supply people's needs, and any cuts in the cost of the services must take the form either of a stricter assessment of needs (for example, by raising the standard for entry to higher education) or of discrimination between those who can *and will* provide adequately for their own doctoring and schooling and housing[1] and those who cannot or will not.

The third aim is the promotion of greater equality of incomes. No social service was ever set up with the avowed object of promoting income equality, or justified originally on this ground, but there developed, after the war, a substantial body of opinion which opposed any change in social service expenditure which had a 'regressive' effect, that is, did not promote greater equality of incomes; and which judged the social services by that criterion alone. Of course, the relief of poverty must necessarily involve some redistribution of income, but the relief of poverty and the pursuit of income

[1] Cf. W. A. Lewis: *The Principles of Economic Planning*, 1949, pp. 31–32: 'If the Government simultaneously abolished housing subsidies and cut working-class taxation by an amount exactly equal to the subsidies the working classes would be no worse off financially, but they would then without doubt prefer to spend the money in other ways than on housing, and would live in overcrowded and inadequately provided houses, some because they do not know the advantage of better housing, and others because they value these advantages too lightly in comparison with other ways of spending their money.'

equality are not the same thing, and if the latter is accepted as an over-riding aim, much more severe limitations are imposed on the Chancellor when he has to decide to spend more or less on the social services, or modify their structure in any way.

Fourthly, it is possible to regard the social services as a means of socialising the national income. It is maintained in some quarters that the State should not merely ensure that no citizen lacks a certain minimum income, but should actually provide the whole of that income from public funds as a 'basic ration' or 'social dividend'. By this criterion, the most efficient form of social service is that which provides free, universal and equal benefits for all, irrespective of their differences of need and means. On this basis, no social service can be called wasteful or inefficient on the ground that it benefits the rich as well as the poor. If the social services have to be cut, the ration must be reduced all round; if expanded, it must be increased all round.

Finally, the social services may be used for the support of general economic policy, in which case they must be subordinated to it, and the other criteria (relief of poverty, etc.) may have to take second place or be abandoned. It can be argued that the social services ought to stand in their own right and not become the handmaid of general economic policy, except in the broad sense that they must not become too large in relation to the national income. But it is doubtful if this is possible as long as the social services are, as one writer puts it, 'hearty spenders of public money'. The National Insurance Fund, for example, because of its size and its parallel operation with the budget, is inextricably bound up with general economic policy, and, in particular, employment policy.

The importance of distinguishing these different aims may be illustrated by a simple example. Suppose that the community consists of four persons, Smith, Baker, Turner and Jones; that their incomes are, respectively, £4, £5, £6 and £7 a week; that their needs, because of physical, occupational, family and other differences, are respectively £3, £7, £8 and

£7 a week; and that there is available for distribution, in the form of social services, a total sum of £4 a week. The allocation of these services would vary, according to whether the aim were relief of poverty, promotion of equality of incomes, or the provision of a basic ration, as follows:

| | Income | Needs | Alternative additions to income for: | | |
			1 Relief of Poverty	2 Promotion of Equality	3 Basic Ration
Smith	4	3	$+0=4$	$+2\frac{1}{3}=6\frac{1}{3}$	$+1=5$
Baker	5	7	$+2=7$	$+1\frac{1}{3}=6\frac{1}{3}$	$+1=6$
Turner	6	8	$+2=8$	$+\frac{1}{3}=6\frac{1}{3}$	$+1=7$
Jones	7	7	$+0=7$	$+0\ =7$	$+1=8$

The first allocation would abolish poverty, but the second and third would not. The second allocation would significantly reduce inequality, but the first and third would hardly affect it. The third would put uniformity of provision before either relief of poverty or promotion of equality.

Nevertheless, although some of these aims may be mutually incompatible, they are not mutually exclusive. It is always possible to adopt compromise policies in regard to the social services which blend discriminate and indiscriminate benefits, which combine a measure of poverty relief with concessions to economic policy or equalitarianism, and so on. The purpose of separating the different aims is simply to clarify discussion and avoid the kind of argument in which people uphold different policies because, without realising it, they are making different assumptions about the aims of policy.

Beyond the short-term and intermediate aims there is the long-term question: What is to be the eventual place and purpose of the social services in society? There are four possible points of view on this matter. The first is that the social services should, in the long run, be self-liquidating. The second is that they should be a permanent but not a pervasive feature of society, a means of dealing with problems of mal-adjustment and abnormality, like a police force in a largely law-abiding country. The third is that they should be a fluctuating element in society, expanding or contracting according to changing circumstances and changing public opinion regarding the respective merits of private provision, voluntary association, and public social services for supplying certain needs. The fourth is that the social services should be a growing and, eventually, an all-pervasive feature of economic and social life.

Fifty or a hundred years ago, some economists would have assumed the first of these four long-term aims. Nassau Senior, for example, while admitting that there should be permanent State help for certain special classes, such as the blind and the insane, regarded other forms of State relief as justifiable only if they brought people as quickly as possible to a condition in which they would no longer require State relief. He regarded even State aid to education as self-liquidating in the sense that after the first generation or two had received education, parents would appreciate its value for their children and give it due importance with food, clothing and shelter in the family budget:

'We may look forward to the time when the labouring population may be safely entrusted with the education of their children; but no Protestant country believes that this time has come and I see no reason to hope for it until generation after generation has been better and better educated. . . . If the continuance of the assistance and superintendence, in one form or another, of the Government is necessary for that purpose—and I think I have shown it to be so—we must recommend that continuance, although we may treat it only as a means of preparing the labouring classes for a better, but remote state of things, when that assistance and superintendence shall no longer be necessary."[1]

Senior thought that the 'remote state of things' would come about 'in the latter part of the twentieth century'.

[1] N. W. Senior: *Suggestions on Popular Education*, 1861, p. 37.

Marshall held similar views, but for an additional reason. He clearly believed that economic progress would soon raise the whole gamut of incomes above the poverty line and that with it would come moral progress sufficient to ensure a wise expenditure of those incomes. In his evidence before the Royal Commission on the Aged Poor in 1893 he was asked:

'Have you given any consideration or formed any opinions as to the possibility of a universal scheme of pensions?'

His answer was:

'Yes, there are two especially that I think have a great deal to be said for them, Mr. Charles Booth's and Mr. Moore Ede's modification of Mr. Charles Booth's. My objections to them are that their educational effect, though a true one, would be indirect; that they would be expensive; and that they do not contain, in themselves, the seeds of their own disappearance. I am afraid that, if started, they would tend to become perpetual. *I regard all this problem of poverty as a mere passing evil in the progress of man upwards; and I should not like any institution started which did not contain in itself the causes which would make it shrivel up, as the causes of poverty itself shrivelled up.*'[1]

In recent years the ground has shifted through the second and third of the long-term aims of policy which we distinguished; and there have developed a number of pointers which suggest an approach to the fourth aim: that, so far from being self-liquidating, the social services are becoming self-propagating. We can usefully conclude our analysis by picking out these pointers.

In the first place, it was noticed earlier that social insurance is in some ways a more efficient way of relieving poverty than social assistance, provided that the insurance categories continue to represent causes of poverty. There is, however, no mechanism for undoing any part of the compulsory insurance

[1] *Official Papers by Alfred Marshall*, 1926, p. 244 (not his italics).

scheme, and it seems likely that even if normal earnings were to rise to the point at which most people could afford to make their own provision for periods of illness, unemployment, maternity and old age, they would still be bound to the compulsory national scheme. People would continue to take in each other's washing, even though each were able, and would much prefer, to do his own.

In the second place, there is the tendency for the definition of the subsistence level to become more generous as standards of living rise. Consequently, social services designed to provide a subsistence level income, so far from becoming unnecessary as standards of living improve and the whole range of income rises, find the target receding as fast as they pursue it.

In the third place, the growing predominance of health, education and similar services which aim at providing, not minimum standards, but the 'best possible' standards, suggests that a large part of the field is, for this reason, destined to increase.

In the fourth place, the supporters of the idea of socialising the national income, whether by providing a basic ration, by making participation in the social services the 'mark of citizenship', or by simply pursuing the political conviction that communal provision is always better than private provision, are clearly pressing for a continuous and uninterrupted growth of social services.

It is evident that there is abundant scope for divergent views on these highly important matters; but only too often the campaigners on different sides are unaware of the implications either of their own arguments or of those of their opponents. A clearer understanding of the underlying issues would avoid much fruitless controversy.

21

SUGGESTIONS FOR FURTHER READING

NOTE: The books, etc., are selected for their interest, relevance and readability. The list is a reading list, not a reference list or a list of sources.

GENERAL

J. R. Hicks: *The Social Framework* (2nd Edn., 1952)

A. M. Carr-Saunders, D. Caradog Jones & C. A. Moser: *Social Conditions in England & Wales* (1958)

T. S. Ashton: *The Industrial Revolution* (1948)

J. L. & Barbara Hammond: *Lord Shaftesbury* (1933)

B. S. Rowntree & G. R. Lavers: *English Life and Leisure* (1951)

F. Zweig: *Labour, Life and Poverty* (1948)

CHAPTER I   SOCIAL ECONOMICS

A. Marshall: *Principles of Economics* (8th Edn., 1920), Book I and Appendix C

A. C. Pigou: *Income* (1946)

J. E. Meade and Richard Stone: *National Income and Expenditure* (pamphlet, 4th Edn., 1957)

A. C. Pigou: *Economics of Welfare* (4th Edn., 1932), Part I

D. H. Robertson: 'Utility and All That' (Chapter I of *Utility and All That and other Essays*, 1952)

CHAPTER II   POPULATION

E. Cannan: *Wealth* (3rd Edn., 1928), Ch. III

I. Bowen: *Population* (Cambridge Economic Handbooks, 1954)

W. B. Reddaway: *The Economics of a Declining Population* (1939)

Report of the Royal Commission on Population (1949)

Report of the Economics Committee (Papers of the Royal Commission on Population, Vol. III, 1950)

Report of the (Phillips) Committee on the Economic and Financial Problem of the Provision for Old Age (1954)

CHAPTER III HOUSING

Marian Bowley: *Housing and the State* (1945)

F. W. Paish: 'The Economics of Rent Restriction' (chapter in *The Post-War Financial Problem and Other Essays*, 1950)

C. F. Carter & W. B. Reddaway: 'Houses—The Next Step' (article in the *London & Cambridge Economic Bulletin*, March 1954)

W. B. Reddaway: 'Housing Problems' (article in *The Three Banks Review*, Sept. 1954)

Geoffrey Howe & Colin Jones: *Houses to Let* (Bow Group Pamphlet, 1956)

CHAPTER IV WORKING CONDITIONS

A. Marshall: *Principles of Economics* (8th Edn., 1920), Book VI, Ch. III

G. P. Jones & A. G. Pool: *A Hundred Years of Economic Development* (1940), Chs. VII, XIII and XIX

G. D. H. Cole: *A Short History of the British Working Class Movement 1787–1947* (1948), Part I, Ch. IX; Part II, Ch. X; Part III, Ch. XII

B. L. Hutchins & A. Harrison: *A History of Factory Legislation* (1911)

M. Penelope Hall: *The Social Services of Modern England* (1952), Ch. XV

CHAPTER V UNEMPLOYMENT

Pilgrim Trust Report: *Men Without Work* (1938)

Employment Policy (White Paper, May 1944)

W. H. Beveridge: *Full Employment in a Free Society* (1944)

E. V. Morgan: *The Conquest of Unemployment* (1947)

The Economic Implications of Full Employment (White Paper, March 1956)

CHAPTER VI   POVERTY

D. Caradog Jones: *Social Surveys* (1949)

B. S. Rowntree: *Poverty and Progress* (1941)

Mark Abrams: *Social Surveys and Social Action* (1951)

CHAPTER VII   VOLUNTARY SOCIAL SERVICES

H. A. Mess (Ed.): *Voluntary Social Services since 1918* (1948)

Lord Beveridge: *Voluntary Action* (1948)

CHAPTERS VIII–X   PUBLIC SOCIAL SERVICES

K. de Schweinitz: *England's Road to Social Security* (Revised Edn., 1947)

Sidney & Beatrice Webb: *English Poor Law Policy* (1910)

(*Beveridge*) *Report on Social Insurance and Allied Services* (1942)

W. A. Robson (Ed.): *Social Security* (3rd Edn., 1948)

Hardy & Margaret Wickwar: *The Social Services* (Revised Edn., 1949)

M. Penelope Hall: *The Social Services of Modern England* (1952)

Central Office of Information: *Social Services in Britain* (pamphlet, 1955)

(*Guillebaud*) *Report on the Cost of the National Health Service* (1956)

Central Office of Information: *Health Services in Britain* (pamphlet, 1957)

B. E. Shenfield: *Social Policies for Old Age* (1957)

INDEX

Made and printed in Great Britain by William Clowes and Sons, Limited, London and Beccles